I0300472

Al-Fārābī

Syllogism:
An Abridgement of Aristotle's Prior Analytics

Ancient Commentators on Aristotle

GENERAL EDITORS: Richard Sorabji, Honorary Fellow, Wolfson College, University of Oxford, and Emeritus Professor, King's College London, UK; and Michael Griffin, Assistant Professor, Departments of Philosophy and Classics, University of British Columbia, Canada.

This prestigious series translates the extant ancient Greek philosophical commentaries on Aristotle. Written mostly between 200 and 600 AD, the works represent the classroom teaching of the Aristotelian and Neoplatonic schools in a crucial period during which pagan and Christian thought were reacting to each other. The translation in each volume is accompanied by an introduction, comprehensive commentary notes, bibliography, glossary of translated terms and a subject index. Making these key philosophical works accessible to the modern scholar, this series fills an important gap in the history of European thought.

A webpage for the Ancient Commentators Project is maintained at ancientcommentators.org.uk and readers are encouraged to consult the site for details about the series as well as for addenda and corrigenda to published volumes.

Al-Fārābī

Syllogism: *An Abridgement of Aristotle's Prior Analytics*

Translated by
Saloua Chatti and Wilfrid Hodges
with an Introduction by
Wilfrid Hodges

BLOOMSBURY ACADEMIC
LONDON • NEW YORK • OXFORD • NEW DELHI • SYDNEY

BLOOMSBURY ACADEMIC
Bloomsbury Publishing Plc
50 Bedford Square, London, WC1B 3DP, UK
1385 Broadway, New York, NY 10018, USA
29 Earlsfort Terrace, Dublin 2, Ireland

BLOOMSBURY, BLOOMSBURY ACADEMIC and the Diana logo are trademarks of Bloomsbury Publishing Plc

First published in Great Britain 2020
This paperback edition published in 2022

Copyright © Saloua Chatti and Wilfrid Hodges, 2020

Saloua Chatti and Wilfrid Hodges have asserted their right under the Copyright, Designs and Patents Act, 1988, to be identified as Editors of this work.

For legal purposes the Acknowledgements below constitute an extension of this copyright page.

All rights reserved. No part of this publication may be reproduced or transmitted in any form or by any means, electronic or mechanical, including photocopying, recording, or any information storage or retrieval system, without prior permission in writing from the publishers.

Bloomsbury Publishing Plc does not have any control over, or responsibility for, any third-party websites referred to or in this book. All internet addresses given in this book were correct at the time of going to press. The author and publisher regret any inconvenience caused if addresses have changed or sites have ceased to exist, but can accept no responsibility for any such changes.

A catalogue record for this book is available from the British Library.

Library of Congress Cataloging-in-Publication Data
Names: Fârâbî, author. | Chatti, Saloua, translator. | Hodges, Wilfrid, translator.
Title: Al-Farabi, Syllogism : an abridgement of Aristotle's Prior analytics / translated by Saloua Chatti and Wilfrid Hodges ; with an introduction by Wilfrid Hodges
Other titles: Falsafat Aflâṭûn. Selections. English | Farabi, syllogism : an abridgement of Aristotle's Prior analytics
Description: New York : Bloomsbury Academic, 2020. | Series: Ancient commentators on Aristotle | Includes bibliographical references and index. | Summary: "The philosopher Abu Nasr al-Farabi (c. 870-c. 950 CE) is a key Arabic intermediary figure. He knew Aristotle, and in particular Aristotle's logic, through Greek Neoplatonist interpretations translated into Arabic via Syriac and possibly Persian. For example, he revised a general description of Aristotle's logic by the 6th century Paul the Persian, and further influenced famous later philosophers and theologians writing in Arabic in the 11th to 12th centuries: Avicenna, Al-Ghazali, Avempace and Averroes. Averroes' reports on Farabi were subsequently transmitted to the West in Latin translation. This book is an abridgement of Aristotle's Prior Analytics, rather than a commentary on successive passages. In it Farabi discusses Aristotle's invention, the syllogism, and aims to codify the deductively valid arguments in all disciplines. He describes Aristotle's categorical syllogisms in detail; these are syllogisms with premises such as 'Every A is a B' and 'No A is a B'. He adds a discussion of how categorical syllogisms can codify arguments by induction from known examples or by analogy, and also some kinds of theological argument from perceived facts to conclusions lying beyond perception. He also describes post-Aristotelian hypothetical syllogisms, which draw conclusions from premises such as 'If P then Q' and 'Either P or Q'. His treatment of categorical syllogisms is one of the first to recognise logically productive pairs of premises by using 'conditions of productivity', a device that had appeared in the Greek Philoponus in 6th century Alexandria"– Provided by publisher. Identifiers: LCCN 2020019750 (print) | LCCN 2020019751 (ebook) | ISBN 9781350126992 (hardback) | ISBN 9781350127012 (ebook) | ISBN 9781350127036 (epub)
Subjects: LCSH: Aristotle. Prior analytics. | Logic. Classification: LCC PA3891.A2 F37 2020 (print) | LCC PA3891.A2 (ebook) | DDC 160–dc23
LC record available at https://lccn.loc.gov/2020019750
LC ebook record available at https://lccn.loc.gov/2020019751

ISBN: HB: 978-1-3501-2699-2
PB: 978-1-3501-9489-2
EPUB: 978-1-3501-2703-6
ePDF: 978-1-3501-2701-2

Series: Ancient Commentators on Aristotle

Typeset by RefineCatch Limited, Bungay, Suffolk

To find out more about our authors and books visit www.bloomsbury.com and sign up for our newsletters.

Acknowledgements

The present translations have been made possible by generous and imaginative funding from the following sources: the National Endowment for the Humanities, Divison of Research Programs, an independent federal agency of the USA; the Leverhulme Trust; the British Academy; the BA/Leverhulme Small Research Grant; the Jowett Copyright Trustees; the Royal Society (UK); Centro Internazionale A. Beltrame di Storia dello Spazio e del Tempo (Padua); Mario Mignucci; Liverpool University; the Leventis Foundation; the Arts and Humanities Research Council; Gresham College; the Esmée Fairbairn Charitable Trust; the Henry Brown Trust; Mr and Mrs N. Egon; the Netherlands Organisation for Scientific Research (NOW/GW); the Ashdown Trust; the Lorne Thyssen Research Fund for Ancient World Topics at Wolfson College, Oxford; Dr Victoria Solomonides, the Cultural Attaché of the Greek Embassy in London; and the Social Sciences and Humanities Research Council of Canada. The editors wish to thank Dawn Sellars for preparing the volume for press; and Alice Wright, Publisher, along with Georgina Leighton at Bloomsbury Academic, for their diligence in seeing each volume of the series to press.

To the memory of Béchir
Saloua Chatti

To Helen with thanks for all the flowers
Wilfrid Hodges

Contents

Preface *Richard Sorabji* viii
Conventions ix
Acknowledgements x

Introduction *Wilfrid Hodges* 1
1. A brief guide to categorical syllogisms 1
2. Al-Fārābī and his writings 7
3. The Book *Syllogism* 27

Textual Emendations 113

Translation *Saloua Chatti and Wilfrid Hodges* 115

Notes 165
Bibliography 181
English–Arabic–Greek glossary 191

Arabic–English index 195
Index of Passages from Aristotle 201
Subject Index 203

Preface

Richard Sorabji

Readers of our translations from Greek will wish to know how the text translated here from the later Arabic of al-Fārābī relates to the more familiar Greek commentaries on successive passages of Aristotle. Even though al-Fārābī also wrote long commentaries of the type more familiar in Greek, this text of his is instead a loose abridgement of the contents of Aristotle's *Prior Analytics* on syllogism and other forms of argument. I believe this latter kind of format derives indirectly from the general style of introduction that Ammonius provided in sixth-century CE Alexandria to his commentary on the earlier introduction (*Isagōgē*) to Aristotle's logic written by Porphyry (232/3–309 CE). Later in the sixth century CE, Paul of Persia, a native Syriac speaker, wrote an introduction to Aristotle's logic either in Syriac, or, as more commonly thought, in Middle Persian and dedicated it to the king of Persia, Khushru I Anushiruwān.[1] It too is a continuous abridgement, rather than a commentary on successive passages of Aristotle, and the translators compare it from time to time with al-Fārābī. I believe we can identify the post-Ammonian class that Paul attended in Alexandria and on which he drew for part of his text, although I shall leave the argument for that to another time. The point relevant for now is that a sixth-century student of commentary on Aristotle could already write an abridgement of Aristotle's logic, as opposed to a commentary on successive passages of Aristotle's text.

The translators' lucid introduction to al-Fārābī's text rightly takes a different form from the annotation and notes supplied in our standard translations of commentaries on Aristotle, because those commentaries supply or presuppose extracts from Aristotle himself which call for the translators' comments on those extracts, whereas here what needs elucidating is the abridgement of Aristotle's doctrine.

Note

1 J. P. N. Land, *Anecdota Syriaca* (Leiden: Brill, 1855), vol. 4, online at http://dbooks.bodleian.ox.ac.uk/books/PDFs/555081467.pdf

Conventions

This book is divided into chapters which in turn are sometimes divided into sections and then into subsections. Displayed text is referenced on the lefthand side, for example (1.2.3) is the third displayed text in the second section of Chapter 1.

Al-Fārābī's book *Syllogism* is divided into parts which are subdivided into paragraphs; for example paragraph 10.3 is the third paragraph in Part 10. Below that level it is referenced by pages and lines. Thus [66] 36,5–7 is lines 5 to 7 on page 36 of the edition [66] of *Syllogism*. The labelling by pages and lines is shown in the margin of the translation. We use a similar style for referring to pages and lines of other classical or medieval texts. A reference such as 36,5–7 with no book mentioned is a reference to *Syllogism*.

The division of al-Fārābī's text into parts is given by al-Fārābī himself in his introduction, for Parts 1 to 18. The labelling of Parts 19 and 20 is modern, and the subdivision of Part 18 into 18a–18d is our own.

In the translation, square brackets [...] enclose words or phrases that have been added to the translation for purposes of clarity. Round brackets (...), besides being used for ordinary parentheses, contain transliterated Arabic words.

Acknowledgements

We thank Sir Richard Sorabji for his invitation to write this volume, and for his steady interest, encouragement and suggestions. We also thank Dawn Sellars for her very thorough and helpful advice on editorial matters. We have benefitted from discussions with many people, including Rosabel Ansari, Nacéra Bensaou, Susanne Bobzien, Michael Carter, Besma Nouha Chaouch, Greg Cherlin, Thérèse-Anne Druart, Asadollah Fallahi, Manuela E. B. Giolfo, Ahmad Hasnawi, Daniel King, Joep Lameer, John P. McCaskey, Mokdad Arfa Mensia, Seyed N. Mousavian, Jamal Ouhalla, Riccardo Strobino, Jalila Tritar. Of course none of these people should be blamed for any of our mistakes or misjudgements.

Introduction

Wilfrid Hodges

1 A brief guide to categorical syllogisms

We begin our discussion of al-Fārābī's book *Syllogism* [66] with a short description of Aristotle's theory of syllogisms as al-Fārābī will have known it from the Arabic sources available to him.

1.1 Categorical sentences

There are four main kinds of quantified categorical sentence, as in the following examples:

Universal affirmative Every human is an animal.

Universal negative No human is a horse.

Particular affirmative Some animal is a human.

Particular negative Some animal is not a horse. Or, Not every animal is a horse.

These sentences all happen to be true, but of course there are false categorical sentences too, like 'Every human is a horse'.

The noun immediately after the quantifier expression 'Every', 'No', 'Some' or 'Not every' is known as the subject, and the noun at the end of the sentence is known as the predicate. In the examples above, the subject comes before the predicate, or as we will say, the sentences are written in SP ordering. But al-Fārābī was aware that some logicians wrote the sentences in PS ordering, i.e. with predicate before subject. The PS ordering is almost as artificial in Arabic as it is in English. Al-Fārābī illustrates it with sentences that we translate as:

Animal is true of every human.
Animal holds of every human.
Animal is in every human.

There are similar examples for the other categorical forms. As PS versions of 'Not every animal is a horse' al-Fārābī writes sentences that we translate as

Horse doesn't hold of every animal.
Horse fails to hold of some animal.
Horse is absent from some animal.

These three sentences are read as synonymous – so the scope of 'some' in the last two is the whole sentence.

The subject and predicate of a categorical sentence are called its terms. Aristotelian logic is relaxed about the syntactic form of terms. For example the sentence 'Every philosopher laughs' is acceptable as a universal affirmative sentence with 'laughs' as predicate. If you want to you can paraphrase it as 'Every philosopher is a laugher', so as to replace the verb by a noun. In PS form that becomes 'Laugher is true of every philosopher'. Al-Fārābī observed (22,11f) that in logic Aristotle generally replaced the term words and phrases by single letters of the alphabet: 'No *B* is an *A*' and so on.

Aristotle recognized two kinds of categorical sentence that have no quantifier. One is singular sentences with a proper name subject, such as 'Zayd is an animal'. The other, called indeterminate sentences, would be illustrated by 'Horse is animal' if English allowed such a sentence. Al-Fārābī believes that indeterminate sentences have a role to play in explaining how arguments that are not logically valid can still have a limited form of cogency; see the discussion of Tolerance in Section 3.21 below. Otherwise sentences with no quantifier play a very minor role in *Syllogism*.

1.2 Syllogisms

When we take two categorical sentences, we sometimes find ourselves committed to a third sentence. If this happens, we say that the first two sentences are premises, the third is the conclusion, and the premises form a syllogism.

For example the pair of premises 'Every human is an animal' and 'Every animal is sentient' produces the conclusion 'Every human is sentient'. But the pair of premises 'Every human is an animal' and 'Some animals fly' has no conclusion and doesn't form a syllogism.

What exactly does it mean to say that if we 'take' a certain pair of sentences then we are 'committed to' a third sentence? Aristotelian logicians tended to treat this relationship between premises and conclusion as undefined but recognizable from examples, so that part of the task of logic was to build up a description of the properties of the relationship by studying examples. Al-Fārābī believed that Aristotle and the other Greek philosophers had bequeathed two main kinds of example.[1]

In the first kind of example we have a scientific or philosophical question which we want to answer, for example 'Is it the case or not that the moon is spherical?' Al-Fārābī calls a two-way question of this kind an objective (*maṭlūb*). A scholar will try to resolve the question by finding a fact already known about the moon, and a fact already known about sphericity, such that when these two facts are put together they prove either that the moon is spherical or that it is not spherical. Resolving the question in this way is called 'verifying the objective' (*taṣḥīḥ al-maṭlūb*), or 'proving the objective' (*bayān al-maṭlūb*). Al-Fārābī takes from Aristotle the point that the already known facts could be either things previously proved by syllogisms, or self-evident things. In order for anything to be known at all, some things must be self-evident; al-Fārābī has his own catalogue of the ways in which a thing can be self-evident (cf. Part 7). Al-Fārābī also notes that if a syllogism uses facts proved by other syllogisms, then the syllogisms involved can be combined into a compound syllogism (cf. Part 18b).

The second kind of example occurs when two people find that they disagree about something. Disagreements are resolved by debate according to an established protocol. The two debaters are respectively the Questioner and the Responder. The Questioner begins the debate by posing an objective, which is a two-way question as in the previous paragraph. The Responder is required to choose one of the two answers to the objective, an action called concession or commitment (both *taslīm*), since it concedes a proposition to the Questioner and commits the Responder to trying to defend the conceded proposition against attacks by the Questioner. For example the Questioner can attack by inviting the Responder to make two further commitments, to premises of a syllogism whose conclusion is incompatible with the chosen proposition. Or the Responder can do the same in reverse, enticing the Questioner to commit to the premises of a syllogism which has the chosen proposition as its conclusion. Ideally this to-and-fro will eventually lead the two debaters to an agreement about which arm of the objective is true; when this happens, the debate is again said to verify the objective. (The objective may also be posed as a single sentence which the Responder can accept or reject. This sentence is said to be 'put up for consideration' (*mafrūḍ*).)

Al-Fārābī observes that in the first kind of case the outcome is new knowledge, ideally knowledge with certainty (which he calls demonstrative knowledge and studies in his book *Demonstration* [71]). In the second kind of case the outcome is only the resolution of a dispute, and the proposition that the debaters come to agree on could well be false. Nevertheless both contexts use the same rules about what propositions do or don't follow from what other propositions, rules which al-Fārābī believes were known to Plato but formalized by Aristotle. Before the rules of debate were established, the best that one could do by way of arguments was to use rhetorical devices that had the power to persuade people but no power to resolve disputes or reach the truth. Al-Fārābī gives the impression of believing that the rules of debate, which implicitly contain the rules of syllogism, came into being as a socially accepted device for settling disputes – so that the rules of syllogism are a kind of intellectual counterpart of the Marquess of Queensberry Rules of boxing. Believing this, al-Fārābī can avoid having any further views on the foundations of logic.

1.3 Figures

Al-Fārābī accepted the classification given by Aristotle for all syllogisms with two quantified categorical premises. These syllogisms are classified into moods: two syllogisms are in the same mood if they differ at most in their choice of terms. Accordingly one can describe the moods using letters for the terms; the choice of letters in the listing below became standard but not universal. There are fourteen moods, classified into three figures that are distinguished by the relative positions of the letters.

The Arabic logicians named the moods as 'first mood of the first figure', 'second mood of the first figure' etc. This relied on logicians to agree the order of listing; which they normally did, except for slight variations in the third figure. Also al-Fārābī in *Syllogism* defied the consensus by switching the second and third moods of the first figure.

The list below takes the moods in the order that al-Fārābī used in *Syllogism*. We write the premises and conclusions in the SP form, as al-Fārābī himself usually did. The Latin Scholastics later gave bespoke names *Barbara* etc. to the moods; these Latin names were unknown to al-Fārābī, but for convenience we include them below.

First figure:

Barbara (first mood of first figure). Every *C* is a *B*; every *B* is an *A*. Therefore every *C* is an *A*.

Darii (second mood of first figure). Some *C* is a *B*; every *B* is an *A*. Therefore some *C* is an *A*.

Celarent (third mood of first figure). Every *C* is a *B*; no *B* is an *A*. Therefore no *C* is an *A*.

Ferio (fourth mood of first figure). Some *C* is a *B*; no *B* is an *A*. Therefore not every *C* is an *A*.

Second figure:

Cesare (first mood of second figure). Every *C* is a *B*; no *A* is a *B*. Therefore no *C* is an *A*.

Camestres (second mood of second figure). No *C* is a *B*; every *A* is a *B*. Therefore no *C* is an *A*.

Festino (third mood of second figure). Some *C* is a *B*; no *A* is a *B*. Therefore some *C* is not an *A*.

Baroco (fourth mood of second figure). Some *C* is not a *B*; every *A* is a *B*. Therefore some *C* is not an *A*.

Third figure:

Darapti (first mood of third figure). Every *B* is a *C*; every *B* is an *A*. Therefore some *C* is an *A*.

Felapton (second mood of third figure). Every *B* is a *C*; no *B* is an *A*. Therefore some *C* is not an *A*.

Datisi (third mood of third figure). Some *B* is a *C*; every *B* is an *A*. Therefore some *C* is an *A*.

Disamis (fourth mood of third figure). Every *B* is a *C*; some *B* is an *A*. Therefore some *C* is an *A*.

Ferison (fifth mood of third figure). Some *B* is a *C*; no *B* is an *A*. Therefore some *C* is not an *A*.

Bocardo (sixth mood of third figure). Every *B* is a *C*; some *B* is not an *A*. Therefore some *C* is not an *A*.

The understanding is that if we choose any three nouns to put for *A*, *B*, *C* respectively in one of these moods, the result will be two material (i.e.

ordinary-language) premises and one material conclusion, and this conclusion will follow from these two premises.

1.4 Perfect and imperfect syllogisms

Following Aristotle, al-Fārābī believed that the moods in the first figure are perfect, i.e. self-evidently correct. The moods of the other figures are not perfect, and so we need to do extra work to show that the conclusion does follow from the premises. Aristotle showed that the moods in the second and third figures can be justified by reducing them to moods in the first figure. He suggested three procedures for doing this: conversion, ecthesis and proof by absurdity.

The method of conversion is to start with the premises of the mood being justified, but then apply one or more of the following inferences:

(*a*-conversion) Every *B* is an *A*. Therefore some *A* is a *B*.
(*e*-conversion) No *B* is an *A*. Therefore no *A* is a *B*.
(*i*-conversion) Some *B* is an *A*. Therefore some *A* is a *B*.

(Note that both *e*-conversion and *i*-conversion are the same backwards as forwards, but *a*-conversion is not.) For example we justify the mood *Cesare* in second figure by moving from the premise 'No *A* is a *B*' to 'No *B* is an *A*' by *e*-conversion, and then applying *Celarent* in first figure. In some cases we also need to apply a conversion to the conclusion in order to get the terms into the right order for the figure.

The method of ecthesis involves introducing a fourth letter. Further details of this method are best left to the Introduction to Part 12 (Section 3.12).

Aristotle's method of using proof by absurdity to reduce to first figure is never mentioned in *Syllogism*. The argument that al-Fārābī describes as syllogism of absurdity in Part 15 is not connected with reduction to first figure, though otherwise it is broadly similar to Aristotle's method; the main differences will be described in Section 3.15. As al-Fārābī presents it, the idea of the proof is to assume the contradictory opposite of the conclusion that we want to draw, and then use this assumption to deduce something 'clearly false'.

1.5 Productive versus unproductive premise-pairs

Some Aristotelian logicians count the conclusion of a syllogism as part of the syllogism; others don't. (Aristotle is unclear on the point.) Al-Fārābī is sometimes listed as one of those who didn't count the conclusion as part of the syllogism. But his real position was subtler than this: he normally assumed that any premise-pair (i.e. pair of premises) comes with an objective, as in Section 1.2 above. As a result, any premise-pair has a place in one of the three figures, and this limits its possible conclusions to four candidates. A premise-pair from which one of these candidates follows is a syllogism, and it is also said to be productive. If none of the four candidates follow from the premises, the premise-pair is unproductive.

Although Aristotle's definitions were a little different from al-Fārābī's, Aristotle had the same distinction between productive and unproductive premise-pairs. In *Analytica Priora* 1.4–6 he classified the possible categorical premise-pairs into forty-eight moods, and proved that all of these premise-pairs except those in the fourteen moods listed above were unproductive. Hence one can speak of productive moods and unproductive moods. Before modern times, logicians found Aristotle's procedure for proving non-productivity very difficult. Certainly al-Fārābī misreports it at 20,2–5. (Aristotle's procedure is discussed in Note 68 to Section 3.8 below, under the name of 'method of pseudoconclusions'.)

So instead of following Aristotle's methods, some logical authors of the first millennium AD gathered up his results on productivity into a set of jointly necessary and sufficient conditions for a categorical premise-pair in a given figure to be productive. Such a list allowed the readers to confirm that they had a complete list of productive categorical moods, without their ever having to cast their eyes over an unproductive premise-pair. But the 'conditions of productivity' (to give them their Arabic name) were presented without proofs, either Aristotle's or any other, so that they had to be taken on trust. Books using this approach were presumably written for readers who could make use of a list of categorical syllogisms – perhaps as hints for constructing lectures or arguments – but had no interest in the scientific underpinnings of logic. Al-Fārābī's *Syllogism* uses this approach.

2 Al-Fārābī and his writings

2.1 Al-Fārābī the person

The work translated in Chapter 5 below is *Syllogism* (Arabic *Qiyās*), an elementary introduction to logic by Abū Naṣr al-Fārābī.[2]

Very little is known about al-Fārābī personally. The historians begin to take note of him only a century or so after his death, and much of what they report may be gossip, guesswork or gush. But there is a consensus that he was born around AD 870, that he spent much of his life in Baghdad with visits to Aleppo, Damascus and Egypt, and that he died in AD 950.[3]

The earliest explicit reference that we have to him is his entry in the *Catalogue* (*Fihrist* [126], cf. [21] under 'Ibn al-Nadīm') of the Baghdad bookseller Ibn al-Nadīm in 988. It describes him as

(2.1.1) Abū Naṣr Muḥammad bin Muḥammad bin Muḥammad bin Ṭurkhān, whose origin is Fāriyāb in the land of Khurāsān, a leading figure in the art of logic and in ancient sciences. ([126] p. 423)

'Origin' here may be the origin of his family rather than his own birthplace. His writings give no hint that he was connected with Khurāsān (an area overlapping north-east Iran and Afghanistan), apart from occasional references in his *Letters/Particles* [75] to the vocabulary of Sogdian, the language of the Silk Road.

On the personal side, what was al-Fārābī's religion? We know from his *Letters/Particles* [75] 131,6–132,4 that he took a rationalist view of religions: the claims of all religions are philosophical claims, but presented in a form that appeals to the imagination, so as to be acceptable to the general populace. This view is unlikely to have endeared him to strict orthodox Muslims, but he could hold such a view and still regard himself as a Muslim. Probably the most that we can learn from *Syllogism* about his religious views is that he regarded religious arguments as open to assessment for their logical cogency, just like any other arguments. He urges that we should apply logic 'with tolerance' when assessing arguments in religious jurisprudence (61,4–11); but his reason lies in a general theory of arguments and is not limited to religion.

Al-Fārābī's standing in the history of music is as high as it is in philosophy. Farmer [78] p. 460 describes his *Great Book of Music* [57] as 'the greatest work on music which had been written up to his time'. In *Proportion* [73] al-Fārābī brings together logic and music in relation to the 'poetical syllogism' – though this type of syllogism is not mentioned in *Syllogism*.[4]

2.2 Neoplatonic academies and Christian schools

The passage of Aristotelian philosophy from Greek into Arabic via Syriac is well documented.[5] In this section we trace a route from the Roman Empire to the

Christian Syriac schools, for the documents that are likely to have had the most influence on al-Fārābī's logic.

Aristotle's *Organon* was publicly available in Greek from the first century BC. By the early third century AD one could consult some introductions and commentaries on logic; we discuss those due to Galen and Alexander of Aphrodisias in Section 2.3 below.

The Roman Empire boasted several academies where Greek learning was preserved and taught. From the mid third century onwards, the main academies tended towards a form of philosophy known today as Neoplatonism; it followed Plato rather than Aristotle and had strong religious overtones. But Neoplatonists were happy to include Aristotle's *Organon* as an introductory part of their teaching syllabus. The academy in Alexandria in particular, under the leadership of Ammonius Hermiou, set up a tradition of composing teaching material based on Aristotle's *Organon*.

There is no evidence of original research in logic within the Neoplatonic academies. Probably al-Fārābī reflects their view when he tells us that in the time of Aristotle

(2.2.1) scientific study reaches its limit, all of its methods are distinguished, theoretical and general universal philosophy are perfected, and there remains in it no place for research, so that it becomes an art that is purely learned and taught. ([75] 151,18–152,2)

Al-Fārābī probably saw his own logical innovations as developments in teaching or applying logic.

There were a few Aristotelian philosophers studying logic outside the Neoplatonic academies. Two in particular were Themistius and Boethius. Boethius wrote in Latin and his work was unknown to the Arabic scholars. But Themistius, who wrote in Greek, was translated into Arabic; see Section 2.3 below.

By the sixth century there were Christian theological schools in several towns of the Middle East. These schools operated in the language Syriac, a relative of Arabic but not mutually comprehensible with it. The framework of Christian theological debate was heavily indebted to Greek philosophy, and Alexandria was the leading centre for Greek philosophy. As a result, a good deal of material from the Alexandrian academy made its way to these Syriac schools, including texts of the *Organon*, commentaries and related teaching materials. Some of these texts were translated into Syriac; also new commentaries were written in Syriac. Within the *Organon*, the Syriac scholars concentrated on *Categories*, *De Interpretatione* and *Analytica Priora*, generally ignoring *Analytica Posteriora* and the later books of the *Organon*. They also recognized the *Eisagōgē* of Porphyry as an introduction to the *Organon*.[6]

Among the Syriac works that survive today are two elementary introductions to logic, the *Logic* of Paul the Persian ([128] with editor's Latin translation) and the *Treatise* of Proba ([161] with French translation). Paul the Persian's *Logic* is from the mid sixth century, and Proba's *Treatise* is dated to the mid to late sixth century.[7] Along with these two there is a work that survives only in an Arabic translation from the mid eighth century, namely the *Logic* of Ibn al-Muqaffa^c [125]. The format and style of Muqaffa^c's *Logic* are so similar to the works of Paul and Proba – particularly that of Paul – that it must have a similar origin. Moreover the colophon to Muqaffa^c's text tells us that his *Logic* is a translation of a work that had already been translated by 'Haylā al-Malkānī the Christian'; this makes it highly likely that Muqaffa^c's *Logic* is a translation of a work originally in Syriac.[8] On that basis we will refer to these works of Proba, Paul and Muqaffa^c as 'the three Syriac introductions'. No comparable Greek elementary introductions to syllogistic logic from the Neoplatonic academies survive, though they must have existed.

It's interesting to see what aspects of *Analytica Priora* the three Syriac introductions reckoned they should teach. All three introductions finish with the categorical syllogisms, i.e. at the end of *Analytica Priora* 1.7.[9] Muqaffa^c has a few remarks on conversion of modal propositions ([125] 68,13–24), but none of the three works mention modal syllogisms at all.

All three Syriac introductions differ from Aristotle by giving ordinary-language sentences of Syriac or Arabic to illustrate each of the syllogistic moods that they discuss. They use lettered sentence forms too, so that in effect they define each mood twice over. Almost certainly their reason for this redundancy is educational: the ordinary-language sentences make it easier for the students to internalize the moods.

Both Paul and Muqaffa^c follow Aristotle in listing all forty-eight categorical moods and determining which of them are productive. They distinguish between syllogistic conclusions of productive moods (which they call 'necessary' or 'sound' conclusions) and pseudoconclusions of unproductive moods (which they call 'non-necessary' or 'broken' conclusions – see Section 1.5 above). Proba by contrast never mentions the unproductive moods.

All three Syriac introductions state the conditions of productivity (cf. again Section 1.5). In Paul and Muqaffa^c these are no more than a useful mnemonic device. But for Proba, after he has removed all mention of the unproductive moods, the conditions of productivity are his only means of distinguishing which moods are productive. The effect is to elevate the conditions of productivity into an essential part of the syllogistic system.

2.3 Sources available to al-Fārābī

The main resource available to al-Fārābī for his studies of Aristotle was one that he strangely never mentions. This was the Arabic translation of all the books of the *Organon*, including *Rhetorica* and *Poetry*, and with Porphyry's *Eisagōgē* added at the beginning. This translation was a major achievement of a coordinated team of (mainly) Baghdad Christian Syriac scholars over a period of more than a hundred years. The team was led in the early years by Ḥunayn bin Isḥāq and at the end by Al-Ḥasan bin Suwār al-Khammār (Ibn Suwār). The outcome was an eleventh-century manuscript copied directly from the autograph of Ibn Suwār. It is now lodged in the Paris Bibliothèque Nationale as the manuscript Arabe 2346. The manuscript Istanbul Topkapı Sarayı Ahmad III 3362 appears to be a slightly earlier version of the same text.[10]

We will refer to the text of Arabe 2346 as the Baghdad Standard. It has been published by Badawi [14] and Jabre [109]. The text was being annotated, and presumably revised where necessary, until late in the tenth century. The translations were in most cases made from Syriac translations of Aristotle's Greek. But each book of the *Organon* had its own translation history. The translation of *Analytica Priora* used in the Baghdad Standard was first made in the mid ninth century by Theodorus.[11] The annotations to the manuscript Arabe 2346 refer to two other translations of *Analytica Priora*, one of them by the early ninth century scholar Ibn al-Biṭrīq, but neither of these translations survives.

In his long commentaries (on which see Section 2.4 below) al-Fārābī follows the text of the Baghdad Standard.[12] But al-Fārābī's dependence on the Baghdad Standard is not always apparent in *Syllogism*, which quotes Aristotle in general sense rather than verbatim.[13]

Besides the text of *Analytica Priora*, al-Fārābī will also have had access to commentaries on this work. The *Catalogue* of Nadīm, published in 988, mentions half a dozen commentaries on *Analytica Priora*, all presumably in Arabic, as follows ([126] p. 405f).

(a) The *Catalogue* mentions two commentaries by Alexander of Aphrodisias, one of them incomplete and the other running 'to the end of the three categorical figures'. Very likely these were two copies of the same Arabic translation of Alexander's *Commentary on Book One of Prior Analytics* [5]. The phrase about the three categorical figures seems to mean that the commentary went only as far as *Analytica Priora* 1.22, or perhaps only 1.7. But since we know that the Greek original ran to the end of *Analytica Priora* i, this may refer only to the copies that Nadīm happened to have. Al-Fārābī could have had access to the whole work.

(b) The *Catalogue* mentions a commentary on *Analytica Priora* by Themistius. This commentary survives in part, in a Hebrew translation or paraphrase probably made from an Arabic version; see Rosenberg and Manekin [136]. There are clear indications that the commentary was used later by Avicenna and Averroes, and that it was their main source of information about the logic of Theophrastus.[14] Al-Fārābī cites Themistius by name in his *Long Commentary on Prior Analytics* [74] at 473,9f and 487,14–18.

(c) A commentary by John 'the Grammarian' (i.e. Philoponus). We have no direct evidence that al-Fārābī used this commentary.

(d) A commentary by Abū Isḥāq Ibrāhīm Quwayrī 'in the form of a tree' (i.e. presumably based on Platonic division in a style favoured by late Neoplatonists).[15] Al-Fārābī never mentions this work, and it is now lost.

(e) A commentary by Mattā. We have no further information about this.

(f) A commentary by al-Kindī. Kindī was the leading Aristotelian scholar of the mid ninth century, and a keen supporter of the moves to translate classical Greek philosophy into Arabic. But this item is probably a misattribution, since a commentary on *Analytica Priora* hardly fits his known interests.[16]

Another work relevant to *Syllogism* is reported in the *Catalogue* with the words 'Themistius commented on some of the topics [in Aristotle's *Topica*]' [126] p. 406. Hasnawi [97], working from quotations by Averroes and passages of Boethius and Abū al-Barakāt, argues that Themistius wrote both a *Commentary on Topics* and a more free-standing work discussing some topics, and he is able to make a partial reconstruction of these two works.

There are also two works of Galen that would almost certainly have been relevant to *Syllogism* if al-Fārābī had them. These are his *Institutio Logica* [83] and his *De Demonstratione*. The first never appears in Arabic records. In the ninth century the translator Ḥunayn bin Isḥāq knew of the second work and invested years of effort searching for a copy. He did eventually find a poor copy of about half the work ([23] Arabic text p. 47). Maimonides [139] 80,9–81,5 quotes al-Fārābī's *Long Commentary on Prior Analytics* as criticizing this work, but it is not clear how much of the work al-Fārābī had, particularly since his quoted comments address only a single brief quotation from the book.

An essay by Alexander of Aphrodisias on conversions [7] and an essay of Themistius on reduction of second and third figure syllogisms to first figure [154] survive only in medieval Arabic translations. Al-Fārābī could well have known both of them, and they both have something to do with syllogisms, though we see nothing in them directly relevant to *Syllogism*.

In one interesting case, detective work by modern scholars uncovered a Persian (or possibly Syriac) work on logic that al-Fārābī borrowed from without acknowledgement. The Persian Neoplatonist philosopher Ibn Miskawayh wrote a work [123] entitled *Ranking of Happiness*. In it ([123] 49,6f) he quoted extensively from a work which 'Paul wrote to Anushirvan' (the Persian emperor Khosraw I). Paul must be Paul the Persian whom we know from Section 2.2. Gutas [89] compares Miskawayh's text in detail with the section on logic in al-Fārābī's *Catalogue of the Sciences* [76], and establishes that al-Fārābī has used Paul's text at the very least as a template for his own work. The template includes passages of the *Catalogue* that have sometimes been quoted as expressing distinctive views of al-Fārābī.

This example with al-Fārābī and Paul is unlikely to be the only case where an Arabic writer borrowed heavily from Neoplatonic sources. For example Gutas [90] p. 45 comments that Abū al-Faraj bin al-Ṭayyib in the early eleventh century 'could do no better than write commentaries on the *Eisagoge* and the *Categories* that are practically translations of those produced five centuries earlier by David and Elias'.

From a fragment of al-Fārābī's work *The Rise of Philosophy* quoted by Uṣaybiᶜa,[17] we learn that two Christian Syriac scholars, Yūḥannā ibn Ḥaylān and Ibrāhīm al-Marwazī, moved to Baghdad and began teaching there. Al-Fārābī tells us that he and Mattā learned Aristotle's logic under these two scholars, al-Fārābī under Yūḥannā and Mattā under Ibrāhīm. He tells us also that under the Romans, Christian authorities had forbidden the teaching of later parts of *Analytica Priora*, for fear that they might be a threat to Christian doctrine; he adds that the Muslims had no such inhibitions. He also remarks pointedly that while Mattā followed the long-established Christian custom of reading only as far as the categorical syllogisms, al-Fārābī read with his tutor as far as the end of the *Analytica Posteriora*.

Al-Fārābī must have had some reasons for making these various points, though we may not be able to recover all of them. There seem to be an anti-

Christian animus and a suggestion that his contemporary Mattā had a defective education in Aristotle's logic. Perhaps there was poor chemistry between al-Fārābī and the Baghdad Christians; perhaps also al-Fārābī wanted to dispel the suggestion that he had been a pupil of Mattā.[18]

But more positively, al-Fārābī is claiming that through Yūḥannā he had access to the Syriac tradition of scholarship and what it inherited from the Neoplatonist academies. Probably he knew works from this tradition that we have no record of.[19]

2.4 Al-Fārābī's writings on logic

Al-Fārābī's logical writings fall roughly under three heads: long commentaries, abridgements, and others. Long commentaries and abridgements are both tied to particular books of the *Organon*; the other writings are free-standing.

A long commentary (*sharḥ*) is a substantial work, maybe running to several hundred pages. The author splits the work being commented on into paragraphs. Each paragraph in turn is quoted or identified, and the author runs through it phrase by phrase, making explanatory comments. Short essays on particular issues may also be included. The style was taken over from Greek examples such as Alexander's *Commentary on Book One of Prior Analytics* [5]. This kind of commentary is sometimes also called 'marginal annotations' (*ta*ᶜ*līqāt*), with reference to a format where the paragraphs being commented on were written as the central text and the comments were put in the margin. (This format can still be seen in some older printed Arabic books.)

Al-Fārābī wrote enough long commentaries to suggest that he aimed to write one for each book of the *Organon* (which for purposes of this section we take to include the *Eisagōgē*). But only one of his long commentaries survives in full. This is his *Long Commentary on De Interpretatione* [59]. Zimmermann [165] published a translation of it, edited with a large amount of useful background information.

We also have perhaps a third of al-Fārābī's *Long Commentary on Prior Analytics*, published in a non-critical edition by Dāneshpazhūh [74]. This text covers *Analytica Priora* 2.11, 61b1 to 2.27, 70a21. A small amount of the missing content can be reconstructed from references in Avicenna, Maimonides and Averroes.[20, 21]

Our evidence for al-Fārābī's other long commentaries is largely from Hebrew or Latin translations. For *Categories* see Zonta [166]; for *Analytica Posteriora* see

Chase [36]; for *Topica* see Zonta [167]; for *Rhetorica* see the partial Latin translation *Didascalia* in [60].

An abridgement (*mukhtaṣar*), also called an epitome, is a more free-flowing kind of commentary. In al-Fārābī's case it usually picks up some points from the book being commented on, and develops them from al-Fārābī's own point of view.

The books of al-Fārābī that are commonly taken to be abridgements are the following;

	Organon	**al-Fārābī's abridgement**
	Eisagōgḗ	[63] (*Eisagōgḗ*)
	Categories	[64] (*Categories*)
	De Interpretatione	[65] (*Short Interpretation*)
	Analytica Priora	[66] (*Syllogism*)
(2.4.1)	"	[67] (*Short Syllogism*)
	Analytica Posteriora	[71] (*Demonstration*)
	Topica	[68] (*Analysis*)
	"	[70] (*Debate*)
	Sophistical Refutations	[69] (*Sophistry*)
	Rhetorica	[60] (Rhetoric)
	Poetics	[119] (*Poetics*)

The list shows that al-Fārābī wrote at least one abridgement for each book of the *Organon*. This can hardly be an accident. The list also shows that for two books of the *Organon*, namely *Analytica Priora* and *Topica*, he wrote two abridgements each. But the two cases are different, in the following way.

Al-Fārābī judged that the *Topica* is not a homogeneous book. It contains material of three different kinds. First there is material on the nature and construction of syllogisms; his abridgement *Analysis* [68] comments on this material. Second there is material on the purpose and conduct of debates; his abridgement *Debate* [70] answers to this material. And third there is a discussion of definition; he moves this to join other material on definition in *Analytica Posteriora*. So there is no real duplication in having both *Analysis* and *Debate*.[22]

By contrast *Syllogism* and *Short Syllogism* are alternative treatments of the same material. In Section 2.7 below we compare them in detail.

A number of writers, both medieval and modern, have assumed that al-Fārābī intended his abridgements of all the books of the *Organon* to be published as a single book. This hypothetical work is sometimes referred to as the Summary (*talkhīs*) or the Synopsis (*jawāmi*ᶜ). Nadīm may have been referring to a collection of this kind when in his *Catalogue* [126] p. 423 he attributed to al-Fārābī a 'synopsis of the books of logic'. Likewise Uṣaybiᶜa reports that al-Fārābī wrote an 'abridgement of all the books of logic'. Averroes believed that he had such an abridgement written by al-Fārābī, and he made his own abstract (*tajrīd*) of the whole book.[23]

Whether or not al-Fārābī intended his abridgements as a single book, it was convenient for copyists to assemble them as a single manuscript. As we will see in the next section, the main manuscripts of *Syllogism* all come from collections of this kind. The earliest known witness to this arrangement is the manuscript Escurial, Real Biblioteca, Derenbourg 612, dated to AD 1269, which contains commentaries attributed to Avempace; the commentaries run through a string of al-Fārābī's abridgements, finishing with that on *Analytica Posteriora*.[24]

However, the evidence from Escurial 612 is not all in one direction. Its commentary on *Syllogism* [17] 180,2–5 makes the sound point that *Syllogism* could hardly have been intended as a part of a book that also contained an abridgement of *De Interpretatione*, since *Syllogism* opens with several Parts that simply repeat definitions from this earlier book of the *Organon*.

The evidence that al-Fārābī's own texts offer us for this 'synopsis of the books of logic' is frankly negative. Within a single book al-Fārābī quite often refers back to things he has said earlier in the book. (Thus in *Syllogism* we have 'as we said' (*ᶜalā mā qulnā*) at 43,7; 44,8 and 44,15.[25]) By contrast there are almost no links of this kind between separate abridgements. Worse still, al-Fārābī's abridgement of *Analytica Posteriora* opens with a reference back to material that al-Fārābī says has already been given, about means of achieving knowledge ([71] 19,5–13), but al-Fārābī's description doesn't correlate with any of his surviving abridgements of earlier books of the *Organon*. In fact the relevant commentary in Escurial 612 points out this discrepancy ([45] vol. 3 p. 294,10–13). So the abridgement of *Analytica Posteriora* may well have been written to be part of a collection, but if so the collection didn't consist of abridgements that we have today.

Henceforth we will treat *Syllogism* as an independent abridgement of *Analytica Priora*.

There remain al-Fārābī's writings on logic which are not commentaries on Greek books. Most of these were written to prepare the student for study of the *Organon*; in this they reflect the profusion of prolegomena in the tradition of the Alexandrian academy. Examples are his *Introductory Risala* [61] and *Five*

Sections [62]. Another work of this genre is al-Fārābī's *Indication of the Way to Happiness* [72], which concludes that the way to happiness is through logic, and that logic needs to be approached through a preliminary study of language. Mahdī ([58] Introduction 24–8) has argued that al-Fārābī expected the reader of this book to move on to al-Fārābī's book *Expressions* [58], which introduces the vocabulary of logic, and then on to a study of the *Categories* through al-Fārābī's abridgement [64].

Al-Fārābī has another book which is relevant to logic but far too original to be pigeonholed within Alexandrian traditions. This is his *Letters/Particles* [75]. Note 34 to Section 2.8 below will comment on its contribution to the philosophy of language. The book also contains a theory of the historical origins of logic.

2.5 The manuscripts of *Syllogism*

Our translation of *Syllogism* follows the text given by Rafīq al-ᶜAjam in the second volume of his edition [3] of logical works of al-Fārābī. On pages 40–9 of his first volume al-ᶜAjam explains his choice and use of the manuscripts. He lists eighteen manuscripts of *Syllogism* that he consulted. All of them are from the eighteenth century or thereabouts. Of these he chose to work with five manuscripts *B*, *H*, *E*, *M* and *K* as follows:

***B* = Bratislava 231 (also numbered TE 41)** This manuscript is in the Bašagić Collection at the University Library in Bratislava. At the time of writing there is a web page <http://retrobib.ulib.sk/Basagic/frames.htm> with some information about this collection. A note in the text of the manuscript indicates that the copying was begun in the year 1115 h = AD 1703/4.

***H* = Süleymaniye Ḥamidiye 812** in the Süleymaniye Library in Istanbul. The manuscript is dated 1133 h = AD 1720/1.

***E* = Emanet Hazinesi 1730** in the Topkapı Palace Museum in Istanbul. The manuscript is dated 1089 h = AD 1678/9.

***M* = Tehran 595** in the Majles-e Shurā-ye Melli (Library of the Iranian National Assembly) in Tehran. The date of the manuscript is not recorded.

***K* = Kermān 211** in the Kermān collection of the University of Tehran. The manuscript is dated 1100 h = AD 1688/9.

Pages of all five of these manuscripts are reproduced in [3] volume two.

Grignaschi ([88] Appendix I A) sets out charts comparing the contents of several manuscripts, including the five above. Grignaschi's charts split the five into three groups: a group *B* and *H*, a second group *M* and *K*, and a third group consisting of just *E*. All three groups carry some introductory material before the books of the *Organon*; for example they all contain an abridgement of Porphyry's *Eisagōgḗ*. Of the books of the *Organon*, all three groups contain abridgements of *Categories, De Interpretatione, Analytica Priora* and *Analytica Posteriora* in this order. The groups differ in what they add immediately before or immediately after the abridgement of *Analytica Posteriora*. These differences seem to be at least partly a response to al-Fārābī's rearrangement of the material in *Topica*. Here is the material added between *Syllogism* and the abridgement of *Analytica Posteriora*:

B,H	***M,K***	***E***
'transfer' and 'jurisprudence' at end of *Syllogism*	–	('transfer' and 'jurisprudence' at end of *Short Syllogism*)
Analysis	–	–
abr of *Soph Refs*	abr of *Soph Refs*	–

And here is the material added after the abridgement of *Analytica Posteriora*:

B,H	***M,K***	***E***
Debate	–	*Debate*
abr of *Rhetorica*	–	–
abr of *Poetics*	–	–

Grignaschi's charts indicate that the manuscripts *B* and *H* contain all the abridgements found in *M*, *K* or *E*, and moreover they include extra material in *Syllogism*. This extra material consists of Parts 19 and 20 on Transfer and on Jurisprudential Syllogisms respectively; these two Parts are in *E*, but attached to *Short Syllogism* instead of *Syllogism*. We will refer to them as the Tailpiece.

Al-ᶜAjam ([3] vol. 2, pp. 11–64) provides a critical edition of *Syllogism*, giving precedence to the readings of the manuscript *B*. Türker [157] has published a text of *Short Syllogism* including the Tailpiece, based on four manuscripts available to her in Istanbul. Al-ᶜAjam's critical apparatus for the Tailpiece includes readings of *E*, together with the main differences between Türker's edition and his own text.

2.6 The structure of *Syllogism*

In terms of its relationship to Aristotle's *Organon*, *Syllogism* falls naturally into four segments as follows:

Segment	Part	*Syllogism*	Aristotle
First	1,2	Propositions	*De Interpretatione*
	3–5	Opposites	
Second			*Analytica Priora*
	6	Conversion	1.2
	7	Known without syllogism	
	8	Syllogism	1.1
	9	Categorical syllogisms	
	10	The figures	
	11	First figure	1.4
	12	Second figure	1.5
	13	Third figure	1.6
Third	14	Hypothetical syllogisms	1.29,44
	15	Syllogism of absurdity	1.23,29
	16	Induction	2.23,25
	17	Likening	2.24
	18a	Syllogisms in general	
	18b–d	Kinds of compound syllogism	1.25,42
Fourth = Tailpiece	19	Transfer	
	20	Jurisprudential syllogisms	

This division into numbered segments is ours, not al-Fārābī's. He gives the numbering of Parts, up to Part 18 (which he doesn't subdivide). The numbering of Parts 19 and 20 in the Tailpiece is a modern convention.

The double line through the middle of the table, separating Part 13 from Part 14, marks the point where al-Fārābī moves beyond the categorical syllogisms. Up to this point he is covering the same range of material as the three Syriac introductions (cf. Section 2.2), so that he could have used these or similar works as models to follow. Below the double line al-Fārābī is sailing free in the open ocean with no earlier textbooks to serve as maps.

The first of the four segments consists of material that correlates with *De Interpretatione*, and the second segment keeps broadly in step with *Analytica*

Priora 1.1–7. In the first segment a difference between al-Fārābī and the earlier writers is apparent. All of the Syriac introductions begin with an introduction to logic, and Muqaffa[c] includes so much material from *Categories* and *De Interpretatione* that his work is sometimes described as containing abridgements of these works. Al-Fārābī by contrast dives straight into the material from *De Interpretatione* that is a prerequisite for syllogisms, in particular the definitions of the different kinds of proposition.

The second segment runs in parallel with the three Syriac introductions, allowing us to compare the four works. Paul and Muqaffa[c] review all forty-eight categorical moods, and show in each case that it is productive or that it is not. Proba and al-Fārābī omit all the unproductive moods. Also all four authors include the conditions of productivity, but Paul and Muqaffa[c] put them *after* the listing of moods, whereas Proba and al-Fārābī put them *before* the listing. All four writers depart from Aristotle by using natural language sentences to illustrate the moods that they are discussing; this reduces the artificiality of the sentence forms, and no doubt the readers will be grateful. Al-Fārābī takes this move a step further: like the Syriac introductions he uses the Aristotelian PS ordering to express the moods, but then he departs from the Syriac introductions by repeating each mood in SP form.

We move on beyond the double line and into the third and fourth segments. Although most of the material below the double line does correlate with some later parts of *Analytica Priora*, very little here can be seen as any kind of exposition of Aristotle's text.

The material in Parts 14, 15 and 18b, all of it in the third segment, is a natural continuation of the preceding treatment of categorical syllogisms. We are given some rules of reasoning and some conditions on their use. Part 15 on *reductio ad absurdum* gives a new way of using categorical syllogisms; Part 18b explains how several categorical syllogisms can be fitted together into a single argument. Both these parts loosely reflect material that is in *Analytica Priora* but later than the listing of syllogisms. The hypothetical syllogisms of Part 14 have a different origin, as we will see in Section 3.14 below. But al-Fārābī would probably have excused their presence here by pointing to Aristotle's unfulfilled promise at *Analytica Priora* 1.44, 50a40–50b2 to write later about the number of syllogisms 'from a hypothesis'.

The remainder of the third and fourth segments, amounting to about half of *Syllogism*, moves away from the description of syllogisms and towards the analysis of written or spoken arguments. Part 18a is a brief introduction to analysis of arguments and would more sensibly have been put before Part 16.

A theme that recurs through all of the six Parts 16, 17, 18c, 18d, 19 and 20 is a pair of argument forms, induction (*istiqrā'*) and likening (*tamthīl*). These two forms of argument clearly correlate with *Analytica Priora* 2.23f on induction and analogy. In his *Long Commentary on Prior Analytics* [74] al-Fārābī studies these two sections of *Analytica Priora* in detail; but what he says in the six Parts of *Syllogism* is not close to Aristotle, and it is probably unhelpful to try to draw *Syllogism* together with this section of the *Long Commentary on Prior Analytics.*

One can detect a second theme running through these six parts of *Syllogism*, namely the range of nonsyllogistic operations that are available to a logician. Al-Fārābī mentions a method for proving universal affirmative sentences, under the name of Accepting and Rejecting; in his *Analysis* [68] he relates this method not to syllogisms but to topics of consequence as discussed in Aristotle's *Topica.* Also in these six parts of *Syllogism* al-Fārābī mentions methods of searching, for terms or families of terms that will allow some proofs to be constructed. The search procedures required for induction are not the same as those required for likening, and al-Fārābī finds himself discussing how these procedures interact. He also discusses what is the syllogistic content, or the 'syllogistic potential' as he calls it, of proofs constructed using any or all of these procedures.

What is the structure of Parts 16, 17, 18c, 18d, 19 and 20? There is no satisfactory answer. For example Parts 18d and 19 cover very much the same points, but in a slightly different vocabulary; also the account in Part 19 is both more coherent and more readable than that in Part 18d. This is one of several indications that the Tailpiece (Parts 19 and 20) was not written to be read as a part of *Syllogism*. Even with the Tailpiece removed, Parts 16, 17, 18c and 18d fail to present a convincing structure (for example why are Parts 15 and 18c separated, since they both concentrate on induction?). To cast more light, we have to change the question and ask how the Tailpiece was intended to be related to the remaining parts of *Syllogism* and *Short Syllogism*, and how these remaining parts relate to each other.

2.7 *Syllogism* and *Short Syllogism*

Al-Fārābī has given us two abridgements of *Analytica Priora*, namely *Syllogism* [66] and *Short Syllogism* [67].[26] The Tailpiece (Parts 19 and 20 in *Syllogism*) is found attached sometimes to *Syllogism*, but more often to *Short Syllogism*; it is set apart from both of them by its slower and more discursive style. When the

Tailpiece is removed we will speak of the curtailed *Syllogism* and the curtailed *Short Syllogism*.

In ᶜAjam's edition ([3] vol. 2) the curtailed *Syllogism* takes up thirty-five pages, the curtailed *Short Syllogism* takes up twenty-nine, and the Tailpiece takes up twenty. The two curtailed texts cover very much the same topics and in the same way, though they have little text in common. Lameer [116] p. 14 is surely right that they read like two editions of the same work, with the later edition substantially reworked from the earlier.

Here is a chart of the correspondences between the two curtailed texts:

Curtailed *Syllogism*	Curtailed *Short Syllogism*
1,2. Propositions	1. Propositions
3–5. Opposites	2. Opposites
6. Conversion	
7. Known without syllogism	3. Kinds of proposition
8. Syllogism	
9. Categorical syllogisms	4. Categorical syllogisms
10. The figures	
11. First figure	
12. Second figure	
13. Third figure	
14. Hypothetical syllogisms	5. Hypothetical syllogisms
15. Syllogism of absurdity	6. Syllogism of absurdity
16. Induction	8. Induction
17. Likening	
18a. Syllogisms in general	
18b–d. Kinds of compound syllogism	7. Compound syllogisms

To judge which of the two is the earlier, we go first to the individual parts where there are the most significant differences between the two. One of these is the section on categorical syllogisms. In *Syllogism* al-Fārābī defines each mood in five different formats; this leads to a large amount of unnecessary repetition. In *Short Syllogism* by contrast he uses only two formats. Also in *Short Syllogism* he avoids mood definitions that use letters instead of material terms; he may be the first logician to defy the authority of Aristotle by not using such definitions. As a result of these changes, the account in *Short Syllogism* contains the same logical information as *Syllogism* but is more readable and has much less redundancy.

Also *Short Syllogism* corrects the eccentric ordering of the first figure moods in *Syllogism*, which puts *Darii* ahead of *Celarent*. Everything points to the *Short Syllogism* version of this material being a tidied-up and improved version of that in *Syllogism*.

Another case is the two sections that discuss the syllogism of absurdity. We will see that the account in *Syllogism* makes false claims about impossibility; these false claims are removed in *Short Syllogism*.[27] Again the only plausible way round is that *Short Syllogism* is an improvement of *Syllogism*.

In the curtailed *Syllogism* the treatment of induction is split between two parts, Part 16 and Part 18c, with some extraneous material between them (notably Part 18a, which seems misplaced). In the curtailed *Short Syllogism* the same information about induction is gathered together in a single section, and nothing corresponds to the misplaced Part 18a. Again *Short Syllogism* is the version that shows clear editorial improvements. There is a similar pattern in the material on opposite pairs of sentences; in *Syllogism* this is needlessly split between three Parts, but *Short Syllogism* brings it together as an integrated whole.

Note 88 to Section 3.14 below mentions an advance in the development of hypothetical syllogisms; on present evidence this advance appears first in *Short Syllogism*, and it is not found in *Syllogism*.

Since the comparisons above send a clear message and there seems to be nothing pointing in the opposite direction, we can take it as established that the curtailed *Syllogism* is the earlier version and the curtailed *Short Syllogism* is the later.[28, 29]

Turning to the Tailpiece, we note first that it cannot have been written as a part of *Syllogism*. There is an unacceptable amount of repetition between Parts 17 and 18d in *Syllogism* on the one hand and the Tailpiece on the other hand.[30] The repetition between Part 18d and Part 19 is particularly severe. Also the exposition in Part 18d is poor; it gives an impression that al-Fārābī is trying to cram the contents of his source text into a space too small to hold them. In fact this comparison shows that the Tailpiece was almost certainly written *after* the curtailed *Syllogism*.

This raises the question whether the Tailpiece was originally written as a self-standing essay, or whether it was always intended to be attached to a work that classified the moods of syllogisms. The evidence on this is mixed. On the one hand there are features of the language of the Tailpiece that set it apart from both the curtailed *Syllogism* and the curtailed *Short Syllogism*.[31] At any rate the

Tailpiece does hang together; the way that its final paragraphs return to its opening topic of transfer gives it a kind of literary unity.

On the other hand the Tailpiece is largely non-syllogistic, but there are references to some specific moods, for example *Barbara* (45,9), *Darapti* (52,18), *Felapton* (49,10) and a connected hypothetical mood (50,17). Some references to syllogistic moods are accompanied by phrases such as 'the aforementioned' or 'as we said above' (47,13; 50,17; 57,16.20; 59,10). So in its present form the Tailpiece certainly belongs with a work that lists syllogistic moods. This is not a decisive point, because the Tailpiece will have been adjusted to fit a text that it had become attached to; we can point to at least one place where this happened.[32]

A possible scenario is that after writing the curtailed *Syllogism*, al-Fārābī felt that Part 18 contained interesting ideas that deserved to be expounded at greater leisure. In the course of thinking about this, he could have hit on the idea that what he calls the Synthesis version of likening would also give a framework for understanding some well-known examples of analogy (*qiyās*) in Arabic jurisprudence; this idea is prominent in Part 20. The result was a draft of the Tailpiece. Perhaps he decided that this essay would work best if it was attached to a version of the curtailed *Syllogism* that was revised and trimmed-down and used fewer innovations in technical vocabulary. But all of this scenario is speculation.[33]

2.8 Al-Fārābī's use of language

What languages did al-Fārābī know? His written Arabic is fluent and not unstylish. As a cultured resident of Baghdad he probably knew Persian. But he didn't know Greek; see Zimmermann [165] p. xlvii on his errors in describing basic Greek words. He could have picked up some Syriac from his professional associates in Baghdad, but there is no positive evidence that he did. There is nothing to indicate that he knew any Turkic language.

The historian Ibn Abī Uṣaybiʿa [158] p. 606 reports that al-Fārābī exchanged lessons in logic and linguistics with the linguist Abū Bakr bin al-Sarrāj al-Baghdādī. Uṣaybiʿa's report could be an inference from three facts: first, Sarrāj was known to be interested in logic; second, al-Fārābī was known to be interested in linguistics; and third, the two scholars were near contemporaries, both living in Baghdad, and were the leading innovators of the time in their respective disciplines. There are issues here that are important for assessing al-Fārābī's contribution in general; but they are only marginally related to *Syllogism*, so we relegate them to a note.[34]

When we turn to al-Fārābī's use of Arabic, our first port of call has to be the vocabulary of the Baghdad Standard translation of the *Organon*. From this source al-Fārābī took *qaḍīya* 'proposition', *mūjib* 'affirmative', *sālib* 'negative', *kullī* 'universal', *juz'ī* 'particular', *kayfīya* 'quality', *kammīya* 'quantity', *sūr* 'quantifier', *muhmal* 'indeterminate', *mawḍūᶜ* 'subject', *maḥmūl* 'predicate', *ḍarūrī* 'necessary', *mumkin* 'possible/contingent', *maᶜdūl* 'metathetic', *qiyās* 'syllogism', *muqaddama* 'premise', *natīja* 'conclusion', *antaja* 'entails', *lazima* 'follows from', *wujūd* 'truth' or 'existence', *khalf* 'absurdity', *istiqrā'* 'induction', *maqbūl* 'accepted'. (Zimmermann [164] discusses many of these words and finds Syriac origins for some of them. See also Hugonnard-Roche [107].)

Syllogism shows some moves beyond this established vocabulary. One example is the word *ḍarb*; as we note in Section 3.10, this word seems to transmogrify during the course of the book, from its normal Arabic sense of 'kind' or 'type' to the technical name for syllogistic mood. We note also the appearance at 12,2 of the new word *muntij* 'productive'. As a participle of the verb *yuntiju* (in the sense 'producing that ...') this word is found in the Baghdad Standard at [109] 357,17 and 373,10; but at *Syllogism* 12,2 it is an adjective naming a class of premise-pairs, and this is new. Also al-Fārābī speaks of categorical propositions and syllogisms as *ḥamlī*, a derivative from the already known *ḥaml* 'predication' (as in *maḥmūl*); this replaces the name *jazmī* used in the Baghdad Standard for non-hypothetical syllogisms. Through al-Fārābī's influence *ḥamlī* became widely accepted; in fact when he did use the old word *jazmī* in Parts 19 and 20 of *Syllogism*, some copyist found it unintelligible and assumed it must be a mistake for *juz'ī* 'particular'. Another newly derived adjective that is found in *Syllogism* and became widespread through al-Fārābī's influence was *wujūdī*; normally he used it of non-modalized propositions, but in *Syllogism* 12,18 and in *Long Commentary on De Interpretatione* [59] 17,9 it is given the more specialized meaning of copular verb.

It's interesting to find that the new words *muntij* as 'productive', *ḍarb* as 'mood', *ḥamlī* as 'categorical' and *wujūdī* as 'non-modal' all appear in the translation by Abū ᶜUthmān al-Dimashqī of Alexander of Aphrodisias's essay *On Conversion* [7]. (Cf. also *dā'iman* 'permanently' in Note 59 to Section 3.6.) The exact dates of al-Dimashqī are unknown, but he was appointed chief physician at a hospital in Baghdad in 914, which makes it likely that he and al-Fārābī were close contemporaries. He read Greek (Peters [129] pp. 21f) and was a leading translator of Greek logic. It would make sense for him and al-Fārābī, the most progressive logician of that era, to discuss translations and make some joint decisions.[35]

Almost certainly al-Fārābī imported into logic from Arabic linguistics the term *istithnā'* 'exception', by a route which we explain in Section 3.14 below. Another word that he may have borrowed from the linguists is *ḍamīr* for 'implicit'; see Section 3.3 below. It also seems likely that the use of the root *fyd* in the sense of providing information came into logic from linguistics through al-Fārābī; see Note 34.

Also the evidence is that al-Fārābī was responsible for the widespread use in logic and philosophy more generally of the phrase *min ḥaythu* 'insofar as' or 'because'. The word *ḥaythu* originally meant 'where', so that *min ḥaythu* should mean 'from where'; but already Qur'ānic interpreters had started to weaken the literal sense of 'from' in this phrase. In *Syllogism* the phrase is not very common; it means 'whenever' at 44,15 and 'because' at 50,15. In later works of al-Fārābī it becomes very much more frequent, with an abstract meaning.[36]

The word *ḥukm* 'judgement' is frequent in the Baghdad Standard version of *De Interpretatione* as a name for subject-predicate propositions, but we will note in Section 3.1 below that in *Syllogism* it nearly always means the content, i.e. the part of a subject-predicate proposition that is asserted of the subject. In al-Fārābī's writings this usage seems to be mainly restricted to *Syllogism* and *Short Syllogism*, and to the Tailpiece in particular. Al-Fārābī's use of *irtifā'* follows suit: the Arabic Aristotle used it for rejecting propositions, whereas al-Fārābī uses it for denying that a given *ḥukm* (in the new sense) holds of a given subject.

Three other usages seem personal to al-Fārābī; none of them had much effect on later writers. One is his use of *ṣaḥḥa* and *yaṣiḥḥu*, both of which literally mean 'is true', to mean 'is verified'. This seems to be an abbreviation of a phrase that he uses several times, *yaṣiḥḥu la-nā* 'it is true for us', in the sense that we have confirmed its truth. The second is his use of *mafrūḍ* to mean not 'assumed' (as in the Baghdad Standard) but 'put up for consideration' (as at the opening of a debate). This is of a piece with his tendency to use debate as a setting that gives a structure to logical moves. The third is his use of the verb *inṭawā*, which he uses in a broad sense of 'involve' (as at 34,5; 38,11; 39,10); apart from Averroes in his [137], later logicians made no use of it.

With the possible exception of *ḍamīr*, none of al-Fārābī's terminological innovations mentioned above rely on metaphor. This accords with his statement at *Letters/Particles* [75] 165,3–5, that philosophy never uses metaphors. One curious example is the word *natīja*, which was imported into logic from the vocabulary of reproduction of camels and sheep. Other logicians, including Avicenna, Averroes and the Brethren of Purity, were happy to exploit the implications of the biological metaphor, but al-Fārābī seems not even to notice it.

3 The Book *Syllogism*

Syllogism begins with a list of contents, which we count as Part 0. This Part may not be by al-Fārābī; the list of contents in the parallel work *Short Syllogism* is followed by a phrase telling us where we start reading the words of al-Fārābī himself.

3.1 Introducing Part 1: Sentences

Parts 1 to 5 of *Syllogism* collect up information about sentences, the forms of sentences, and kinds of opposition between sentences. This is material that Aristotle placed in *De Interpretatione*. But al-Fārābī makes no reference here to *Short Interpretation* [65], his own abridgement of *De Interpretatione*. So Parts 1 to 5 seem to be designed to make *Syllogism* a self-contained work.

Al-Fārābī opens Part 1 by defining proposition (*qaḍīya*) or declarative sentence (*qawl jāzim*). The Arabic Aristotle had defined sentence (*qawl*) in *De Interpretatione* [147] 113,2–114,2 essentially as a minimal piece of meaningful discourse, and a declarative sentence as one that 'contains either truth or falsity' – as opposed to requests, commands etc.

Al-Fārābī ignores these definitions given in *De Interpretatione*.[37] Instead his definition of proposition in Part 1 reads like a revision of the definition of 'premise' that the Baghdad Standard gives in *Analytica Priora* 1.1, 24a16f:

(3.1.1) A premise is a sentence which affirms one concept of another or denies one concept of another. ([109] 180,6)

Here 'concept' is *shay'*, literally 'thing'; but the things in question are meaningful parts of a sentence, in effect the concepts expressed by terms of the sentence. Al-Fārābī borrows this usage from the Baghdad Standard, and very often 'concept' is the best translation of his *shay'*. In fact Arabic has two common words for 'thing', namely *shay'* and *amr*; al-Fārābī likes to use *amr* for the concept that is affirmed or denied of another concept, and *shay'* for the other concept.[38]

In his definition of proposition al-Fārābī combines Aristotle's 'affirms' and 'denies' into the single notion 'judges', which in this context could also be translated 'asserts'; to affirm is to assert affirmatively and to deny is to assert negatively. On our present evidence it was al-Fārābī who introduced the notion of judgement (*ḥukm*) into the toolkit of Arabic logic. The notion appears only occasionally in the first half of *Syllogism*, but from Part 16 onwards it is one of al-Fārābī's favourite words, appearing over 140 times. So we should dwell on it for a moment.

'Judgement' is a literal translation of *ḥukm*, and sometimes it is the best translation in logic (for example at 13,6f, where 'The sun is up' expresses a judgement). But al-Fārābī's more usual idiom is that a proposition 'judges' one concept *A* 'of' another concept *B* (*ḥakama bi A ᶜalā B*), meaning that the proposition applies *A* affirmatively or negatively to *B*. Al-Fārābī will often speak of 'transferring' the *ḥukm* from *B* to some other concept, say *D*. So strictly the *ḥukm* is not the whole proposition, but what the proposition expresses about *B* or *D*. For example in '*B* is not four-legged', the *ḥukm* is what is expressed by the part of the sentence 'is not four-legged'. We will read *ḥukm* in this sense as 'content', and in this context we will speak of a proposition expressing that 'the content *A* is true of the subject *B*'.

In the second part of his definition of proposition, al-Fārābī goes on to express the same idea using a notion from Arabic grammar. Arabic is sometimes described as at least partly 'topic-prominent';[39] this means that the grammar is set up to make it easy for me to start a sentence by identifying an object known to you and me (the topic), and then to complete the sentence by giving you a piece of information (the *khabar*) about the topic. Al-Fārābī identifies the topic of a simple sentence with the logical subject (*mawḍūᶜ*). He also identifies the piece of information with the logical predicate (*maḥmūl*); but this is careless. In the sentence 'Zayd is not four-legged' the Peripatetic logicians, including al-Fārābī, would take the predicate to be just 'four-legged', whereas the piece of information also includes the negative copula 'is not'. So al-Fārābī should have identified the linguistic *khabar* with the content (the *ḥukm*) rather than the predicate. But al-Fārābī tends to prefer affirmative sentences to negative ones, and in simple affirmative sentences there is no harm in identifying the content with the predicate.

Al-Fārābī moves on to introduce at 13,8 the notion of a 'hypothetical sentence', i.e. one that judges something under a condition. He takes 'If *p* then *q*' as judging *q* under the condition *p*, and 'Either *p* or *q*' as judging *q* in a way that depends on *p*. So al-Fārābī needs a word for those sentences that are not hypothetical, i.e. that make a judgement without any condition. For this he chooses the word *ḥamlī*, which may be his own coinage (cf. Section 2.8 above); we translate it as 'categorical', though it could also be translated as 'predicative'.[40]

Besides the word 'proposition' (*qaḍīya*) al-Fārābī also uses 'sentence' (*qawl*). It would make sense for him to use *qawl* for the syntactic object and *qaḍīya* for the meaning expressed by the syntactic object. But at least in *Syllogism* he never uses the two words to make this distinction. He is certainly aware of the difference between syntactic expressions and meanings, but he finds it convenient to pass freely between the two. As a result he is not always careful to distinguish between two sentences with the same meaning, and he sometimes deliberately overlooks the difference between two arguments with the same meaning (cf. Part 18a).

Paragraph 1.2 of Part 1 is an interloper: it discusses the temporal properties of verbs, which play no role in the rest of *Syllogism*. Probably a mention of verbs in paragraph 1.1 distracted al-Fārābī by reminding him of his abiding interest in Arabic grammar.

3.2 Introducing Part 2: Categorical sentences

For logical purposes al-Fārābī recognizes four main forms of categorical sentence, as follows:

symbol	**abstract description**	**material instance**
(*a*)	universal affirmative	Every human is an animal.
(*e*)	universal negative	No human is an animal.
(*i*)	particular affirmative	Some animal is a human.
(*o*)	particular negative	Not every animal is a human. or: Some animal is not a human.

The symbols (*a*) etc. are a later Latin convenience; they should be read as shorthand for the abstract descriptions. The distinction universal/particular is called quantity, and the distinction affirmative/negative is called quality. 'Material' here means 'in a natural language', as explained later in this section.

These four forms are said to be quantified (*maḥṣūr*, 13,17), because each of them contains one of the four quantifiers, namely 'every' (*kull*), 'none' (*lā wāḥida*, literally 'not one'), 'some' (*ba*ᶜ*ḍ*) and 'not every' (*laysa kull*); cf. 14,1f. The quantifier is applied to the subject, which is 'human' in the first two examples above and 'animal' in the last two.[41]

For the quantifier to make sense, the subject has to express a concept of a kind that al-Fārābī describes as universal (*kullī*); this is a different sense of 'universal' from the one used to classify sentences, as in (*a*) and (*e*) above. For al-Fārābī in *Syllogism* a universal concept, or more briefly a universal, is a meaning that is true of many different things.[42] By contrast some concepts, such as those expressed by proper names like 'Zayd', are true of only one thing; these concepts are said to be individuals (*shakhṣ*).

Al-Fārābī often talks of 'falling under' (*dākhil taḥta*), which is a relationship between concepts. Suppose *A* and *B* are universals and *C* is an individual. Then at first approximation, *B* falls under *A* if every individual satisfying the concept *B* also satisfies the concept *A*; and *C* falls under *A* if the individual *C* satisfies the concept *A*. The reason for the caution about first approximation is that in his *Expressions* [58] pages 67–73, where al-Fārābī gives several examples to illustrate these notions, all of his examples illustrate permanent or essential properties: for example date palm falls under plant. He never says, for example, that Zayd falls under sitting at those times when Zayd is sitting. Hence we should probably add to the definition of 'falling under' a requirement that the relationship is permanent or essential. But in practice all of al-Fārābī's examples in *Syllogism* satisfy this condition anyway, so we will ignore it in what follows.

Al-Fārābī is not always explicit about whether a given concept is an individual or a universal, so that he conflates these two kinds of falling under. For example he sometimes says '*C* is an *A*', and we don't know whether *C* is an individual or a universal; if it is a universal, he means us to understand the sentence as 'Every *C* is an *A*'. Where *C* falls under *B* and al-Fārābī doesn't seem to care whether *C* is an individual or a universal, we will follow al-Fārābī in speaking of *C* as a 'particular case' (*juz'ī*) of *B*.

Al-Fārābī also speaks of a concept *A* being 'true of' (*ṣaḥḥa* ᶜ*alā*) a concept *B*. This again means that *B* falls under *A*. We sometimes paraphrase '*A* is true of *B*' as '*B* satisfies *A*' where this is stylistically easier. When al-Fārābī says that *A* is false of *B*, he may mean either that not all *B*s are As or that no *B*s are As; we have to decide from the context.

Besides the four quantified sentence forms above, al-Fārābī also considers two kinds of categorical sentence that have no quantifier. The first of these is the singular sentence, whose subject is an individual, as in 'Zayd is walking' and 'Zayd is not walking'; it can be either affirmative or negative. Al-Fārābī never mentions singular sentences in his account of syllogisms in Parts 8 to 13, but he may be allowing them in his discussion of types of reasoning in Parts 16 to 20 (where he speaks of particular cases).

The second kind of sentence with no quantifier has a universal concept as its subject. This corresponds to Aristotle's *adióriston* 'indeterminate' as in 'Pleasure is not good' (*Analytica Priora* 1.1, 24a19) – but only up to a point. In practice Arabic grammar requires the subject noun to be either quantified or marked with an expression such as 'the' or 'this' or 'that'. The Arabic logicians translated *adióriston* rather fancifully as *muhmal*, literally '(sheep or camels) left unsupervised'.[43] Al-Fārābī borrows from *Analytica Priora* 1.4, 26a29f the principle that indeterminate sentences behave in syllogisms exactly like particular sentences (17,8). This should make it redundant to mention them in connection with syllogisms, though al-Fārābī does still discuss syllogisms using them in his Part 10.

In his treatment of likening in Parts 18 to 20 al-Fārābī comes back to indeterminate sentences with a novel suggestion. Perhaps the indeterminate sentence 'The *B* is an *A*' is easier to verify than the universal sentence 'Every *B* is an *A*', and for this reason indeterminate sentences could play a distinguished role in certain forms of argument that fall short of logical rigour. See Section 3.21 on logical tolerance.

In practice al-Fārābī, like other Arabic logicians, often uses letters in place of the subject and the predicate in categorical sentences. This usage is copied from Aristotle. Al-Fārābī delays mentioning the usage until Part 10; but several things that he says before Part 10 will be easier to explain if we introduce the usage at once.

A categorical sentence with letters for subject and predicate, as in 'Every *B* is an *A*', will be called a formal sentence. (This is a modern name; al-Fārābī has no distinguishing name for these sentences.) Aristotle sometimes writes a formal sentence and then indicates a pair of material (i.e. natural-language) words, one for the subject letter and the other for the predicate letter. Aristotle himself describes such an assignment of words to letters just as 'terms', but it is convenient to follow Alexander of Aphrodisias and call it a 'matter' (*húlē*, [5] 52,19–25). If we put the words in place of the corresponding letters, the result is a material sentence which we will call a material instance of the formal sentence. For example, using a modern notation, the matter (*A* four-legged; *B* horse) applied to the formal sentence 'Every *B* is an *A*' gives the material sentence 'Every horse is four-legged', so that this sentence is a material instance of 'Every *B* is an *A*'. This notion allows us to say more precisely what is meant by a material sentence 'having such-and-such a form'. For example the material sentences of the form (*a*) are just the material instances of 'Every *B* is an *A*'.[44]

Introducing another convenient definition from modern logic, we say that a matter satisfies (or makes true) a formal sentence if the resulting material instance is a true sentence. For example the matter (*A* = four-legged; *B* = horse) satisfies 'Every *B* is an *A*', and also 'Some *B* is an *A*'; but the matter (*A* bird; *B* stone) doesn't satisfy 'Some *B* is an *A*'. We will find this notion useful in Part 5, and also for explaining al-Fārābī's brief discussion of unproductive moods in Part 10.

As we noted in Section 1.1, categorical sentences can be written in SP ordering, i.e. with subject before predicate; but they can also be paraphrased in PS ordering with predicate first. Aristotle preferred the PS ordering. Al-Fārābī, like most Arabic logicians, has a clear preference for the SP ordering; but he also uses the PS ordering when he introduces syllogisms in his Part 11. We illustrated in Section 1.1 how the PS versions are generally less natural than the SP ones, particularly in the case of sentences of the form (*o*).

Al-Fārābī also allows some variation in the sentences with SP ordering. For example 'No *B* is an *A*' can appear as 'Every *B* is not an *A*' (39,13f). The sentence 'The human is an animal' is used to mean 'Every human is an animal' at 13,14, though elsewhere it could be an indeterminate sentence.[45]

The two letters in a formal categorical sentence must be distinct. In his formal PS sentences Aristotle puts the letters in alphabetical order, for example with *A* before *B* so that *A* is predicate and *B* is subject. When the Arabic logicians switched to the SP ordering they kept Aristotle's letters for subject and predicate, which is why the letters tend to appear in reverse alphabetical order in Arabic logic.

It is sometimes claimed that al-Fārābī 'ampliates to the possible' in modal sentences; the claim means that in sentences about possibility or necessity he takes 'Every *B*' to mean 'everything that actually is or could possibly be a *B*'. The book *Syllogism* may not be the most appropriate context for discussing this issue, since it contains almost no modal logic. But Hodges [102] examines the evidence and concludes that al-Fārābī made no such claim on his own behalf, though he did believe that Aristotle ampliated to the possible in some circumstances. The statements of some later Arabic logicians about al-Fārābī ampliating in modal sentences are likely to be their interpretations of a rather vague remark of Avicenna.

3.3 Introducing Part 3: Opposites

Al-Fārābī devotes Parts 3, 4 and 5 of *Syllogism* to 'opposite' pairs of categorical sentences, i.e. pairs of categorical sentences that have the same subject and predicate as each other but say something different about them. Part 3 takes up the point made by Aristotle, that in order to establish whether the two sentences do say something different, we need first to bring to the surface anything that is implicit in either of the sentences. Part 4 assumes that the implicit has been made explicit, and classifies the possible logical relationships between the two sentences; the classification follows the lines of what is commonly known as the Square of Opposition. Part 5 repeats the information in Part 4, but in terms of the separate contributions made to a material sentence by its form and its matter, where matter is understood in Alexander's sense as in Section 3.2 above. Matters are classified into three types according to how they contribute to the truth-values of sentences.

In *Short Syllogism* al-Fārābī brings the contents of the present Parts 3 and 4 together into a single Part. Also *Short Syllogism* drops any mention of matter, so that the contents of the present Part 5 disappear. Al-Fārābī could have removed this material because he came to realize that the information given in Part 5 is essentially the same as that given in Part 4 by the relations of the Square of Opposition.

The nearest that Aristotle comes to a discussion of opposite pairs of sentences is Section 6 of his *De Interpretatione*, where he defines contradictory (in the Arabic translation – in Greek he defines contradiction, *antíphasis*, 17a33). There he also defines a pair of sentences to be opposing (*antikeiménai*, 17a34) if they have the same subject and the same predicate, but one is affirmative and the other is negative. In Section 14 of *De Interpretatione* he defines what it is for two sentences to be contrary (*enantíai*, 23a27).[46]

There are discussions of opposite pairs in both Paul the Persian ([128] Latin 13–15) and Muqaffa^c ([125] 29–31); this is unsurprising since both these books aim to cover the contents of *De Interpretatione*. Proba [161] omits the topic.

One reason why an account of Aristotelian logic needs to introduce contradictory pairs early is that contradiction is how sentence negation was understood. Arabic has a common word *laysa* that can be put at the beginning of sentences and in this position behaves very much like a sentence negation; if Arabic speakers had invented logic they might have decided that we negate a sentence by adding a negative particle at the beginning.[47] But Greek had nothing corresponding, and so Aristotle negated a sentence by the more complicated process of passing to its contradictory opposite.[48] We will sometimes write $\overline{p}$ for the contradictory opposite of a sentence or proposition *p*.

Aristotle says in *De Interpretatione* 6, 17a36f that it is necessary to spell out the conditions for two sentences to be a contradictory pair, 'because of the troublesome objections of sophists'. From early times the commentators understood him to be saying that the sophistical arguments analysed in *Sophistical Refutations* contain examples of sentence-pairs that are falsely taken to be contradictory, and so they expanded Aristotle's remark in *De Interpretatione* 6 with examples taken from *Sophistical Refutations*. In all of these examples there is an implied qualification in one of the sentences but not in the other; so it was natural to list the kinds of qualification that one should be aware of. The lists given by Ammonius, Stephanus and Boethius in their respective commentaries on *De Interpretatione* are so close that a common ancestor has been assumed, and the finger points at Porphyry's now lost commentary on *De Interpretatione*. Ebbesen ([53] p. 172) reconstructs Porphyry's list of conditions as follows (in our words):

(1) a personal name must refer to the same individual in both sentences;
(2) if a common noun refers to a specific individual in one sentence, it must refer to the same individual in both;
(3) if the sentences express that a thing is true or false of a part of the subject, it must be the same part in both sentences;
(4) if the sentences express that a thing is true or false in relation to some other thing, it must be the same other thing in both cases;
(5) the sentences must not differ in modality, for example one speaking of what is actual and the other of what is possible;
(6) the two sentences must not speak of different times.

Our notes to the translation of Part 3 compare al-Fārābī's examples with Ebbesen's list.[49]

Aristotle's conditions for contradiction were just one of al-Fārābī's sources for the notion that in logic we need to make explicit (*fī al-lafẓ*) things that are implicit (*fī al-ḍamīr*). Another source was the notion of an enthymeme (again *ḍamīr* in Arabic), as it appears in Aristotle's *Rhetorica*, viz. a syllogism with one premise suppressed. Another was the use of *ḍamīr* in Arabic linguistics to mean 'personal pronoun'; al-Fārābī recognizes this use at his *Expressions* [58] 53,16f:

(3.3.1) … like the sentence 'Why did he go out?', when the pronoun (*ḍamīr*) is understood to mean Zayd.

Taken together, these sources raise the question what *ḍamīr* means in Part 3 of *Syllogism*.

The root *ḍmr* carries the meaning 'hidden'. Metaphorically it was often used to mean 'mind' or 'heart', and the use for personal pronouns was another metaphorical extension. But what metaphor does al-Fārābī intend here? Is the meaning hidden, or is the hidden thing the mind of the speaker? Apparently both, according to al-Fārābī's explanation of enthymeme (*ḍamīr*) in his *Rhetoric* [60] 63,5–7:

(3.3.2) the user hides (*yuḍmiru*) one of the premises and doesn't state it explicitly, and also it is used in accordance with what is in the mind (*ḍamīr*) of the listener.

This looks like his own explanation, and it raises the possibility that the use of the word *ḍamīr* in logic is his own coinage. It is not found in the Baghdad Standard translation of Aristotle's *Rhetorica* [12]. He may have been alerted to the word by its use in linguistics.

3.4 Introducing Part 4: Pairs of opposites

During the Roman Empire period, commentators tended to offer classifications of the different types of opposite pair; see Lee [117] p. 69. The basic classification, which appears first in Apuleius *Peri hermeneias* [118] paragraph V, is the Square of Opposition:

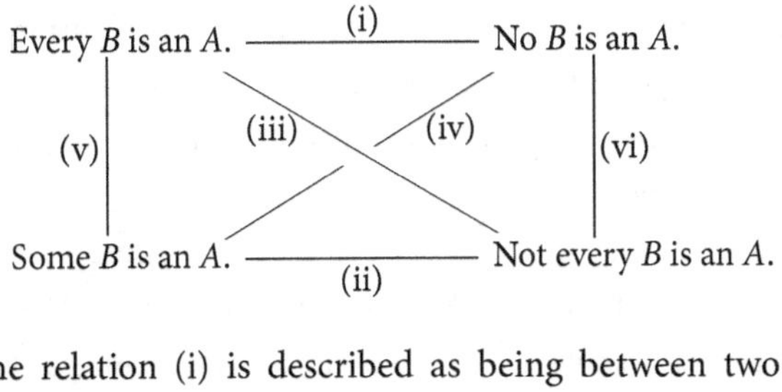

The relation (i) is described as being between two contraries. The relations (iii) and (iv) are both between two contradictories; these are the 'two kinds of contradictory pair' referred to in paragraph 4.2. The two sentences related by (ii) are said to be subcontraries and those related by (v) or (vi) are said to be subalterns.

Two other basic cases are commonly added, one where the two opposite sentences are singular and one where they are unquantified:

Socrates is an *A*. ——(vii)—— Socrates is not an *A*.
(The) human is an *A*. ——(viii)—— (The) human is not an *A*.

Paul the Persian ([128] Latin 13–15) and Muqaffa[c] ([125] 29–31) mention all eight of these relations as forms of opposition.

Al-Fārābī has all except subalternation ((v) and (vi)). The reason for the exception is probably that subalternation is the only one of these relations which holds between two sentences of the same quality. Al-Fārābī may have gone back to Aristotle and noticed that for Aristotle a pair of opposite sentences must be one affirmative and one negative.

This classification of types of opposite pairs is defined purely in terms of the syntax of the propositions: for quantified propositions, their quantity and quality, and for other propositions, the presence or absence of negations and proper names. In this respect it follows Aristotle's practice in *De Interpretatione.* At least from Ammonius onwards, commentators who gave the classification would go on to explain its meaning semantically, in terms of a three-way classification of matters. Al-Fārābī will turn to this topic in his Part 5.

3.5 Introducing Part 5: Contraries and contradictories

In this Part al-Fārābī redescribes the kinds of opposite pair that he listed in Part 4. His new description is semantic, i.e. in terms of which instances of the formal sentences are true and which are false. But the line of his thought is not always easy to follow, because he assumes without any explanation that the reader understands what a matter is, and that the reader accepts a classification of matters into three kinds. This classification carries the same information as the semantic description of the Square of Opposition, so that his explanations as they stand are circular.[50] We will try to avoid this circularity.

In Section 3.2 we explained what a matter is according to Alexander of Aphrodisias, and that explanation fits what al-Fārābī does in his Part 5. We are considering formal sentences with subject *B* and predicate *A*, so a matter will consist of an assignment of a word or phrase to *B* and a word or phrase to *A*. At 16,11f al-Fārābī speaks of 'things and matters' (*umūr wa-mawādd*); since he tends to use 'thing' to mean 'concept', he is probably reminding us that the word or phrase assigned to a letter can be changed to any other word or phrase expressing the same concept (because a true sentence stays true if we change a word to another word with the same meaning).

Al-Fārābī introduces three semantic relationships between a pair of formal sentences with subject *B* and predicate *A*. The first is that the two sentences are semantic contradictories; this means that every matter makes one of the two sentences true and the other one false – or in al-Fārābī's words, the two formal sentences are 'distinguished by truth and falsehood'. The second semantic relationship is that the two formal sentences are semantic contraries; this means that no matter makes both the sentences true. The third is that the two sentences are semantic subcontraries; this means that no matter makes both the sentences false.

To apply these notions to the kinds of opposite pair defined in Part 4, al-Fārābī begins with (vii), a pair of singular sentences, one affirmative and the other negative. For a singular formal sentence the matter must assign to the subject letter a phrase expressing a singular concept; by Part 2 this concept is true of just one thing. Al-Fārābī states without explanation that in this case the two formal sentences are semantic contradictories. But we can verify this: for example exactly one of the two sentences 'Baghdad is in Iraq' and 'Baghdad is not in Iraq' is true. So (vii) expresses a relationship between semantic contradictories.

Al-Fārābī then turns to the relationships (iii) and (iv), which are the two kinds of contradictory relationship between quantified formal sentences. This is where he assumes that we already have a classification of matters. But we need not assume this; instead we can use what he has already established about the case (vii). Suppose for example that we are considering the pair 'Every *B* is an *A*', 'Some *B* is not an *A*'. Take any matter, for instance (*B* = horse; *A* = perissodactyl). If this matter makes 'Some *B* is not an *A*' true, then some horse is not a perissodactyl; putting a name of this horse for *C*, we get a matter that makes the singular sentence '*C* is not an *A*' true. So by the result on (vii) this same matter makes '*C* is an *A*' false; but that implies that 'Every horse is a perissodactyl' is false, so the original matter makes 'Every *B* is an *A*' false as required. On the other hand if our matter (*B* = horse; *A* = perissodactyl) makes 'Every *B* is an *A*' true, then every matter that comes from this one by putting a name of a horse for *C* makes '*C* is an *A*' true, and hence again by the result on (vii) makes '*C* is not an *A*' false, so that the original matter makes 'Some *B* is not an *A*' false. This shows that (iii) is a relationship between semantic contradictories. A closely similar argument shows that (iv) is a relationship between semantic contradictories too.[51]

Next al-Fārābī turns attention to (i), the relationship between 'Every *B* is an *A*' and 'No *B* is an *A*'. Again he assumes we have the three-way classification of matters. And again we can replace his argument by an appeal to his result on (vii), the singular case. Recall from his Part 2 that every universal is true of 'many things'. So suppose we have a matter; the word put for *B* is a universal, so it is true of at least one thing *X*. Assign *X* to the letter *C* in '*C* is an *A*' and '*C* is not an *A*'; the resulting matter makes one of these two sentences false, so it makes at least one of 'Every *B* is an *A*', 'No *B* is an *A*' false. This shows that (i) is a relationship between semantic contraries.

The rest is automatic. Every matter makes at least one of 'Every *B* is an *A*'. 'No *B* is an *A*' false by the fact that (i) is between semantic contraries, and hence at least one of 'Some *B* is not an *A*', 'Some *B* is an *A*' true by the fact that (iii) and (iv) are between semantic contradictories. So (ii) is between semantic subcontraries. Finally (viii) is between indeterminates, which behave like particulars (22,8), and so (viii) likewise is between semantic subcontraries.[52]

So al-Fārābī has set up a semantic Square of Opposition.[53] From this point it is easy to explain and justify his three-way classification of matters. Since (i) is between contraries, there is no matter that makes both 'Every *B* is an *A*' and 'No *B* is an *A*' true.[54] So we have three kinds of matter. First there are those matters that make 'Every *B* is an *A*' true and 'No *B* is an *A*' false; al-Fārābī calls these necessary. Second there are those matters that make 'Every *B* is an *A*' false and 'No *B* is an *A*' true; al-Fārābī calls these prevented. Third there are those matters that make both 'Every *B* is an *A*' and 'No *B* is an *A*' false; al-Fārābī calls these possible. The fact that (iii) and (iv) are between semantic contradictories allows us to complete the following table:

	necessary	**prevented**	**possible**
Every *B* is an *A*	true	false	false
No *B* is an *A*	false	true	false
Some *B* is an *A*	true	false	true
Not every *B* is an *A*	false	true	true

Al-Fārābī adds one further terminological point. Every quantified material categorical sentence can be regarded as the result of applying a matter to one of the four formal sentences of the Square, and this matter is uniquely determined by the sentence. So we can transfer the classification of matters to the sentences themselves. For example if a given material sentence determines a matter that is necessary under the classification of matters, then we can speak of the sentence as being 'in necessary matter', as al-Fārābī does.[55]

The semantic Square of Opposition and its corresponding table of three kinds of matter are deceptively simple. By the time he came to write *Categories* [64] 120,14–126,19, al-Fārābī had become aware of several complications.[56] One is that there are borderline cases: if Zayd is neither white nor black, does he have to be classified as either white or non-white? Another complication is that logic should be independent of contingent facts, and hence should be prepared to handle terms that happen to be empty, i.e. not in fact true of any individual – for example '*N*-sided house' where *N* is any large enough number. This is not the place to expound al-Fārābī's solutions to these problems, particularly since he takes no notice of them in *Syllogism*. But the decisions that he made impinge on the rules for syllogisms, as in Parts 12 and 13 below, and on his use of topics in Part 19; so we should at least sketch them.

As in the present Part 5, his policy in *Categories* 120,14–126,19 is to deal first with singular sentences and then draw out analogous conclusions for quantified sentences. He aims to preserve the semantic relationships of the Square. For example, beginning with the singular sentences, if Zayd doesn't exist then 'Zayd is white' is false; since we want the relationship (vii) to be between semantic contradictories, we have to take 'Zayd is not white' as true. Passing to the quantified case, the analogous position is that if *B* is empty then 'Every *B* is an *A*' and 'Some *B* is an *A*' must be false, and hence both 'No *B* is an *A*' and 'Some *B* is not an *A*' must be true since the relationships (iii) and (iv) are between semantic contradictories. Many later readers have found it paradoxical that 'Some *B* is not an *A*' counts as true when there are no *B*s. At least in his surviving works, al-Fārābī never discusses the paradox; nor does he explain the implications of these decisions for the theory of syllogisms.

When we are dealing with a version of Aristotelian logic that allows empty terms, the reading of 'Every *B* is an *A*' as false when there are no *B*s is known today as existential import. The statements of existential import in *Categories* are a little indirect, but clear enough for us to credit al-Fārābī with being the first logician to state that affirmative universal sentences have existential import.[57] But in *Syllogism* al-Fārābī shows no awareness of empty terms, so that the question of existential import doesn't yet arise.

3.6 Introducing Part 6: Conversion

The Aristotelian terminology of conversion is confused almost beyond repair, often throwing us on the mercy of context and common sense.[58] This confusion affected all logicians, at least up to and including Avicenna.

In Arabic there are two main words involved, *ᶜaks* ('conversion' or 'converse') and *munᶜakis* ('convertible'). Conversion is the operation of taking a categorical sentence (material or formal) and transposing the two terms, so that for example we convert 'Every horse is an animal' to 'Every animal is a horse'. Often it is required that some feature of the sentence (such as truth) is preserved by this operation; in some cases we may also change the quantity from universal to particular, so that for example 'Every horse is an animal' is converted to 'Some animal is a horse'. The converse is the sentence that results from this operation. A sentence is convertible if this operation can be performed so as to preserve certain features of the sentence.

There are three main levels of conversion, according to how much has to be preserved in the operation. We can call them neutral, truth-preserving, and permanently truth-preserving. In the neutral case the operation simply alters the syntax of the sentence. Al-Fārābī introduces a term to distinguish this case: he calls it 'reversal' (*inqilāb*) of the sentence (17,14). But in the heat of the battle he forgets that he has this term, and simply uses 'converse' to name the result of reversal (e.g. 52,3).

The second level is where truth is preserved; this applies only to material sentences, since formal sentences have no truth value. At this level we say that the sentence 'Every human is a laugher' is convertible, meaning that it is true and so is its converse 'Every laugher is a human' (e.g. 44,19). When al-Fārābī applies 'convertible' in this sense to a universal affirmative sentence, he says also that the two terms of the sentence are 'convertible in predication' (as at 51,11; see also *Expressions* [58] 75,16–76,8 where he discusses this notion). In passages where 'convertible in predication' is used, it would often have been better to introduce a new sentence form meaning 'A thing is a *B* if and only if it is an *A*'. In fact al-Fārābī almost does this at 50,12 when he speaks of the statement '*A* and *B* are true of each other' as a 'kind of predication'. But in general al-Fārābī prefers to reinterpret or qualify Aristotle's sentence forms rather than introduce new ones.

The third level is the one we meet most often in practice, because of its importance in Aristotle's theory of syllogisms. In fact the definition of conversion that al-Fārābī gives at *Syllogism* 17,10–12 applies only to this case. As that definition says, the requirement on the operation is that 'truth is preserved permanently (*dā'iman*) in whatever matter (*mādda*) it is in'; the quantity is allowed to change. Conversion at this level is a kind of formal entailment from the original sentence to its converse. So for example 'No *B* is an *A*' converts to 'No *A* is a *B*' because we can see that regardless of what *B* and *A* are taken to mean, if it is true that no *B* is an *A* then it is true that no *A* is a *B*. The entailment remains valid if we replace *B* and *A* by any material terms; this is what al-Fārābī means by 'permanently in whatever matter'.[59] Al-Fārābī uses 'permanently' in this sense at 16,8.10; 18,2.4.5.13; in several of these passages the whole phrase is 'permanently and in all matters'.

Aristotelian logicians reckon that there are three valid conversions at this third level. One of them is from 'No *B* is an *A*' to 'No *A* is a *B*' as above; this is known today as *e*-conversion.[60] Another is from 'Some *B* is an *A*' to 'Some *A* is a *B*'; this is known as *i*-conversion. The third is from 'Every *B* is an *A*' to 'Some *A* is a *B*; this is known as *a*-conversion.[61]

Paragraph 6.2 of Part 6 repeats facts stated in paragraph 6.1, but adds justifications. For both *e*-conversion and *i*-conversion it shows that the original proposition and its converse can be paraphrased into a form that is symmetrical between the two terms. For example 'No *B* is an *A*' is paraphrased as '*B* and *A* are totally disjoint', where presumably it is self-evident that *B* and *A* being totally disjoint is the same thing as *A* and *B* being totally disjoint. This proof for *e*-conversion is very like the one that Alexander of Aphrodisias [5] 31,4–10 attributes to Theophrastus and Eudemus.

In his *Analysis* [68] 114,16–19 al-Fārābī points to a connection between *e*-conversion and a contraposition of connected hypothetical propositions. (See Fallahi [56] for details and context.) This is indirectly relevant to *Syllogism* because it is one of several places where al-Fārābī uses an Aristotelian topic to justify both a hypothetical inference and a categorical proposition. Another such place will be in Part 19 of *Syllogism* where he exploits the topic of Accepting and Rejecting.

3.7 Introducing Part 7: Known without syllogism

In Section 7 al-Fārābī tells us that all knowledge available to us comes to us either from a syllogism or not from a syllogism. This statement can hardly be challenged; but we want to know what kinds of knowledge al-Fārābī believes we can obtain without syllogism. Al-Fārābī lists four kinds.

The first two kinds of thing 'known without syllogism' are the accepted (*maqbūl*) propositions and the standard (*mashhūr*) propositions. According to al-Fārābī's accounts elsewhere, these are two classes of propositions that a debater or an orator can call on without having to justify them. If a proposition is standard, i.e. accepted as true by the consensus, then an orator can use it as a basis for an argument to persuade his audience (*Rhetoric* [60] 105,20–107,2). But as al-Fārābī says at [60] 53,1f, the consensus sometimes adopts a statement until somebody comes across a counterexample to it.[62] So these are kinds of belief, not of knowledge, and strictly they should not be in the list in Part 7 at all.[63] *Short Syllogism* says the same as *Syllogism* about these first two kinds.

In *Syllogism* the third kind of thing known without syllogism is what is known by sense-perception. *Syllogism* offers no examples; but some manuscripts of *Short Syllogism* supply the example 'Zayd is walking', and one suggests 'The sun is bright and the night is dark' ([157] 250,8, [67] 75,10f, see their critical apparatus).

Syllogism adds a fourth category, consisting of things known by the intellect, such as that three is odd and five is half of ten. Most manuscripts of *Short Syllogism* give similar mathematical examples. Manuscript *E* of *Short Syllogism* omits this fourth category, for no obvious reason; we know no evidence that al-Fārābī ever had doubts about whether 'three is odd' is known without syllogism.

But there may be a discrepancy, or at least a failure to tie up loose ends, between the list in this Part and a passage in Part 19 in the Tailpiece, at 49,11–19. In this latter passage al-Fārābī claims he has a method for establishing the proposition 'Everything attached to created things is created' incontrovertibly and in a purely conceptual way, by confirming that from '*X* is attached to created things' we can infer '*X* is created', where *X* is arbitrary. He is claiming that in this case we know the truth of a proposition through recognizing the validity of an inference. The claim is much clearer in Part 19 than it is in the earlier version in Part 18d. Since the proposition 'Everything attached to created things is created' is recognized through an inference, it is presumably not primary; but the inference is not one that appears in al-Fārābī's lists of syllogistic moods. This issue has to do with the relationship between syllogisms and topics; we will not pursue it further here.[64]

Turning to the propositions that we know by syllogism, we can assume that 'syllogism' here includes the moods of categorical or hypothetical syllogism that are listed in *Syllogism* Parts 11 to 14; the same list appears in *Short Syllogism*. We will see that in Part 16 al-Fārābī claims to reduce induction to a first figure syllogism in *Barbara*.

3.8 Introducing Part 8: Syllogisms

Al-Fārābī defines syllogism at the beginning of Part 8,19,8f, as follows:

(3.8.1) A syllogism is a discourse in which more than one thing is posited, such that when [these things] are composed, something other than them follows from them, by themselves, and not by accident but necessarily.

This definition should be set alongside two others. In *Expressions* al-Fārābī gives a slightly more elaborate description of syllogism:

(3.8.2) Syllogisms in general are things that are arranged in the mind in an order such that when the things have been put in this order, the mind as a result finds itself unavoidably looking down at something else of which it was ignorant before, so that it knows it now. (*Expressions* [58] 100,3–5)

In the background of both of these is the definition given by the Arabic Aristotle:

(3.8.3) The syllogism is a discourse such that when more than one thing is posited in it, there follows something else, of necessity, through the truth[65] of those posited things, by themselves. ([109] 184,3f, translating *Analytica Priora* 1.1, 24b18–20)

Definitions (3.8.1) and (3.8.3) make clear that the genus of syllogism is 'discourse' (*qawl*), so in particular the things that are posited or arranged in the mind are pieces of discourse. All the examples given later in this book and elsewhere in al-Fārābī's writings indicate that he takes these 'things' to be propositions. The posited propositions are called 'premises' (*muqaddama*, literally 'thing put in front', 20,8).

The definitions (3.8.1)–(3.8.3) leave it open whether a syllogism is an occurrence of discourse on a particular occasion, or a pattern of meaningful language that could occur on many occasions or on none. For definiteness we will assume the latter, since al-Fārābī says nothing to imply the former. At 37,12–15 al-Fārābī tells us that what makes a piece of discourse a syllogism is the intended and understood meaning; the linguistic expression can vary widely.

The definitions above also indicate that the pattern involves some successive events. The premises are posited or composed, and then after that – and presumably as a result of it – 'something else' follows or comes into the mind. This something else is called the 'conclusion' (*natīja*, 19,9) of the syllogism, and all of al-Fārābī's examples of conclusions are in fact propositions. The syllogism is said to 'produce' (*yuntiju*) the conclusion; this means the same as saying that the conclusion 'follows from' (*lazima* ᶜ*an*) the premises.

In some places, though not in the three definitions above, al-Fārābī says (19,10; 34,20) or implies that a syllogism involves another event which takes place 'first' (*awwalan*), i.e. already before the positing or composing of the premises. This first event is that a question (*mas'ala*) or objective (*maṭlūb*) is put up for consideration (*furiḍa*). The objective can take the form of asking which of two contradictory alternatives is true; it can also be a single sentence put up for a decision about whether the sentence is true or false. Al-Fārābī speaks of the objective as giving the 'aim' (*qaṣd*, 19,12) of the syllogism. The general picture is that a syllogism is a piece of purposive discourse, so that the person performing the discourse must have chosen a purpose for it. (See Section 1.2 on the role of the objective.)

All this complexity leads us to ask exactly how much of the events described above counts as the syllogism itself. Modern writers sometimes list al-Fārābī among those Aristotelian logicians who don't count the conclusion as a part of the syllogism.[66] This is technically correct, but two points should be added. The first is that at least with categorical syllogisms, al-Fārābī always assumes that the syllogism comes labelled as being in such-and-such a figure (which implies, as we will see in the next Section, that the conclusion must be one of four candidates determined by the figure). He justifies this assumption by the further assumption that every syllogism comes with an objective. The second point is that under al-Fārābī's assumptions (though he never states it explicitly), every categorical syllogism has a unique logically strongest candidate conclusion that follows from it, and this unique candidate can be described as 'the conclusion' of the syllogism.[67]

Like Aristotle, al-Fārābī leaves open the possibility that a syllogism could have more than two premises. In fact at 20,9–11 and in Part 18b he describes how a syllogism with many premises can be built up out of smaller syllogisms, forming what he calls a 'compound syllogism'. But his default assumption is that a syllogism has exactly two premises.

Al-Fārābī also needs a vocabulary for describing a discourse where we get as far as positing or composing propositions, but then nothing follows. In this case there is no syllogism, but al-Fārābī still speaks of the composed propositions as 'premises'. He also speaks of the pair of premises as a 'composition' (*ta'līf*) or a 'premise-pair' (*iqtirān*, literally 'joining-up'). We will normally write a premise-pair as two sentences with a semicolon between them. For example at 30,7 he gives the premise-pair

(3.8.4) Every human is an animal; some human is white.

A premise-pair that does produce a conclusion, and hence forms a syllogism, is said to be 'productive' (*muntij*); otherwise it is 'unproductive' (*ghayr muntij*).

In paragraph 8.2 at 20,2–5 al-Fārābī attempts unsuccessfully to explain Aristotle's method of pseudoconclusions,[68] a method for proving that a given premise-pair is unproductive. In fact he fails to appreciate that the method makes sense only for categorical premise-pairs in a given figure, and he misstates the requirements on the pseudoconclusions. He may not have understood the method at all. But as we saw in Section 1.5, he arranges his treatment of categorical syllogisms in such a way that his reader need never know about the method.

Al-Fārābī claims that Aristotle placed a further restriction on syllogisms. It is not mentioned in any of (3.8.1)–(3.8.3) above, though al-Fārābī does belatedly introduce it at the end of Part 10 below. This is that the conclusion should follow formally, i.e. not 'because of the matters that the expressions signified' (22,13–23,1). Since this affects our understanding of the definitions of syllogism, we take up this issue at once.

Al-Fārābī notes that when Aristotle lists the categorical syllogisms in *Analytica Priora* 1.4–6, he always takes the sentences involved to be formal sentences, not material ones. Al-Fārābī's further comments on this fact are too brief to allow us to be sure how he understands it, but here follows an interpretation that involves as few silent assumptions as possible. Al-Fārābī believes that the definitions (3.8.1)–(3.8.3) can be applied also when the sentences involved are formal, because we understand the relation 'follows from' in this case too, even though formal sentences are strictly not meaningful. For example we understand that from the formal premise-pair 'Every *C* is a *B*; and every *B* is an *A*' there follows 'Every *C* is an *A*'. On this basis we can list and classify the formal categorical syllogisms. We also have the notion of a 'material instance' of a formal syllogism, got by applying a suitable matter to replace the letters by words. The unspoken restriction of the previous paragraph is that when the definition of syllogism is applied to a material syllogism, the material syllogism must be a material instance of a formal syllogism that meets the definition. This restriction implies that the material syllogism can be shown to be a syllogism by considering the formal syllogism of which it is an instance, and this formal syllogism is independent of the matter.

That said, al-Fārābī himself doesn't restrict himself to formal syllogisms. In fact in parts of *Syllogism*, and in all of his treatment of categorical syllogisms in *Short Syllogism*, al-Fārābī goes to the opposite extreme from Aristotle and lists only material syllogisms. Also he sometimes justifies both syllogisms and conversions by appealing to facts about particular material instances – as for example with the mood *Baroco* in Section 3.12 below. Al-Fārābī recognizes the intention behind Aristotle's use of term letters, but it is probably a mistake to describe al-Fārābī himself as a formal logician.

3.9 Introducing Part 9: Categorical syllogisms

As al-Fārābī told us at 20,6, the premises of a categorical syllogism are categorical propositions. By 20,8f each of these premises has two components or terms, namely its subject and its predicate. The same holds for the premises of any categorical premise-pair. In paragraph 9.1 al-Fārābī restricts himself to the case where the two premises share one term (called the 'middle term') and their other two terms are distinct.[69] In paragraph 9.2 al-Fārābī follows Alexander [5] 44,14–45,13 and 47,27–48,12 in assuming that each categorical syllogism has an objective (which Alexander calls *próblēma*), and then in defining major and minor extremes and premises in terms of this objective.

One of al-Fārābī's favourite words is 'arrangement' (*tartīb*). In this book he applies it to syllogisms in three ways.

(1) *Figures*. In paragraph 9.2 al-Fārābī defines the major and minor terms and premises of a syllogism in terms of its objective. The major extreme is in the major premise and the minor extreme is in the minor premise, but there are different arrangements (*tartīb*) according as each of these extremes is subject or predicate in the premise containing it. These arrangements are called 'figures' (*shakl*). In paragraph 9.2 al-Fārābī recognizes three figures:

First figure: the middle term is subject in one premise and predicate in the other.

Second figure: the middle term is predicate in both premises.

Third figure: the middle term is subject in both premises.

Al-Fārābī's definition of the first figure at 21,8f in this Part disagrees with the definition assumed in Part 11 below. At 21,8f he tells us that the middle term is subject in one of the premises and predicate in the other; but the examples in Part 11 show that he makes the stronger requirement that the middle term is subject in the major premise and predicate in the minor premise. Equivalently, in Part 11 he requires that the minor extreme is subject in the minor premise and the major extreme is predicate in the major premise. The syllogisms that meet the requirement of Part 9 but not that of Part 11 were gathered up and studied in the early twelfth century by Ibn Ṣalāḥ Hamadānī ([43] 107–168, translated in [135]) and Majd al-Dīn Jīlī [43] 169–220 under the name of 'fourth figure'. An example of a fourth figure syllogism is: 'Every *C* is a *B*; every *B* is an *A*. Therefore some *A* is a *C*.'

In the calculations of Part 10 we will see that al-Fārābī assigns categorical premise-pairs to figures, regardless of whether they are productive (i.e. are syllogisms). So he is silently assuming that all categorical premise-pairs, productive and unproductive alike, have attached objectives.

(2) *Listings*. Within each figure there are several moods, distinguished by the forms of the premises. Al-Fārābī also speaks of the order in which the moods are listed as an 'arrangement' (*tartīb*). This order is important because the Arabic logicians identified the moods as, for example, the third mood of the first figure. (So it is very odd that in *Syllogism* al-Fārābī adopts his own eccentric listing of the first figure moods; see paragraph 11.1 below.) To distinguish this kind of arrangement from that in (1), we refer to the 'listing' of the moods.

(3) *Orderings*. Within each categorical proposition there are two arrangements (again *tartīb*) of the terms: the predicate can come either before the subject (as usually in Aristotle) or after the subject (as usual in Arabic logic). We will describe this kind of arrangement as the 'ordering' of the proposition. Al-Fārābī uses either ordering in premise-pairs, but in any one premise-pair he always uses the same ordering for both premises.[70]

3.10 Introducing Part 10: Figures

In this Part al-Fārābī counts the number of moods (*ḍarb*) of categorical premise-pairs in each figure, and the number of those moods that are productive. ('Mood' is understood as in Section 1.3 above.) The word *ḍarb* is a common Arabic word for 'kind', and it is not found in this narrower logical sense before this book of al-Fārābī.[71] Even in this book, al-Fārābī gives no definition of 'mood'.

At first he says he is counting premise-pairs (22,1) or syllogisms (22,9f). But on reflection it is clear that premise-pairs and syllogisms are beyond counting, because there is no bound to the number of words that could appear as terms in them. So at 22.10 al-Fārābī becomes more careful and claims only to be counting the 'kinds' (*ḍarb*) of syllogisms. Though he never explains what he means by 'kind', we can infer it from his use of the expression in Parts 11 to 13. At the end of these three parts *ḍarb* has become a fully-fledged technical term of logic meaning 'mood'. Are we capturing a technical term at its moment of birth?

It remains unclear whether al-Fārābī allows the word *ḍarb* to apply to unproductive premise-pairs as well as productive ones (i.e. syllogisms). For convenience we will assume he does. On that assumption, al-Fārābī counts two material premise-pairs as having the same mood if they are instances of the same formal premise-pair. So the moods can be counted by counting formal premise-pairs, provided that we agree a convention on what letters to use for the three terms of a premise-pair. In paragraph 10.3 al-Fārābī points out that Aristotle has such a convention, using *A, B, C* for major, middle and minor terms respectively.

In paragraph 10.1 al-Fārābī counts the moods of premise-pairs in each figure. Since the placing of *A*, *B* and *C* is fixed by the figure, it remains only to fix the quantity (universal, particular or indeterminate) and the quality (affirmative or negative) of each of the two premises, allowing $(3 \times 2)^2 = 6^2 = 36$ moods in each figure (22,1). This makes a grand total of $36 \times 3 = 108$ premise-pairs. Since the indeterminate premises supposedly behave like the particular ones (17,8), many logicians ignore indeterminate premises, and on this reckoning there are only sixteen moods in each figure and a total of forty-eight across the figures. Al-Fārābī sometimes slips into ignoring the indeterminates.

In paragraph 10.2 al-Fārābī counts the moods of syllogisms (i.e. productive premise-pairs) in each figure. This is a harder calculation, because one must first determine which formal premise-pairs are productive. Aristotle made this determination in *Analytica Priora* 1.4–6, applying his methods to the forty-eight moods one by one. But as he went through them, he noted some general rules as they came to light; these general rules came to be known as laws of syllogism, or (among the Arabic logicians) conditions of productivity. Al-Fārābī, like some other logicians, simply listed the conditions of productivity and used them instead of Aristotle's method of pseudoconclusions to eliminate the unproductive moods.[72]

According to al-Fārābī there are four productive moods in the first figure, four in the second and six in the third. This agrees with the listing in Section 1.3 above, which ignores indeterminate sentences. But the calculations that he sets out include indeterminate sentences, which is misleading. We relegate further details of the calculations to a footnote.[73]

3.11 Introducing Part 11: First figure

In Part 11 al-Fārābī spells out the four productive categorical syllogisms in the first figure, as listed in Section 1.3. He takes them in the order *Barbara, Darii,*

Celarent, Ferio. The usual order is *Barbara, Celarent, Darii, Ferio*; this is Aristotle's ordering in *Analytica Priora* 1.4, 25b32–26a21, and it is followed by Paul the Persian, Proba, Ibn al-Muqaffaᶜ, Avicenna and al-Fārābī himself in his *Short Syllogism* [67]. Al-Fārābī's reason for switching *Celarent* and *Darii* in *Syllogism* is unknown.

Al-Fārābī runs through the list five times, once in each of the paragraphs 11.1 to 11.5, using different formats as follows.

Format 1 The moods are described using formal sentences in the PS ordering (cf. Section 1.1, and 23,10 'if you go from the first extreme to the last'). The major premise is given before the minor. This is in paragraph 11.1.

Format 2 As Format 1, but using the SP ordering (23,10f 'if you go from the last to the first'). The minor premise is given before the major. This is in paragraph 11.2.

Format 3 As Format 1, but using material sentences in the SP ordering. The minor premise is given before the major. This is in paragraph 11.3.

Format 4 Again with material sentences but using the PS ordering. The major premise is given before the minor. This is in paragraph 11.4.

Format 5 The moods are listed with abstract descriptions, for example 'the major premise is affirmative universal'. Generally the major premise is described before the minor. This is in paragraph 11.5.

Format 1 represents Aristotle's usual practice in listing the moods, except that Aristotle lists productive and unproductive moods together. He allows some mild variations; for example he may say 'first extreme' and 'last extreme' rather than *A* and *C*. The Baghdad Standard text follows Aristotle's format faithfully.

Format 3 appears already in the second century AD, in Galen's *Institutio Logica* [83] 13.1, 29,15f, where two premises for *Barbara* are given in SP ordering with the minor premise first: 'The human is an animal; the animal is a being'. He has already described the first figure categorical syllogisms at [83] 8.3, 20,1–15, in the abstract Format 5 with the major premise listed before the minor.

Coming closer to al-Fārābī, Paul the Persian [128] in the sixth century gives only a single list, including both productive and unproductive moods. Each mood is described in three formats. The first is abstract as in Format 5, with the major premise described before the minor. The second is as in Format 1. After this he gives an example (or two examples for unproductive moods) with material sentences in PS ordering, as in Format 4. Proba [161] does likewise, except that he lists only productive moods. When he gives material examples, he gives them first in SP ordering (as in Format 3) and with minor premise before major, and then in PS ordering with the major premise before the minor. (See for example [161] 110,8–12; van Hoonacker's French translation follows the ordering of the Syriac.) The one new format in al-Fārābī is Format 2, using formal sentences in the SP ordering with the minor premise before the major.

The amount of repetition between these five formats used in *Syllogism* is excessive. In *Short Syllogism* al-Fārābī cuts down to just two formats; he uses material examples in the SP ordering (i.e. Format 3), together with abstract descriptions (Format 5) but with minor premise before major. This is much more readable. There is a clear educational advantage in giving material examples. On the other hand more rigorous logicians could complain that an explanation using a material example might rest on some unnoticed special feature of the example being used, and so the formal validity of the mood would not be proved. Al-Fārābī's treatment of *Baroco* in Part 12 below will illustrate this danger.

In paragraph 11.5, [66] 24,14–19, al-Fārābī introduces the notion of a 'perfect' mood, which is a mood that self-evidently yields a conclusion, so that nothing else is needed to show that the conclusion follows. Following Aristotle, he says that this is a feature of the moods in the first figure and no others. We infer that the syllogistic moods in the second and third figures, which are productive but not perfect, need something else to prove that the conclusion follows, in spite of the fact that the definition of 'syllogism' at (3.8.1) has already assured us that they already prove the conclusion 'by themselves'. This might seem a subtlety too far. But one way to make the distinction would be to allow the 'something else' to be further steps of reasoning from the information already given by the premises.

3.12 Introducing Part 12: Second figure

In Part 12 al-Fārābī lists the four moods of categorical syllogisms in the second figure. This time he lists them in the standard order. As in Part 11 he runs through the list several times, using the same five formats mentioned in Section 3.12 above, but with two differences. First, Format 4 is reduced to a brief remark 'One can also arrange these examples in the first ordering' (27,12f). And second, in all formats (including 2 and 3) the major premise is given before the minor. In the discussion below we use the SP ordering and we take the major premise before the minor.

Since the second figure syllogistic moods are not perfect, one or more extra steps of reasoning are needed to verify that the conclusion does follow from the premises. In the first three cases, namely *Cesare, Camestres* and *Festino*, a conversion is applied to one premise so as to bring the premise-pair to a mood of the first figure. This implies a small amount of further rearrangement, as in the proofs for *Cesare* and *Camestres:*[74]

Cesare

1. No *A* is a *B*; and every *C* is a *B*.
2. No *B* is an *A*; and every *C* is a *B*. (By *e*-conversion.)
3. Every *C* is a *B*; and no *B* is an *A*. (Swap the premises.)
4. No *C* is an *A*. (By *Celarent*.)

Camestres

1. Every *A* is a *B*; no *C* is a *B*.
2. Every *A* is a *B*; no *B* is a *C*. (By *e*-conversion.)
3. No *A* is a *C*. (By *Celarent*.)
4. No *C* is an *A*. (By another *e*-conversion.)

The proof of *Baroco* raises some difficult issues. The consensus among both ancient and modern logicians has been that the mood is valid: its premises do entail its conclusion. But there has been less agreement about how one can demonstrate the validity. Since neither of the premises has the form (*e*) or (*i*), neither *e*-conversion nor *i*-conversion can be used. Also *a*-conversion is useless since it creates a premise-pair where both premises are particular, contravening the conditions of productivity. Aristotle justifies the mood by *reductio ad absurdum*.[75] Most Aristotelian logicians followed Aristotle down this road, some adding that this is the only way that *Baroco* can be justified.[76]

But there is one other tool in Aristotle's toolkit, namely the method known as ecthesis. To apply ecthesis to *Baroco*, we use the premise 'Some *C* is not a *B*' to justify introducing a fourth term *D* with the properties 'Every *D* is a *C*' (or 'Some *D* is a *C*') and 'No *D* is a *B*'.[77] These two premises can then be added to the premise 'Every *A* is a *B*' so as to yield the conclusion. Before al-Fārābī, Galen had already claimed to justify *Baroco* by this route in his *Institutio Logica* [83] 9.6, 22, 6–12. Al-Fārābī offers in his paragraphs 12.1, 12.2 and 12.3 a justification of *Baroco* that agrees with Galen fairly closely, as follows.

Baroco

1. Every *A* is a *B*; some *C* is not a *B*.
2. Let *D* be the part of *C* that is not a *B*. Then no *D* is a *B*.
3. Every *A* is a *B*; no *B* is a *D*. (From 1, 2 by *e*-conversion.)
4. No *A* is a *D*. (From 3 by *Celarent*.)

5. No *D* is an *A*. (From 4 by *e*-conversion.)
??6. No some *C* is an *A*. (By 5 since *D* is some *C*.)
7. Some *C* is not an *A*. (6 rearranged.)

Al-Fārābī jumps straight from 5 to 7, citing as reason that '*D* is some *C*'. If he had written 'Some *C* is a *D*' then we could have read him as assuming 'Some *C* is a *D*' from the definition of *D*, and then deducing 7 from this and 5 by *Ferio*. This is the route that Galen took in *Institutio Logica*. This route assumes that 'Some *C* is not a *B*' entails that there are some *C*s.

Closer examination of al-Fārābī's text raises a doubt whether he did intend to follow Galen's route via *Ferio*. He writes '*D* is some *C*' rather than 'Some *C* is a *D*', and similarly 'Human is some animal' rather than 'Some animal is human', even in two paragraphs which on his own description use the SP ordering (paragraphs 12.2 and 12.3, cf. 26,5f and 27,12f). This suggests that we should read '*D* is some *C*' not as an (*i*) sentence but as an extract from a definition of D. Al-Fārābī will have known that we can use a definition 'D is such-and-such' to replace 'D' in a sentence by 'such-and-such' or vice versa. It seems he hopes he can stretch this method to use '*D* is some *C*' so as to replace '*D*' by 'some *C*'. Unfortunately this is logical nonsense.

There is a second problem with this proof of *Baroco*, even if we ignore the twist in al-Fārābī's account and rely instead on Galen's route via *Ferio*. As we remarked above, Galen's proof assumes that 'Some *C* is not a *B*' entails that there are some *C*s. The logicians mentioned in Note 76, who believed that there is no proof of *Baroco* by ecthesis, may have doubted that this entailment holds.

In his paragraph 12.3 al-Fārābī appears at first to have a way around this problem, by choosing an illustrative example. He chooses 'animal' as a material term for *C*, and of course we know that there are animals. This choice allows al-Fārābī to deduce the conclusion in the instance of *Baroco* that he gives. But to infer that the conclusion of *Baroco* follows by formal logic, we would need to derive the nonemptiness of *C* from the premises, not from a contingent fact about animals. This would take us back precisely to the dubious point in Galen's argument.

In *Syllogism* al-Fārābī shows no awareness of the issue of relying on contingent facts in logical proofs. But as we saw in Section 3.5, in his *Categories* he did take note of empty terms. There he counted 'Some *C* is not a *B*' as true when there are no *C*s; in short he rejected the implication required by Galen's proof. If at this point he had gone back to the proof of *Baroco* that he gives in *Syllogism*, he would have had to acknowledge that the proof is faulty; it needs to be rewritten, or at least given a new justification. But there is no evidence that he did ever reconsider this proof.[78]

3.13 Introducing Part 13: Third figure

In Part 13 al-Fārābī lists the six moods of categorical syllogisms in the third figure, but not quite as in the order familiar today. There are two differences: *Datisi* is put before *Disamis* and *Ferison* is put before *Bocardo*.[79] The formatting of the moods is the same as in Part 11, except that Format 4 is not mentioned at all.

Al-Fārābī justifies the moods *Disamis*, *Datisi* and *Ferison* by *i*-conversions, following *Analytica Priora*. *Bocardo* is similar to *Baroco*, but we will see below that it is safe from the problems raised by al-Fārābī's proof of *Baroco* in second figure. Only *Darapti* and *Felapton* raise a new issue.

The issue is that there is a plausible reading of the categorical sentences which makes both of these moods invalid. Namely, allow terms to be empty, but read 'Every *B* is an *A*' and 'No *B* is an *A*' as both true when *B* is empty. (For modern logicians this is a natural reading.) Then *Felapton* is invalid. To show this, choose any matter for *A* and *C* that makes 'Every *C* is an *A*' true, and read *B* as 'eleven-legged donkey' (or in any other way that makes *B* empty). Then the premises 'Every *B* is a *C*' and 'No *B* is an *A*' are both true but the conclusion 'Some *C* is not an *A*' is false; so *Felapton* is invalid. A slight adjustment of this argument shows that *Darapti* is invalid too under this reading of categorical sentences.

Al-Fārābī needs *Darapti* and *Felapton* to be valid; he cites *Darapti* at 52,17 and *Felapton* at 49,9 and 60,12. But his reasoning is sound. In *Syllogism* he tells us at 13,13–15 that terms are nonempty; by implication this excludes empty terms from use in syllogisms. In *Categories* he interprets 'Every *B* is a *C*' as false when *B* is empty (cf. Section 3.5).[80]

We turn to *Bocardo*. Here al-Fārābī uses ecthesis, in line with Galen *Institutio Logica* [83] 10.8, 24, 1–9. But in this case al-Fārābī's conventions in *Categories* (cf. Section 3.5) create no problems for the ecthesis. By those conventions the premise 'Every *B* is a *C*' has existential import, so it implies that *B* is nonempty Hence al-Fārābī's reading of 'Some *B* is not an A' yields that there is an individual that is a *B* and not an *A*, and so *D* is nonempty The rest is straightforward.

3.14 Introducing Part 14: Hypothetical logic

Al-Fārābī considers hypothetical logic under three separate heads in different parts of the book *Syllogism*.

The first head is to introduce the kinds of hypothetical proposition and distinguish them from the kinds of categorical proposition. He does this in paragraph 14.3, where he classifies the hypothetical propositions as either connected (i.e. of the form 'If *p* then *q*') or separated (i.e. of the form 'Either *p* or *q*'), where *p* and *q* are propositions. In paragraph 14.6 he refines the definition of the separated propositions into two cases: in the complete separated case we read 'Either *p* or *q*' as meaning that exactly one of *p* and *q* is true, and in the incomplete case we read it as meaning that at most one of *p* and *q* is true. In paragraph 14.8 he adds a further sentence form 'Not both *p* and *q*', i.e. a negated conjunction; he never describes this form as hypothetical, but he treats it as a paraphrase of the incomplete separated form.[81]

Under the second head, al-Fārābī introduces hypothetical syllogistic moods as a second kind of syllogistic mood alongside the categorical moods of syllogism. This is the main task of his Part 14. He describes ten moods in all: two moods for connected hypothetical propositions, four for complete separated hypothetical propositions, two for incomplete separated hypothetical propositions, and a final two moods using negated conjunctions.[82]

The third head, in Part 19, is less straightforward. Al-Fārābī is discussing the topics of Accepting and Rejecting, and he makes what seems at first to be a passing reference to hypothetical reasoning. On closer inspection, and comparing with a parallel passage in his *Analysis* [68] 102,4–9, we see that in fact he is describing a form of reasoning that yields a connected hypothetical proposition as *conclusion*, unlike the hypothetical moods of Part 14 where the hypothetical proposition is always a premise.

All of this needs to be put in its historical context. Al-Fārābī in his *Long Commentary on De Interpretatione* 53,6–9 describes that context as follows:

> Aristotle does not in [*De Interpretatione*] pay attention to the composition of hypothetical statements, though he touches upon the subject in *Analytica Priora*. The Stoics, such as Chrysippus and others, have gone into this to the point of exaggeration, by making an exhaustive study of the subject of hypothetical syllogisms, as Theophrastus and Eudemus had done after Aristotle's time.' (Trans. Zimmermann [165] p. 45.)

Clearly al-Fārābī is using a source that is aware of the pre-Stoic efforts of Theophrastus and Eudemus towards a hypothetical logic, and is hostile to the Stoics. That source could be either Galen or Alexander of Aphrodisias, or both.

As Bobzien [27] shows, Alexander in his *Commentary on Prior Analytics i* and his *Topica* presented devices of Stoic logic in a form that implied that Peripatetic logicians had them already before the Stoics. He did this in two ways. First he recast the five Stoic 'indemonstrable' argument forms[83] as kinds of syllogism, but hypothetical rather than categorical. And secondly, he presented the Stoic indemonstrables as in some sense derivable from Aristotelian topics; the exact sense is not entirely clear. The effect was that Alexander provided two different bases for treating hypothetical logic as a Peripatetic logic: first as a system of syllogisms, and second as an application of topics.

Al-Fārābī gives evidence of how these two bases were exploited after Alexander. He sets out the hypothetical syllogisms in *Syllogism* Part 14 and in the parallel passage *Short Syllogism* [67] 82,7–86,1.[84] He develops the connection with topics in *Syllogism* Part 19 and in his work *Analysis*. Al-Fārābī is not our only source in either case. For the hypothetical syllogisms we have above all Boethius *De Hypotheticis Syllogismis* [28] which has much in common with al-Fārābī's account. For the connection with topics we have the evidence collected by Hasnawi [97] of works of Themistius on the topics.[85]

We will come back to the connection with topics in Section 3.21 below. Meanwhile we return to Part 14.

Al-Fārābī tells us in paragraph 14.1 that 'there are five primary hypothetical moods in total', two belonging to connected hypothetical propositions and three belonging to separated. There is nothing in the rest of Part 14 that straightforwardly adds up to five. Presumably the number five comes from the Stoic five indemonstrables, and the adjective 'primary' refers to the Stoic claim that 'all the other arguments are reducible to these'.[86]

Thus in a sense the five primary argument forms correspond to the four perfect moods of categorical syllogisms. But the analogy between categorical and hypothetical moods doesn't go much further than this. For the categorical syllogisms, Aristotle lays out forty-eight premise-pairs and shows that fourteen of them are productive. For the hypothetical syllogisms we are not given a preliminary list of premise-pairs that have to be tested for productiveness; we are simply given the productive premise-pairs with their conclusions. But as we saw in Section 3.10 above, al-Fārābī has hidden this difference between the categorical and hypothetical cases by suppressing the unproductive categorical premise-pairs.

Al-Fārābī points out some common features between the ten argument forms (a)–(j),[82] and introduces some vocabulary for dealing with them. A hypothetical sentence contains two 'parts' (*juz'*), each of which is a categorical sentence, and the two sentences are joined by a connecting phrase. The first and second sentences are respectively the antecedent and the consequent. So we can think of a hypothetical sentence as having the form $(p{*}q)$ where p is the antecedent, q the consequent and $*$ the connecting phrase. If r is a categorical sentence, al-Fārābī distinguishes between r unaltered (*bi-ᶜaynihi*) and the contradictory opposite (*muqābil*, cf. Part 4 above) of r; we will write $\overline{r}$ for the contradictory opposite of r. In every hypothetical mood, the first premise is a hypothetical proposition $(p{*}q)$, and the second premise is either p or $\overline{p}$ or q or $\overline{q}$. If the second premise was one of p and $\overline{p}$ then the conclusion is one of q and $\overline{q}$; and likewise if the second premise was one of q and $\overline{q}$ then the conclusion is one of p and $\overline{p}$. In all cases the effect of the second premise is to detach one of the letters from the first premise and leave the other letter as conclusion, either unaltered or changed to its contradictory negation.[87]

In the separated cases, the symmetry between the parts makes it obvious how to extend these moods to allow three or more alternatives: 'Either p or q or r or s' and so on. At 32,15f al-Fārābī gives two examples, one complete separated and one incomplete separated, that both have three alternatives. Both examples have the form 'This X is either A or B or C', in effect three singular propositions with the same subject term. This is a common pattern both in Stoic examples and in Galen.[88]

Al-Fārābī calls the second premise the *mustathnāt;* we have translated this word as 'detached', to fit what actually happens in the inference. But literally *mustathnāt* means 'excepted', and the reason why al-Fārābī uses the word is interesting as an example of migration of technical terms from one field to another. Arabic linguists had studied a group of sentences described as 'exception' (*istithnā'*) for many years before al-Fārābī. A typical example is the sentence 'I met your brothers except for Zayd'. If your brothers are ᶜAmr, Khalid and Zayd, then the effect of the sentence is to say

> I met ᶜAmr, Khalid and Zayd;
> except for Zayd.
> In short, I met ᶜAmr and Khalid.

In the language of Al-Fārābī's younger contemporary the linguist al-Sīrāfī [143] p. 86, making the exception performs a 'diminution' (*tanaqquṣ*) on the given sentence, leaving the third line as the 'remainder'. Evidently al-Fārābī saw the formal similarity to the inference

> I met either ᶜAmr, Khalid or Zayd;
> except that I didn't meet Zayd.

So I met either ᶜAmr or Khalid.

In both cases the second line (the excepted clause or *mustathnāt*) contradicts a conjunct or disjunct of the first line, and this leads to the conjunct or disjunct being cancelled in the third line. But the analogy stops there.[89, 90]

As one might expect from his debt to the Alexandrian academy, al-Fārābī's account of hypothetical propositions and syllogisms has close similarities to what we find in the commentaries on *Analytica Priora* of Philoponus [130] 240,26–247,32 and pseudo-Ammonius [9] 65–76. Some of al-Fārābī's classifications of hypothetical propositions, in *Syllogism* or elsewhere, are not found in Galen or Alexander, but resemble items in Boethius *On Hypothetical Syllogisms* [28]. Presumably these items come from one or more common sources of al-Fārābī and Boethius; Porphyry and Themistius are natural candidates.[91]

Thus al-Fārābī's distinction in paragraph 14.6 between hypothetical conditions 'by nature' and 'by posit' has several components, some of which appear also in Boethius. There are several classifications involved, and most of them make best sense as classifying hypothetical propositions that are taken to be true, in terms of the grounds for taking them to be true. Neither al-Fārābī nor Boethius relates them to distinctions between syllogistic moods.

For example al-Fārābī speaks at 32,16f of some separated hypothetical propositions expressing a conflict which is 'by nature' (*bi-al-ṭabᶜi*); at *Debate* [70] 102,19f he gives the same description but with 'separation' rather than 'conflict'. Boethius [28] (1.3.6) speaks of some conditional propositions having 'some consequence of nature' (*aliquam naturae consequentiam*). There are several possible readings of 'nature' here. (1) The 'nature' could be the essences of some of the ideas involved. This correlates with al-Fārābī's distinction at *Categories* [64] 127,2–5 between consequences that are 'by accident' (*bi-al-ᶜaraḍi*) and those that are 'by essence' (*bi-al-ḏāti*). (2) The 'nature' could be physical nature (*al-ṭabīᶜāt*), as with Boethius's example 'If the earth is interposed then an eclipse of the moon follows' (*si terrae fuerit obiectus, defectio lunae consequitur*, [28] (1.3.7)). But Boethius himself says that this consequence is caused by 'the position of the terms'; and at *Expressions* [58] 55,2f al-Fārābī gives the same example with 'when' (*lammā*), as an example of a consequence that doesn't express uncertainty about whether the condition holds. (3) In a Peripatetic context it is also possible that the 'nature' is the nature of the human intellect, in the sense that some of our beliefs are innate; though neither Boethius nor al-Fārābī says anything to suggest this reading in the present context.[92]

Both al-Fārābī and Boethius describe some or all non-natural hypothetical truths as being 'by accident'. Thus Boethius [28] (1.3.6) speaks of consequences 'secundum accidens', with the example 'When fire is hot, the sky is round' (*cum ignis calidus sit, coelum rotundum est*). Above in (1) we noted al-Fārābī's use of 'by accident' in *Categories*; his example there is 'If Zayd came, ᶜAmr left'. But al-Fārābī also has other terms to describe the non-natural case; in *Debate* [70] 102,20–103,10 these include 'occurring at a particular time' (*kā'in fī waqtin mā*), 'posit' (*waḍᶜ*), 'convention' (*iṣṭilāḥ*), and finally *ittifāq*, an Arabic word whose meanings include 'random coincidence', 'factual correspondence' and 'agreement made between two or more people'. The third of these meanings is close to 'convention' and to one meaning of *waḍᶜ*. In *Debate* [70] 108,7 al-Fārābī says that the non-natural hypothetical propositions are called 'posited propositions', and that the syllogisms arising from them are called 'syllogisms of posit' (*qiyāsāt al-waḍᶜ*). He also observes correctly that *waḍᶜ* is used for a proposition which two debaters agree to accept as a premise for a syllogism, making the syllogism a 'syllogism of *waḍᶜ*'.

The examples given above by Boethius and al-Fārābī for accidental connected hypothetical propositions illustrate two main types. (i) In Boethius's example of fire and the sky, the truth is permanent and the two clauses are self-standing true sentences. In such cases one might want to read the 'if' as 'even if' or 'whether or not'. Avicenna gives several similar examples; this shows that they are in the Arabic tradition though al-Fārābī misses them. If they are described as true by *ittifāq*, that could mean either that the consequent is in *correspondence* with the facts, or that the two clauses are unrelated and their presence in the same proposition is a *random* coincidence. (ii) Al-Fārābī's example 'Either Zayd will come or ᶜAmr will', which he describes at *Debate* [70] 103,4f as by posit and *ittifāq*, could illustrate an *agreement* made between the two people.

In paragraph 14.2 al-Fārābī begins to compare Arabic expressions which could be put for $*$ in $(p * q)$ so as to yield a connected hypothetical proposition. In paragraphs 14.6 and 14.8 he will do the same for separated hypothetical propositions. There is a fuller discussion for the connected case in *Expressions* [58] 54,10–56,10. There as here he takes the primary expression for $*$ to be 'if' (*in* in Arabic),[93] noting that the use of this word carries an implication that the speaker is uncertain of the truth-value of the condition it is attached to. This theme of the connection between conditionals and uncertainty is found in Arabic linguists of al-Fārābī's time and earlier; the linguistic discussions are quite subtle and point to different kinds of uncertainty (whether? when?).[94]

3.15 Introducing Part 15: Syllogism of absurdity

Al-Fārābī discusses the syllogism of absurdity (*qiyās al-khalf*) in two places in *Syllogism*: in Part 15 he gives a definition and a material example, and in paragraph 18b.6 at the end of Part 18b he gives a second material example as part of a compound syllogism. *Short Syllogism* also has a section on the syllogism of absurdity, and it repeats al-Fārābī's example of a syllogism of absurdity being used in a compound syllogism. Al-Fārābī gives a further account of the syllogism of absurdity at *Debate* [70] 104,18–106,2. His *Long Commentary on Prior Analytics* [74] 263–312 contains a word-by-word analysis of Aristotle's discussion at *Analytica Priora* 2.11–14 of the use of absurdity for reduction to the first figure of categorical syllogisms in the second and third figures.

The basic idea behind the syllogism of absurdity, as al-Fārābī understands it, is that if we show that p is a statement that entails something r that is known to be false, then we can conclude from this that p is false, and hence that the contradictory opposite $\overline{p}$ of p is true. There are two reasons why one has to say more than this. The first is that in practice the inference from p to the known falsehood r normally makes use of some other assumptions, and we have to explain why the outcome is $\overline{p}$ rather than the contradictory opposite of one of these other assumptions. The second is that there are two different arguments in play: first the argument with premise p and false conclusion r, and second the argument that concludes $\overline{p}$. We will refer to the first argument as the 'internal syllogism', and to the second as the 'external argument' (since it is not obvious that the external argument should be counted as a syllogism). We need to understand how the two arguments fit together.

Al-Fārābī's accounts of the syllogism of absurdity contain some inconsistencies. For example he uses the name 'syllogism of absurdity' sometimes to refer to the internal syllogism (as at *Syllogism* 34,3 and *Short Syllogism* 86,7), and sometimes to the external argument (as at *Debate* 104,18 where he describes the syllogism of absurdity as a compound of three syllogisms, one of which is the internal syllogism). So we will rest nothing on al-Fārābī's use of this name. The most coherent of his theoretical accounts is that in *Short Syllogism*, and we will begin with this.

In *Short Syllogism* al-Fārābī describes the internal syllogism as having a premise q that is 'clearly true' and a conclusion r that is 'clearly false'. He describes the other premise p as doubtful (*mashkūk fīhi*) and not known to be true or to be false (86,6). The fact that p is not known to be true or to be false plays no overt role in what follows, so for the moment we set it aside. The name 'doubtful' can be read simply as the name of the premise that is not known to be true. Al-Fārābī goes on to tell us that the internal syllogism can be used to provide $\bar{p}$ as 'conclusion' (*yuntijahu*, *Short Syllogism* 86,15 – presumably the conclusion of the external argument) in the following way. We first put $\bar{p}$ up for consideration (*nafriḍu*) and suppose that *p* is 'taken' (*yu'khadhu*). These are terms from the language of debate; they mean that a Questioner poses $\bar{p}$ as an objective, and the Responder chooses to commit to the option *p* rather than $\bar{p}$. *Syllogism* 34,14 confirms this reading by explaining that $\bar{p}$ has not been 'conceded' to us (we being the Questioner), so that *p* must have been conceded. Then the known truth *q* is added to *p* to form a premise-pair with the known falsehood *r* as its conclusion; this means that we as Questioner force the Responder to accept this syllogism, so that he grants that *p* and *q* entail *r*.

The effect of this division between Questioner and Responder is that the two arguments, the external and the internal, belong to different people who may make different assumptions. The point of the descriptions of *q* and *r* as 'clearly true' and 'clearly false' is that their truth and falsehood are agreed by both Questioner and Responder, so that in particular *q* is a premise of both arguments. But only the Responder needs to assume *p*, in order to carry out the internal syllogism deriving *r* from *p* and *q*. We as Questioner are not committed to accepting *p* as a premise, so we are free to infer from the truth of *q* and the falsehood of *r*, together with the internal syllogism, that *p* is false. Thus *q* and $\bar{r}$ should be counted as premises of the external argument.

So the Questioner's argument, which is the external argument, has premises *q* and $\bar{r}$ but not *p*. This agrees with modern accounts in terms of natural deduction, where the assumption *p* is in force for the internal argument but is 'discharged' in the external. It is possible that the idea of splitting the external and internal arguments between the two participants in a dialogue is new with al-Fārābī; at least it illustrates how he uses dialogue rules to give arguments a formal structure.[95] But al-Fārābī himself never discusses the premises of the external argument, so that it is not clear how he understands the situation.

When we turn from *Short Syllogism* to *Syllogism*, we find that the statement *r* is now said to be 'clearly false and impossible' (34,3). As we saw, the logical facts don't require *r* to be clearly impossible for the argument to work; 'clearly false' is enough. A reason for strengthening 'false' to 'impossible' appears at *Debate* [70] 105,3 where al-Fārābī tries to justify the external argument by relying on a premise that 'Everything from which an impossibility follows is impossible'. His argument is that since an impossibility follows from *p* and *q*, at least one of *p* and *q* must entail an impossibility. (This is a logical error.[96] In *Syllogism* al-Fārābī avoids this error in paragraph 15.1, but at 34,19 in paragraph 15.2 he commits it in the gross form that one of *p* and *q* must entail the *same* impossibility that was entailed by *p* and *q* together.) Since *q* is true it can't entail an impossibility; so *p* must entail an impossibility and hence be false. We remark that if al-Fārābī had used 'false' throughout – as in *Short Syllogism* – rather than 'impossible', his argument would have been valid. It is correct that if *p* and *q* together entail a falsehood, then at least one of *p* and *q* is false.[97]

The dialectical Questioner and Responder don't appear within syllogisms, so we have to ask how al-Fārābī represents an argument by absurdity as a syllogism, either simple or compound. At this point we should look at his material example in *Syllogism* paragraph 18b.6, which appears also in *Short Syllogism*. The example is a compound syllogism proving that the world is created. Al-Fārābī tells us that the compound syllogism contains a syllogism of absurdity, together with a categorical syllogism and two hypothetical syllogisms (one connected and one separated). How does this syllogism of absurdity sit within the compound syllogism?

One clue is that in order to use its first premise ('The world is either eternal or created') al-Fārābī's argument needs to show that the world is not eternal. So we should check whether the argument assumes 'The world is eternal', and derives something impossible from this and other clearly true premises. The following is a conjectural reconstruction. We abbreviate 'attached to created things' as AC, and 'free of created things' as FC.

The world is eternal. If the world is eternal, it is not AC.

The world is a body. The world is not AC.

(3.15.1)

The world is a non-AC body. A non-AC body can't move.

The world can't move.

This is an internal syllogism of absurdity. The doubted premise *p* is 'The world is eternal', and the impossible conclusion *r* is 'The world can't move'. The clearly true premise *q* is in several parts, all of which al-Fārābī states as premises. The first two are 'If the world is not eternal, it is not AC' and 'The world is a body'. The remaining true premises state that a non-AC body is FC, and that nothing FC can move; we have contracted this part of the proof to save space.

Also the top inference in (3.15.1) is a connected hypothetical syllogism (in fact modus ponens), and the bottom inference is an instance of the categorical mood *Barbara* in the first figure. The middle inference is not a syllogism at all, but a rearrangement of the propositions so as to introduce a new term, namely 'body that is not AC'. Al-Fārābī shows no awareness that he is making a non-syllogistic move here.

Curiously the doubted premise *p* is never stated, except as the antecedent of the premise 'If the world is eternal, it is not AC'. This is a place where the dialogue analysis comes into conflict with the aim of presenting the external argument as a syllogism, because *p* is a premise of the internal syllogism but not of the external.[98]

Overall, al-Fārābī's text from 'If the world is eternal . . .' to 'this is impossible' reports the internal syllogism, though with the doubted premise suppressed. At the end of this syllogism al-Fārābī assumes silently that we have proved 'The world is not eternal' (the contradictory opposite of the doubted premise), and deduces the required conclusion 'The world is created' from this and the opening premise, by a separated hypothetical syllogism.

One last point is that the validity of the external argument should be independent of the question which of the premises and conclusion are true and which are false. For the internal syllogism this is not a problem; if it follows valid syllogistic rules then it is valid. But the external argument, as al-Fārābī presents it, depends on *q* being true and *r* being false. In this respect the external argument as al-Fārābī presents it is not an argument in formal logic.

3.16 Introducing Part 16: Induction (*istiqrā'*)

Part 16 marks a major turning-point within *Syllogism*. In Parts 1 to 15 al-Fārābī has studied syntactic arrays of words in sentences and of sentences in syllogisms. With Part 16 on induction he switches to methods and procedures. A sign of the change of direction is that the word 'method' (*ṭarīq*) appears twenty-two times in Parts 16 to 20 but never in Parts 1 to 15. There is also a change of speed, particularly in the Tailpiece, as al-Fārābī allows himself to be very repetitive in discussing how general procedures apply to various kinds of argument.

The methods that al-Fārābī has in mind are all in aid of organizing arguments that are more complex than those in Parts 1 to 15. They often involve searches for terms or families of terms to serve a certain purpose in a complex argument; typically al-Fārābī discusses what we are looking for, where we should look for it, how we test whether we have found it, and how we use it when we have found it. The outcome of a method will generally be one or more syllogisms.[99]

Al-Fārābī organizes his discussion of methods around two argument-forms that he found in late sections of *Analytica Priora*: induction in *Analytica Priora* 2.23 and likening (or analogy or paradigm) in *Analytica Priora* 2.24. In his *Long Commentary on Prior Analytics* al-Fārābī is committed to trying to make sense of the details of Aristotle's descriptions of the two forms. But in *Syllogism* this is not his concern; here he sets out induction and likening on his own terms, first as pure argument-forms, and then as the formal backbones of various other arguments found in the philosophical or religious literature. One of the main things that he takes from Aristotle is the labelling of the components of these argument-forms, both by words and by letters. In fact he makes generous use of Aristotle's labelling by the letters *A, B, C, D*.[100] We think modern readers are likely to find these letters helpful, so we have added them in more places than al-Fārābī himself did. It is also clear that al-Fārābī had other sources besides Aristotle for his treatment of these two argument forms.[101]

We begin with induction (*istiqrā'*), which al-Fārābī also calls examination (*taṣaffuḥ*). His description of induction takes up two separate parts of *Syllogism*, Part 16 and Part 18c; *Short Syllogism* 90,11–93,10 combines the same material into a single Part.[102]

The aim of induction is to verify a universal proposition 'Every *B* is an *A*'. The proposition could also be negative: 'No *B* is an *A*', though al-Fārābī generally leaves it to the reader to work out what details change in the negative case. In both cases the term *A* is called the content (*ḥukm*, cf. Section 3.1). Verifying can include refuting (as with objectives, cf. Section 1.2 above).

The first step of induction is to break down the term *B* into several particular cases, say $B_1, \ldots, B_n$. These particular cases may be individuals that fall under *B*, or they may be subspecies or subclasses of *B*; al-Fārābī hardly distinguishes between these two possibilities.[103]

The aim is to choose the particular cases so that for each one of them, say B_i, we already know without argument whether or not every B_i is an *A*.[104] If we find that for each *i* from 1 to *n*, every B_i is an *A*, then we can infer that every *B* is an *A*. If on the other hand we find some *i* such that not every B_i is an *A*, then we have a refutation (*ibṭāl*) of 'Every *B* is an *A*'. There is a similar situation with 'No *B* is an *A*'; we prove this negative proposition if we find that for every *i*, no B_i is an *A*.

Al-Fārābī doesn't say much in *Syllogism* about how to organize the search for the particular cases $B_1, \ldots, B_n$. Certainly he is aware that different collections of particular cases chosen on different principles might serve the same purpose. For example if *B* is movement, then particular cases could be walking, flying and swimming (*Syllogism* 35,12); but equally they could be flying, being transformed, growing and shrinking (*Long Commentary on Prior Analytics* [74] 515,6f). In *Analysis* [68] 96,3–97,6 he argues that if it is not immediately obvious that every B is an A, we can apply Platonic division[105] to B so as to split it into two subcases B_1 and B_2, and if we are lucky it may be clear both that every B_1 is an A and that every B_2 is an A. Then induction allows us to put the two cases together and conclude that every B is an A as required. If we are unlucky, we can try repeating the procedure, using division to split B_1 into B_{11} and B_{12}, and so on downwards until we are successful. The overall implication is that induction is a way of splitting the problem of showing that every B is an A into a number of smaller problems that are more manageable.[106]

When the particular cases $B_1, \ldots, B_n$ have been found and it has been checked that they lead to a proof of 'Every B is an A', it remains to formalize this outcome as a syllogism. Elsewhere al-Fārābī makes the point that this formalized syllogism will be a self-contained argument with the same conclusion as the procedure as a whole; having made the search, we can discard everything except the premises of the syllogism. (E.g. 43,10–12, which makes this point both about induction and about the parallel situation in likening.) This may be what he means by his unexplained remarks that induction is 'reduced to' syllogism (12,6), or is 'potentially' syllogism (12,6; 35,14).

Al-Fārābī is never at his best on questions of formal detail; in fact he proposes two different ways of formulating the syllogism, neither of them satisfactory. His first attempt, at *Syllogism* 35,16–18, runs as follows:

(3.16.1) Every B is B_1 or B_2 or . . . or $B_1, \ldots, B_n$; (every) B_1 and B_2 and . . . and B_n is an A. Therefore every B is an A.

Short Syllogism 91,5f; 91,10f gives the same account, except that 'or' in the first premise becomes 'and' so that the two premises match. (In both *Syllogism* and *Short Syllogism* al-Fārābī gives (3.16.1) using material terms instead of letters.) He claims that this form (3.16.1) is in the first mood of the first figure, i.e. *Barbara*. Following terminology introduced in *Short Syllogism* (as explained below), we will refer to the first premise of (3.16.1) as the completeness condition.

Al-Fārābī describes the syllogism a little more fully in paragraph 19.15. Thus at 53,16 he tells us that a new middle term is introduced, to represent the particular cases. For example if B is agent and the particular cases of agent are taken to be tailor, mason, cobbler and carpenter, then the new term is

(3.16.2) the tailor and the mason and the cobbler and the carpenter.

Al-Fārābī clearly understands that the individuals falling under this term are the tailors *and* the masons *and* the cobblers *and* the carpenters. But as we would do it today, the new term would be written as a disjunction of terms:

(3.16.3) tailor *or* mason *or* cobbler *or* carpenter.

With hindsight al-Fārābī's indecision about whether to write 'and' or 'or' can be traced to the fact that he lacked any justified formal procedure for defining new terms of this kind.[107]

If we call this new term C, then the syllogism (3.16.1) can be read as a straightforward *Barbara*: 'Every B is a C; every C is an A. Therefore every B is an A'. So we have the right conclusion, but where do these two premises come from? In the examination phase of the procedure, each B_i was examined separately and yielded the information 'Every B_i is an A'. But there is an essential step missing in al-Fārābī's account, namely a rule for bringing all these separate pieces of information together into a single premise, as follows:

(3.16.4)

Every B_1 is an A.
⋮ ⋮
Every B_n is an A.
Therefore every B_1 or . . . or B_n is an A.

The credit for noticing this new rule must go to Avicenna, who in his *Qiyās* [146] 6.6, 349–356.6 (cf. 9.21, 559.5–12) points out that the rule can be incorporated into a tidied-up form of (3.16.1) as a new kind of syllogism with multiple premises:[108]

Every B_1 is an A.
⋮ ⋮
(3.16.5) Every B_n is an A.
Every B is either a B_1 or . . . or a B_n.
Therefore every B is an A.

Today we would describe this argument form as 'syllogism by cases'; Avicenna calls it 'syllogism by division [of cases]' (*al-qiyās al-muqassam*). This syllogism, and indeed most of what Avicenna says about induction in his *Qiyās* 9.21, is a cleaning-up of al-Fārābī's various comments on induction in *Syllogism* and elsewhere.[109]

The completeness condition in (3.16.1), 'Every B is a B_1 or ... or a B_n', is justified by whatever reason we have for believing that $B_1, \ldots, B_n$ is an exhaustive list of particular cases of B, in the sense that every individual falling under B falls under at least one of the B_i. Al-Fārābī never spells this out in *Syllogism*, but at *Short Syllogism* 91,15–17 he proposes a name for the property of $B_1, \ldots, B_n$ expressed by this first premise. Thus he describes the induction as 'complete' (*tāmm*) when the listing of the particular cases exhausts the subject *B*, and 'deficient' (*nāqiṣ*) when it doesn't. This could be the first appearance of the expression 'complete induction' in logic.[110]

In *Analysis* [68] 96,14–17 al-Fārābī suggests a different formalization of induction, using hypothetical rather than categorical logic. The formalization that he is describing seems to be

If every B_1 is an $A, \ldots,$ and every B_n is an A, then every B is an A.
(3.16.6) Every B_1 is an $A, \ldots,$ and every B_n is an A.
So therefore every B is an A.

This is not a very successful formalization. The first premise just says that the conclusion can be derived from the second premise. The reason why it can be derived is not stated; it is the completeness condition, which records that the cases $B_1, \ldots, B_n$ exhaust B.

What can be said when the outcome of the induction is a refutation: 'Not every *B* is an *A*'? Al-Fārābī discusses this case later in some applications (49,9; 60,11f). Suppose we have found a B_i such that 'No B_i is an *A*'. Since B_i is a particular case of *B*, we also have a premise 'Every B_i is a *B*'. From these two premises we can deduce 'Not every *B* is an *A*' by a straightforward application of *Felapton* in the third figure (cf. Section 1.3 and paragraph 19.9 to the translation). A corresponding hypothetical argument could be found, but al-Fārābī doesn't discuss this.

We must note al-Fārābī's passing claim at 35,5–8 that induction can be used to check that for each particular case B_i, *most* B_is are *A*s, leading to the conclusion that *most* *B*s are *A*s. This claim needs to be stated carefully in order to avoid obvious counterexamples.[111] Why does al-Fārābī make the claim? The answer seems to lie in his theory of tolerance, according to which it is permissible in some subject-matters to use Aristotle's syllogistic rules even when the sentence forms have been given nonstandard interpretations. We explore this theory further in Section 3.21 below, in the discussion of paragraph 19.13.

We should say something about al-Fārābī's names for induction. In Part 16 his name for it is *istiqrāʾ*, which is the Baghdad Standard translation of Aristotle's *epagōgḗ* in *Analytica Priora* 2.23, and also – mistakenly – of Aristotle's *apagōgḗ* in *Analytica Priora* 2.25. There is nothing to suggest that al-Fārābī knew the meanings of either of these Greek words, or that they were the words being translated by *istiqrā'*. So his understanding of the word will have been based on his knowledge of it as a word of Arabic, together with what he could glean from Aristotle's explanations.

The normal meaning of *istiqrā'* in classical Arabic is examination, checking, investigating.[112] In *Syllogism* 35,2–10 al-Fārābī describes the whole procedure of induction, from the choosing of the particular cases to the final syllogism, and declares that the induction itself is the examination (*taṣaffuḥ*) of the particular cases one by one.[113] The word *taṣaffuḥ* has not been found in the logical literature before al-Fārābī; but having used it to define induction, he feels free to use it as an alternative name for induction (e.g. in *Syllogism* at 57,21; 58,9; 59,14; 60,3; 61,11, all of these in Part 20).

By contrast in *Long Commentary on Prior Analytics* [74] 514,13 al-Fārābī quotes Aristotle as saying that induction is 'that it is demonstrated by . . .', implying that induction is a form of demonstration. In other places al-Fārābī refers to induction as a 'method' (*ṭarīq*); for example at *Syllogism* 57,20 he speaks of 'the method of examination' and at *Long Commentary* 521,14 he compares induction with experience (*tajriba*, translating *empeiría*) as 'two methods'. Taken as a method, induction would include more than just the examination of particular cases; for example it should include the decision about what particular cases to list, and the drawing of the conclusion after the examination.

Probably there is very little to be made of this discrepancy. Common sense suggests that induction should be described as a method; but the *word* (*istiqrā'*) just means examining to check whether something is the case. Al-Fārābī also speaks of induction as a form of discourse (*qawl*, *Syllogism* 35,14). He may speak this way in order to help comparison of induction with syllogism, which is also a form of discourse (*Syllogism* 19,8).[114]

3.17 Introducing Part 17: Likening (*tamthīl*)

In Part 17 al-Fārābī moves on to the second of the two argument forms that will dominate *Syllogism* from here onwards.[115] He refers to this argument form as the method of likening (*tamthīl*). As with induction, his exposition of likening takes up two parts, Part 17 and Part 18d. But unlike induction, there is no corresponding part of *Short Syllogism* that conflates these two parts. This is because *Short Syllogism* has no mention of likening until the Tailpiece (Parts 19 and 20). In fact Part 19 begins with an exposition of likening that is very close to Part 17, except that it uses different terminology, describing the method as 'inference to the unobserved by means of the observed' (45,10).

On the surface, likening runs as follows. We know that a certain thing *D* has the property *A*, and that another thing *C* – which is not known to have the property *A* – is similar to *D*. So we infer that *C* has the property *A*. The things *C* and *D* may be either individuals or classes; for example at 45,14f *C* is the sky and *D* is animals.

Clearly something must be added in order to make this argument work. Al-Fārābī has a scheme to describe what needs to be added. In a diagram:

(3.17.1)

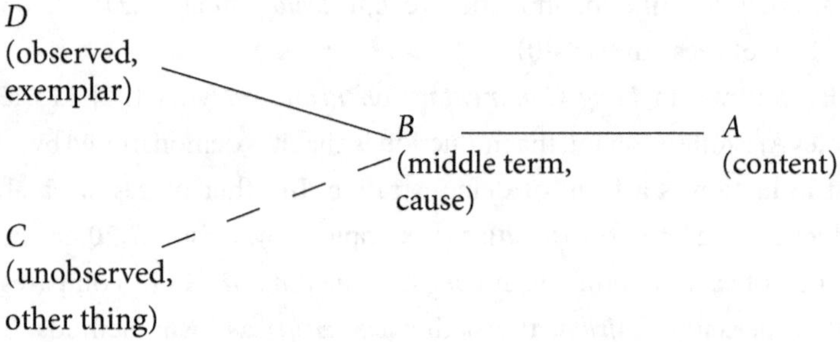

Al-Fārābī is helpfully consistent in his use of these four letters *A, B, C, D*. Also the names put below the letters in this diagram are all taken from al-Fārābī's text.[116]

According to al-Fārābī, we apply likening by finding a concept *B* satisfying the following two conditions:

(3.17.2) *D* is an *A* because it is a *B*

and *C* is a *B*. From the first of these conditions we can deduce

(3.17.3) Every *B* is an *A*.

This proposition (3.17.3) together with the second condition yields the conclusion '*C* is an *A*' by a syllogism in the mood *Barbara*; this conclusion is what likening was intended to deliver.

The syllogism in *Barbara* has (3.17.3) as its major premise, and for this reason al-Fārābī often refers to (3.17.3) simply as 'the major premise'. Also the middle term of the syllogism is *B*, which explains why *B* is labelled 'middle term' in the diagram. The other name for *B*, namely 'cause', is an abbreviation for 'cause of *A*' or 'cause of the content', because (3.17.2) can be read as saying that *B* is the cause of the content *A*.[117]

That's likening in a nutshell. But it has two ingredients that need further study, namely the search for *B* and the derivation of the major premise from (3.17.2). We begin with the search.

The search will consider various candidates for *B* in turn. As each candidate is considered (or to use al-Fārābī's phrase, 'is up for consideration as a cause'), we have to confirm or refute the claim that it meets the required conditions. So there are questions about where to look for the candidates, and also about how to confirm or refute the claim for each candidate.

As to where to look, al-Fārābī postpones his comments to Part 19 where he introduces transfer from the observed to the unobserved, a form of likening. There in paragraphs 19.3 and 19.4 he will describe two ways of proceeding. The first, which he calls Analysis, is to search for *B* satisfying both the conditions above. The second, which he calls Synthesis, is to ignore *C* at the beginning and concentrate on finding *B* so as to satisfy (3.17.2). Then when *B* is found, we can choose any *C* that falls under *B* and take up the argument from that point. So it seems that Analysis here is another name for likening, and Synthesis is a slight adaptation of likening.[118] The dashed line in the diagram above represents the fact that *C* is used in the search for *B* in Analysis but not in Synthesis.

As to how to establish that a particular candidate meets the conditions or fails to meet them, al-Fārābī will begin to consider this question systematically in Part 18d.

We turn to the derivation of the major premise (3.17.3) from (3.17.2). The details of the derivation as he describes it in paragraph 17.2 are not entirely clear. But probably he deduces from (3.17.2) that

(3.17.4) Every *B* is an *A* because it is a *B*.

He seems to regard (3.17.2) as equivalent to the conjunction of (3.17.4) and '*D* is a *B*'. Having deduced (3.17.4), he goes on to derive the major premise (3.17.3) directly from (3.17.4).[119]

Part 17 is the first of several places in which al-Fārābī discusses arguments to the effect that the world or some part of the world is created. His most intricate examples are in Part 18b below, and we postpone a general discussion of these arguments to the Introduction to Part 18b in Section 3.19.

3.18 Introducing Part 18a: General observations

Part 18a is a brief introduction to the logical analysis of real-life arguments. It would more naturally have come between Parts 15 and 16. Al-Fārābī's main source for it is probably *Analytica Priora* 1.32, 46b40–47b14. There Aristotle in the Baghdad Standard translation ([109] 294–297) speaks of analysing arguments found 'either in questioning or in books', and comments on the need to remove redundant material or add premises that have been omitted. Aristotle sees this work as a part of his project to 'reduce syllogizings to the aforementioned figures', a project that he had introduced in *Analytica Priora* 1.23–25. Aristotle also maintains (in 1.25) that some arguments need to be read not as one syllogism but as several interlocking syllogisms; al-Fārābī will pick this up with his notion of 'compound syllogisms' in Part 18b.

The reference to arguments in 'books' will have meant more to al-Fārābī than it did to Aristotle. Presumably Aristotle had in mind philosophical discussions conducted through debates and circulated essays. But by the time of al-Fārābī there had come into being a large literature of commentaries on the works of Aristotle and Plato. Already in the time of the Middle Platonists there were commentaries on Plato's dialogues that undertook to rewrite Plato's arguments in syllogistic form; for example in the second or third century AD Alcinous [4] 159,7–14 claims to find in the dialogue *Parmenides* a three-premise compound hypothetical syllogism. The author of *Harmony* ([77], dubiously attributed to al-Fārābī) quotes at 87,7–10 an analysis of an argument of Plato into a categorical syllogism. Parts 18 to 20 of al-Fārābī's *Syllogism* can be read as making a case that analysis into syllogisms should be applied to rational arguments in general, including biology and Islamic theology.[120]

3.19 Introducing Part 18b: Compound syllogisms

The syllogisms

This Part is built on the observation that several two-premise syllogisms can be built up into a single compound argument by taking the conclusion of one syllogism as premise of another in such a way that all the two-premise syllogisms are connected up. Al-Fārābī calls this compound argument a syllogism too, in fact a compound syllogism (*qiyās murakkab*). In contexts where some syllogisms can be compound, we will refer to the non-compound two-premise syllogisms as 'simple', though al-Fārābī himself doesn't use this expression.

Expressions equivalent to *qiyās murakkab* do occur in the Baghdad Standard, but it is not clear that they ever mean what al-Fārābī means, namely that syllogisms are joined up by taking the conclusion of one as a premise of another. For example the Baghdad Standard applies such a phrase to *Analytica Priora* 36b20 for a syllogism 'compounded from' two premises; or again in the translation of 68a11 two syllogisms are said to be 'compounded' when one is used to prove 'Every *B* is an *A*' and the other to prove 'Every *A* is a *B*'. The meaning of the phrase in the Arabic header to *Analytica Priora* 1.42 is unclear, and in any case the header may have been added after al-Fārābī was dead.

So very probably al-Fārābī should take credit for identifying this branch of study.[121] But compound syllogisms in al-Fārābī's sense are probably present at *Analytica Priora* 1.23–25, 40b17–42b26; 1.42, 50a5–10 and *Analytica Posteriora* 1.12, 78a14–21.

Al-Fārābī gives two examples of compound syllogisms. The first is made up of seven simple syllogisms in the mood *Barbara* with the following formal structure:

(3.20.1)

Every *H* is a *G*. Every *G* is an *F*.

Every *H* is an *F*. Every *F* is an *E*.

Every *H* is an *E*. Every *E* is a *D*.

Every *H* is a *D*. Every *D* is a *C*.

Every *H* is a *C*. Every *C* is a *B*.

Every *H* is a *B*. Every *B* is an *A*.

The *I* is an *H*. **Every *H* is an *A*.**

The *I* is an *A*.

The premises printed in boldface are those which are both premises and conclusions of simple syllogisms. At 39,8–10 al-Fārābī says that we can omit the boldface premises since they are implied. Most likely he means that they can be reconstructed by starting at the top of the diagram with the premises printed in roman, and working downward by logical deduction.

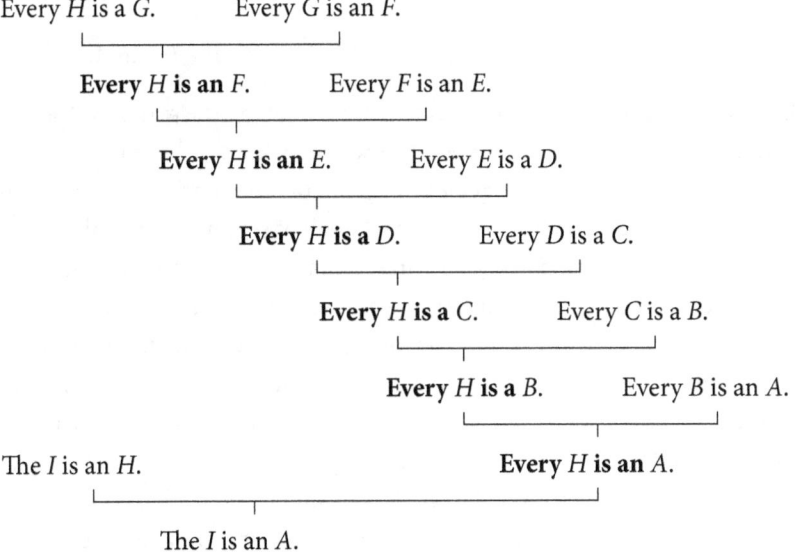

If this is what he means, he is guilty of a slight oversimplification. Here is another compound syllogism with exactly the same roman premises in the same order, and the same conclusion:

(3.20.2)

The *I* is an *H*. Every *H* is a *G*.

The *I* **is a** *G*. Every *G* is an *F*.

The *I* **is an** *F*. Every *F* is an *E*.

The *I* **is an** *E*. Every *E* is a *D*.

The *I* **is a** *D*. Every *D* is a *C*.

The *I* **is a** *C*. Every *C* is a *B*.

The *I* **is a** *B*. Every *B* is an *A*.

The *I* is an *A*.

The boldface premises are completely different from before. The reason is clear: we can reconstruct the boldface premises when we know the conclusion and roman premises *and the shape of the compound syllogism*. But the conclusion and roman premises allow the compound syllogism to take any of several different shapes.

Do the two reconstructions of al-Fārābī's first compound syllogism carry different information about the underlying argument? A century later Avicenna believed that the answer was Yes, and he introduced some useful terminology in order to discuss the point. Namely, Avicenna refers to the bottom simple syllogism in a compound syllogism, i.e. the simple syllogism with the same conclusion as the compound syllogism, as the 'proximate syllogism' (*qiyās qarīb*); the 'proximate premises' are the two premises of the proximate syllogism. ([146] 9.3, 433,10.)

Thus if we look at the two reconstructions above and translate them back into material sentences, we see that the proximate syllogism of the first is what al-Fārābī calls the 'seventh syllogism':

The world is a body;
(3.19.3) every body has a created existence.
Therefore the world has a created existence.

By contrast the proximate syllogism of the second reconstruction is

(3.19.4)
The world exists after having been nonexistent;
everything that exists after having been nonexistent
has a created existence.
Therefore the world has a created existence.

These two proximate syllogisms contain different answers to the heuristic question: If you were aiming to show that the world is created, where would you start your enquiry? Should you begin by laying out the broad landscape as in (3.20.1), or should you go first to the relevant details as in (3.20.2)? In this way the two reconstructed compound syllogisms represent different heuristics. Al-Fārābī himself never mentions this point, and possibly he was not consciously aware of it. But the fact that he complicated the overall shape of (3.20.1) by using the proximate syllogism (3.19.3) is evidence that he felt some need to use (3.19.3) rather than (3.19.4).

Al-Fārābī's second example of a compound syllogism was analysed already in Section 3.15.

Proofs of creation

Al-Fārābī's examples of arguments for analysis include seven arguments proving that the world or some major aspect of it (such as the sky) is created, as follows:

para	**passage**	**to illustrate**
17.2	36,11–37,3	likening
18b.3f	38,14–39,11	compound syllogism
18b.5	40,1–4	nonhomogeneous compound syllogism
19.2	45,12–46,14	likening
19.8	48,15–49,5	failure of likening-with-induction
19.10	49,14–17	method of rejecting
19.12	51,13–52,7	redundancy of accepting+rejecting

Two of these arguments, including the very complex argument at paragraph 18b.3, are in Part 18b.

In al-Fārābī's time, arguments about whether the world is created were familiar both in Aristotelian philosophy and in *kalām* (Islamic philosophical theology).[122] But as the chart indicates, al-Fārābī presents these seven arguments as illustrations of logical structures. The primary message that al-Fārābī sends by using the arguments in this way is that arguments in general can be analysed within the framework of Aristotelian logic; the reader is not likely to learn much here about the creation of the world. But some arguments, particularly the one set out in paragraph 18b.3, use some notions that call for explanation.

All seven arguments use the concept 'created'. This is two related words in Arabic: *ḥādith* and *muḥdath*, the first an active participle and the second a passive participle. But both words are used to cover the same range of ideas.[123] To say that a thing *X* is created could indicate either of the following, among other possibilities:

(i) *X* was made by an agent. The argument at paragraph 17.2 illustrates this. Al-Fārābī says nothing to clarify what counts as an agent. In his argument at 38,15 al-Fārābī mentions that the world is composed; Saadia[124] had argued that a composed thing must have had a composer.

(ii) *X* came into being out of pre-existing matter. This is the claim made at paragraph 19.8. Since the matter was pre-existing, it follows that at some time in the past *X* didn't exist. But that would be the case also if *X* was created out of nothing at some time in the past, a possibility that al-Fārābī doesn't consider. In *Syllogism* al-Fārābī ignores creation out of nothing; but this could simply reflect the fact that he is reviewing arguments based on observation, and creation out of nothing is not something that we observe.

Al-Fārābī's argument in paragraph 18b.3 reflects one type of argument that was used to prove (ii). We wish to show that some substance (either *X* or some part of *X*) didn't always exist. It would be enough to show that this substance has, at all times of its existence, some property that nothing could have had at all times in the past. Such properties appear in the literature under the name 'irremovable accident' (*araḍ lā yanfakku minhu*).[125] The name comes from Islamic theology, though anybody familiar with the Peripatetic notion of an inseparable accident will see a similarity. In al-Fārābī's terminology a substance with an irremovable accident is said to be 'attached to a created thing' – the created thing is the accident. So this line of argument can be summarized as 'Everything attached to a created (*ḥādith*) thing is created (*muḥdath*)'.[126] Al-Fārābī simply reports this as one step in a complex argument, but clearly anybody who wants to make the argument stick will need to spend some time analysing the notion of an irremovable accident.

One further comment may be in order. In *Syllogism* al-Fārābī never connects the notion of creation with that of a divine being. All of his arguments for creation, with the one exception of that in 17.2 which proves the existence of a creative agent, can be read as contributions to philosophical physics. This illustrates al-Fārābī's view in his *Letters/Particles* [75] 131,6–9 that the claims of religion are really philosophical claims, expressed in a language that makes them more appealing to the general population.[127] But one should be cautious about presenting al-Fārābī as a person who championed the claims of philosophy over against those of religion. The broadly Neoplatonist philosophy that he espoused was in its own way a form of religion.

3.20 Introducing Part 18c: Induction and syllogism

In Part 18c al-Fārābī considers the use of an induction not as a self-contained argument, but as a component of a larger argument. More precisely he assumes that we are aiming to perform a syllogism in the first figure, for example

(3.20.1) Every C is a B; every B is an A.
Therefore every C is an A.

and we use induction to verify one of the two premises.[128] If we take for granted from Part 16 the formalization of the induction as a syllogism, then the result will be a compound syllogism. It could have either of two forms, according as the induction is used to verify the minor premise 'Every C is a B' of (3.20.1) or the major premise 'Every B is an A'. Or indeed two separate inductions could be used, one to verify the minor premise and the other to verify the major, though al-Fārābī doesn't consider this possibility.

In *Syllogism* al-Fārābī speaks only about using induction to justify the *major* premise of a syllogism in the first figure.[129] In fact he introduces this compound at 40,5–10 in Part 18c, and he continues to work with it until the end of *Syllogism*. Also at *Debate* [70] 97,16–18,1 he says that in debate, induction is used just to verify the major premise of a syllogism in first figure; he adds that induction is used 'never or hardly at all' as the immediate proof of the desired conclusion of an argument.

In Part 18c of *Syllogism* al-Fārābī gives two examples of induction being used to justify the major premise of a syllogism in the mood *Barbara*. The first example uses letters and the second uses material terms, but their formal content is the same. If we adjust the lettering of the lettered version so as to match Part 16, it takes the following form:

(3.20.2)

Every B_1 is an A.
⋮
Every B_n is an A.
[Every B is a B_1 or . . . or a B_n.]
|
C is a B. Every B is an A.
C is an A.

Al-Fārābī omits the completeness condition; we have added it between square brackets because it is needed to make the argument valid. Al-Fārābī's text doesn't make clear whether $B_1, \ldots, B_n$ is a complete list of cases of *B*; his wording in paragraph 18c.1 suggests it is, but in paragraph 18c.2 he introduces the list with 'such as' (*mithla*). For definiteness we will assume that the listed cases do in fact exhaust *B*, so that the completeness condition is true.

Al-Fārābī claims to find a 'defect' in this proof. He refers to this defect several times later in *Syllogism*.[130] In his description of the defect he alternates between 'we' and 'he' through the course of four paragraphs (18c.1–4), creating a strong impression that 'we' have hired a man to do the verifying for us. This may be a device to objectify the procedure. If so, it works better than al-Fārābī realized, since it calls attention to the fact that al-Fārābī has missed out a vital part of the instructions to our hired man: is he supposed just to be checking cases, or is it also his job to verify the completeness condition?

The defect is presented as a dilemma. The dilemma division is whether or not we are sure that our man has in fact examined all the cases of *B*. Al-Fārābī assumes we know that the man has found that *A* is true of every case that he examined.

The first case of the dilemma is where we are not sure that the man has examined all the cases. Then we don't know that he has verified that every *B* is an *A*; so the conclusion fails. This problem with induction was known already in classical times.[131] It may be significant that at 42,5f al-Fārābī says that in this case no conclusion follows 'necessarily', i.e. logically. This leaves open the possibility that an incomplete induction could still imply that every *B* is an *A*, but with less than logical certainty.

The second case of the dilemma is that we are sure that our man has examined all the cases of *B*. In this case we know that he has examined the case *C* which is the subject term of the minor premise. But then *C* will be one of the particular cases listed, say B_i. Therefore the conclusion '*C* is an *A*' is identical with the premise 'B_i is an *A*', and the proof (3.20.2) is circular. This is a defect because it means that we already knew the conclusion when we knew the premises, and nothing was gained by performing the syllogism.[132]

There are two problems with al-Fārābī's account of this second case. The first was pointed out by Avicenna in his critique of al-Fārābī's theory of induction at *Qiyās* [146] 9.22. The proof in the diagram is a compound, consisting of a simple syllogism and an induction. Although the two parts can be fitted together into one proof, there is no compulsion to use them at the same time;

the induction could have been carried out earlier than the syllogism (*qad tabayyana qablu*, [146] 564,6). But in that case the premises of the induction need not enter the mind of the reasoner at the same time as the simple syllogism (cf. [146] 565,15). So in real time the conclusion of the simple syllogism, 'Every C is an A', need not already be available to the reasoner who uses the simple syllogism.

The second problem is that even assuming we know the completeness condition, C might be not one of $B_1, \ldots, B_n$ but an individual falling under one of them, or even a class whose members are scattered between different B_is. In this case al-Fārābī could fairly say that more reasoning is needed to reach the conclusion, but it wouldn't follow that the compound syllogism (3.20.2) is redundant.

3.21 Introducing Parts 18d and 19: The major premise

Parts 18d and 19 both run over the same material, covering various aspects of likening, induction and the use of the 'major premise'. Part 18d is not well presented. Overall it has a negative feel: we are told how not to verify the major premise, but not what we ought to have done instead. We are told that certain people committed certain errors, but we are not told the context in which these errors occurred. There is confusion about exactly what relationship between B and A is under discussion; it may be helpful to list here the options that are mentioned in Part 18d.[133]

(i) Every B is an A because it is a B (42,16, see Note on translation)
(ii) B is the cause of A. (43,14; 44,2)
(iii) Every B is an A and vice versa. (44,16)
(iv) Necessarily every B is an A. (43,3, cf. [68] 103.8)
(v) Whenever and wherever a thing is a B it is an A. (44,4.8, cf. [68] 103,6)
(vi) Every B is an A. (44,2f and *passim*)
(vii) The B is an A. (42,19)

The account of this same material in Part 19 of *Syllogism* is more leisurely and better organized, and bears all the marks of being a later essay than Part 18d. There is also a parallel account in *Analysis* [68] (al-Fārābī's abridgement of parts of Aristotle's *Topica*), and there are some overlaps with pages 99f of *Debate* [70].

In view of their common subject matter, we introduce Parts 18d and 19 together, picking up themes that appear in both.

1. The names and sources of the methods

In Part 18d al-Fārābī refers only to the methods of reasoning that he has already introduced in Parts 16 and 17: induction and likening, both of them taken originally from *Analytica Priora*. In Part 19 he returns to these same methods, or very closely related ones, but with some new vocabulary. A kind of likening appears under the names of 'transfer from the observed to the unobserved' (*nuqlatu min al-shāhid ilā al-ghā'ib*, 46,14f) and 'inference to the unobserved by means of the observed' (*istidlāl bi al-shāhid ᶜalā al-ghā'ib*, 45,10). Both these names can be traced to the philosophy of medicine that served as a forum for debating issues of rationality and empiricism in the early Roman Empire. Al-Fārābī will have seen Galen as the leading figure in these debates. In fact 'inference to the unobserved by means of the observed' is almost verbatim for *istidlāl bi-mā ẓahara ᶜalā mā khafiya* in Ḥubaysh's rendering of Galen *On Medical Experience* [84] (23,7 and elsewhere); and at *Analysis* [68] 104,8f Galen is described as taking observable things as causes of things not open to observation.[134] Transfer (*nuqla*) is probably a translation of Greek *metábasis*, a term also used in these medical debates.

At 48,7 al-Fārābī introduces the name of another method, 'drawing out the content of the cause with regard to its effects', and at 48,10 he mentions another name 'driving out' for the same or a related method. The source of the method is not known, but both the context of the discussion and the negative connotations of 'driving out' suggest that al-Fārābī is talking about a method of refutation.

A reference to Galen at *Analysis* [68] 104,8 will allow us to pin down Galen as the chief person referred to in Part 18d at 43,13. But it would be rash to assume that Galen himself is one of al-Fārābī's sources here. When we consider Galen and causes later in this Section, we will see that the reference to Galen in *Analysis* makes such a crass distortion of Galen's position that al-Fārābī is unlikely to have had Galen's own words in front of him. More likely al-Fārābī was working from a source that contained criticisms of Galen.

2. The search

Both induction and likening involve some form of search procedure, though it is a different kind of search in the two cases. For induction, a middle term B is given, and we have to (i) divide B into particular cases and (ii) verify that the content A is true of each particular case. For likening, the search is to find a middle term B fitting the condition that it is a cause (or more precisely that D is an *A* because it is a *B*); during the search, each candidate has to be checked to see that it does fit this condition. In both cases the major premise is then used as major premise for a syllogism in the first figure, to prove that the content *A* is true of certain things that are known to be *B*s.

In the case of likening we need to know where to look for candidates to be the middle term. Al-Fārābī tells us in Part 19 that for transfer from observed to unobserved[135] there are two possible strategies. The first, which he calls Analysis, is to consider the observed *D* and the unobserved *C*, and look for concepts *B* that both *D* and *C* fall under. The second strategy, which he calls Synthesis, is to ignore *C* during the search and simply look among concepts that *D* falls under. Then when a suitable middle term *B* is found, we can choose *C* to be anything that falls under *B*. This distinction between Analysis and Synthesis is entirely about the organization of the search for the middle term *B*, and has nothing to do with any prooftheoretic devices used for verifying or applying the major premise.[136]

Since the search in likening and the search in induction are aimed at answering different questions, one could devize a strategy that involves both. Thus one would use likening to set the problem of finding a *B* such that *D* is an *A* because it is a *B*; then for each candidate *B*, induction would be used to try to verify that *B* does meet this condition. The verification will yield a major premise for syllogisms. Al-Fārābī refers at *Debate* [70] 99,12–100,13 to 'people' who made just such a combination of induction, likening and syllogism; he muses about whether it should count as rhetorical, dialectical or scientific. The people that he refers to are not identified.

The claim at *Syllogism* 42,7 that 'likening can be used in place of induction', and the claim that 'likening can be used to verify an objective' six lines below, are both misleading; likening finds a term *B*, but likening by itself does nothing to verify the major premise 'Every *B* is an *A*'. Al-Fārābī is well aware of this and devotes most of Part 18d to explaining it. But his exposition is confused; at 43,13ff he says what he should have said here, namely that 'Some people' claimed to be able to use likening in place of induction, but their claim was unjustified.

Having introduced the topic of search procedures that lead to syllogisms for verifying statements, al-Fārābī points out that the logical force of the procedure rests entirely in the final syllogism, and that this syllogism proves or refutes the statement regardless of how the syllogism was found. For convenience we call this observation the self-sufficiency of syllogism.[137] He makes this observation at

43,10–12 in Part 18d, where he tells us that if likening and/or induction are used to find a syllogism verifying a statement,

> then both the likening and the syllogism would lapse, since the syllogism on its own would do the verifying. The thing that verified that *A* is true of *C* would be a syllogism, and so neither likening nor induction would serve any purpose.[138]

Clearly this is an exaggeration: if likening or induction was used to find the syllogism, then it did serve a purpose. If the induction was used to find the evidence that justifies the major premise, then again it did serve a purpose. Al-Fārābī's reason for downgrading the search element in this way is unclear.

In a similar vein, al-Fārābī describes various proofs or proof procedures as 'potentially' syllogisms or as 'reducing' to syllogisms.[139] The proof or procedure in all these cases can be paraphrased so as to finish with a syllogism that proves the same conclusion as the original argument. (In the case of reduction to the first figure of syllogisms in the second and third figures, a final conversion may be needed to bring the conclusion to this form, as with *Disamis* at 28,14.) Then self-sufficiency of syllogism tells us that the logical force of the argument is unaffected if we delete the preliminaries (including the search) and retain only the syllogism. But of course the syllogism still keeps any feature that the preliminaries fed into its premises. In the case of likening, this includes the introduction of a universal premise that was not there at the outset; this is what al-Fārābī means at 64,11 when he says that the starting point of a likening is potentially, and reduces to, a universal premise.

3. The topics of Accepting and Rejecting

In the opening sentences of his *Analysis* [68] 95,3–8 al-Fārābī explains that a topic (*mawḍiᶜ*) is a means to finding a major premise for a syllogism to verify a given objective. Each topic embraces many specific premises that can be used in rhetoric, debate or science. The remainder of *Analysis* is devoted to reviewing some of the main topics from this point of view. Among them are the topics of consequence ([68] 102,4), which include the topics of Accepting (*wujūd*) and Rejecting (*irtifāᶜ*).[140] As with other topics, al-Fārābī explains first how Accepting and Rejecting can be used to find hypothetical premises, and secondly how they can be used to find universally quantified categorical premises.[141]

Al-Fārābī's disinclination to adopt precise definitions and stick to them creates a kind of scenery where broad shapes emerge from the mist and then subside back into it. What follows is an attempt to give al-Fārābī's shapes some solidity with the help of modern logic. There is an obvious danger of anachronism here, but the alternative is to treat al-Fārābī's text as pure literature, abandoning the attempt to find logical substance in it.

Al-Fārābī's discussion of Accepting and Rejecting as the source of hypothetical premises (*Analysis* [68] 102,6–19) allows us to paraphrase the topics as follows:

Accepting

(Topic) The inference from the truth of *p* to the truth of *q* is valid.

|

(Schematic premise) If *p* then *q*.

Rejecting

(Topic) The inference from the falsehood of *q* to the falsehood of *p* is valid.

|

(Schematic premise) If *p* then *q*.

In other words, if sentences are put for *p* and *q* that make either of these inferences valid, then from this fact we can deduce the proposition 'If *p* then *q*'.[142]

Al-Fārābī mentions the connection between the topics of Accepting and Rejecting and hypothetical premises at *Syllogism* 57,17, but makes no use of it. (The fact that he mentions it at all is a clue that he is reading through a source text on topics.) His main interest in Parts 18d and 19 of *Syllogism* is the major premise, which is a universally quantified categorical sentence. So his use of the topics of Accepting and Rejecting to derive premises of this kind is more directly relevant for us. He slightly revises the topics as follows.[143]

Accepting

(Topic) The inference from '*C* is a *B*' to '*C* is an *A*' is valid.

|

(Schematic premise) Every *B* is an *A*.

Rejecting

(Topic) The inference from '*C* is not an *A*' to '*C* is not a *B*' is valid.

|

(Schematic premise) Every *B* is an *A*.

As in the propositional case, the inferences are allowed to depend on material properties of the terms put for *A* and *B*. But al-Fārābī rightly points out that this is not the case with *C*. If *C* is replaced by any name of an individual, then the 'Every' in 'Every *B* is an *A*' loses its justification. He is not so clear on what should be said about *C* instead. By analogy with the condition on the variable in the natural deduction rule for ∀-introduction, the requirement should be that *C* is completely unspecified. Al-Fārābī comes near this at *Syllogism* 51,2 where he refers to *C* as 'the thing under consideration'. But normally he simply omits any mention of *C*.[144]

Al-Fārābī believes that Accepting and Rejecting are robust rules for deriving 'Every *B* is an *A*'. At *Syllogism* 49,18 he says that the application of these rules to likening is 'sound and it would not be possible to oppose it'. But he moves on to discuss two mistakes that can be made in using these topics to derive a categorical premise 'Every *B* is an *A*'. The first mistake is to use one of these topics in the wrong direction, assuming '*C* is an *A*' to infer '*C* is a *B*', or assuming '*C* is not a *B*' to infer '*C* is not an *A*'.[145]

The second mistake is one of redundancy. If 'Every *B* is an *A*' has been derived by using Accepting from *B* to *A*, nothing is gained by adding another derivation that uses Rejecting from *A* to *B*.

4. Galen and proving cause

In *Syllogism* 43,13f al-Fārābī remarks that 'some people' became aware of a gap in the argument when induction is combined with likening so as to prove that the middle term is the cause. We can guess that the problem was that an induction yields a proof that every *B* is an *A*, but does nothing to ensure that being a *B* is a cause of being an *A*. He says that the people who detected this fault then moved away from induction to another procedure that he doesn't name; but it seems to have involved an inference from 'this is a *B*' to 'this is an *A*', which suggests that it involved the topic of Accepting.

As if to confirm this suggestion, al-Fārābī devotes a section (104,4–107,10) of *Analysis* [68] to the question how the topics of Accepting and Rejecting can be used to derive a causal premise. He says at [68] 105,2–4 that some people thought they could make the derived premise causal by applying both Accepting and Rejecting, so as to show that *B* and *A* are coextensional. Also 'people' are said to have used these topics in the context of induction and likening, so as to prove that the major premise is a necessary truth ([68] 106,2–5). This could reflect a view that if the truth of the sentence 'Every *B* is an *A*' follows from a logical inference, then the sentence has some form of logical necessity. However, al-Fārābī's discussion in this section covers a number of possibilities without reaching any clear conclusion about any of them.[146]

Among these various suggestions for proving cause, al-Fārābī at *Analysis* [68] 104,8 names Galen as a scholar who used the topic of Rejecting as a means to proving a causal statement, but used it in the wrong direction for the causation. Galen knew that if certain nerves in an animal are severed, the animal is unable to move. According to al-Fārābī, Galen deduced from this that the nerves are a cause of movement. He insists that Galen has read the implications in the wrong direction; to prove that intact nerves cause the movement we have to show the implication (intact nerves → movement), not the converse.

We need to place this in the context of Galen's own statements. Galen was interested in voluntary movement, and in particular he wanted to identify the channels by which control of voluntary movement passes from the control centre (the *hēgemonikón*) to the organs that move. He collected evidence that the channels are the tree-like structure of nerves that radiates from the cerebral ventricles where he placed the control centre. Part of his evidence was that if a branch of the nervous system is separated from the main tree, voluntary movement ceases in the organs served by this branch.[147]

It will be clear that al-Fārābī is deploying a notion of cause that is far too crude to represent Galen's claims. A first step in the right direction – but only a first step – would be to distinguish between saying that being a *B* is *a* cause of being an *A* and saying that being a *B* is *the* cause of being an *A*. Al-Fārābī has no interest even in advancing this far towards Galen's viewpoint.[148]

Putting together the texts in *Syllogism* and *Analysis*, we can safely infer that the 'some people' at *Syllogism* 43,13f include Galen.[149] But in view of al-Fārābī's lack of awareness of Galen's real position, it seems likely that al-Fārābī's source for this aspect of Galen's work in both *Syllogism* and *Analysis* was primarily a study of topics, in which the author made reference to various applications of the topics of Accepting and Rejecting, citing Galen as an example.[150]

5. Tolerance (*musāmaḥa*)

The speculative comments that we make below are intended first to put al-Fārābī's remarks about tolerance of inaccurate arguments into their proper context, and second to explain why in an abridgement of *Analytica Priora* al-Fārābī chose not to include a section on modal logic. In both cases the context is al-Fārābī's view of how logic in general relates to Aristotle's listing of categorical moods.

For al-Fārābī, the rules of logic consist of the rules of categorical logic as set out by Aristotle, together with the classical moods of hypothetical logic. In particular the rules of modal logic are simply the rules of categorical logic but applied with a certain spin put on the sentences. There is no known example of al-Fārābī proposing any new rule of logic that is not an example of the classical categorical and hypothetical rules. For al-Fārābī the task of a logician in syllogistic logic is to examine various interpretations of the sentences involved, and determine which of the classical rules are safe to use under each of these interpretations.

Aristotle himself had led the way by introducing modal interpretations and then discussing, mood by mood, which moods would allow these interpretations. Thus Aristotle pointed out that modal sentences could be read in several ways: at *Analytica Priora* 1.15, 34b7f he considers a restriction to a particular time, and at *Analytica Priora* 1.13, 32b3–9 he suggests that 'possibly' could be read as 'in most cases . . . like a human becoming grey-haired'. It would be reasonable to suppose that when Aristotle says such things in the middle of a discussion of syllogisms, he means to imply that the syllogistic rules he is discussing will still apply when 'possibly' is read as 'in most cases'.[151]

So for example when al-Fārābī wants to use premises that talk about 'most cases', it will never occur to him to check what rules could be introduced to fit these sentences. Instead he will assume that it is a good approximation to treat 'in most cases' as a variant of 'in all cases' or 'possibly' and hope for the best. It may not always work out right, but 'the arts in which these sentences are used are of a nature to be highly tolerant in their treatment of the pieces of knowledge that they provide' (64,7f).

There is another kind of situation where al-Fārābī recommends tolerance in reasoning. This is where it is recognized as rational (or in al-Fārābī's preferred description, 'useful') to accept a premise of the form 'Every *C* is an *A*' as being literally true, on the evidence of just a few *C*s. These situations probably include those mentioned by al-Fārābī at 61,16–18, where it is simply not possible to examine all the cases of *C*. The justification for accepting universal premises on the basis of less than total evidence will be some form of incomplete induction, and the 'tolerance' consists of relying on induction rather than logical deduction from the evidence.

Here al-Fārābī's notion of 'useful tolerance' identifies a central problem of epistemology, namely that we often have good reason to believe a statement 'Every *C* is an *A*' on the evidence of a small number of particular cases, too small to deduce this statement logically. But having named the problem, al-Fārābī says little that is helpful for solving it.

Though this laissez-faire view of the laws of logic will astonish most modern logicians, it may have been more widespread in al-Fārābī's time than we realize.[152]

We can see Avicenna beginning to break free from it. For example he prefers to introduce new inference rules (such as the many-premise rule that he defines in order to replace al-Fārābī's attempt to use *Barbara* in induction, cf. Section 3.20 above), rather than blur the old rules to cover new cases. We never hear Avicenna recommending 'tolerant' use of logical rules.[153]

6. Refutation by induction

We can be brief here. At 48,6–13; 49,5–11; 58,13–17; 60,10–13 al-Fārābī points out that a failure to prove the major premise 'Every *B* is an *A*' may throw up an example of a *B* that is not an *A*. In this case we have a refutation of 'Every *B* is an *A*', e. a proof of 'Some *B* is not an *A*'. He shows how the procedure in this case finishes up with a syllogism, just as in the positive case where 'Every *B* is an *A*' is proved. But unlike the positive case, the syllogism will be in third figure. At 49,9 he shows how it can be done in the mood *Felapton*; but in fact *Bocardo* suffices, with a weaker minor premise.

3.22 Introducing Part 20: Jurisprudential syllogisms

Among various titles that we find attached to *Short Syllogism* in the manuscripts, one title describes it as 'about logic in the manner of the theologians'. 'Theologians' here are *mutakallimūn*, specialists in *kalām* which is the philosophical or scholastic theology of Islam. The title is odd: nothing in *Short Syllogism* outside the Tailpiece is theological, the theological content of Part 19 of the Tailpiece is not specifically Islamic, and the theological content of the present part (Part 20) is religious jurisprudence rather than philosophical theology. Al-Fārābī himself would hardly have given this title either to *Short Syllogism* or to *Syllogism*. Probably some readers were impressed by the explicitly Islamic content of Part 20 of the Tailpiece, and they may not have realized that Part 19 has its origins outside Islam.[154]

In fact there are ten examples in Part 20, and all but one of them are sentences taken from the Qur'ān, though not always verbatim.[155] The grammatical forms of the sentences vary. Some of them command us to behave in a certain way in certain situations (3, 4, 5, 8 in Note 155 below); some say that a certain kind of action must be carried out (i.e. by someone somewhere, 6 in Note 155); some say that a certain kind of action is forbidden (1,2,7 in Note 155); some advise against a certain kind of action (10 in Note 155); one is an indicative statement (9 in Note 155).

In order to make all of these sentences premises of syllogisms, al-Fārābī requires us to paraphrase them as declarative (i.e. true or false) sentences; in practice he means categorical sentences. Thus a sentence 'Avoid X' paraphrases into 'All X is to be avoided'.[156] Also al-Fārābī reminds us in paragraph 20.4 that before we apply the paraphrased sentence, we should ensure that its terms are unambiguous.[157]

We will assume that all ten examples, and any other sentences that al-Fārābī wants us to consider in this context, have been brought to the form 'Every *D* is an *A*'. This will bring the discussion below into line with the notation of Section 3.17 above. As in that section, al-Fārābī allows us to replace *D* by a universal term *B* such that every *B* is an *A*. Then we apply *D* indirectly to any particular case *C* of *B* by forming a syllogism in the mood *Barbara*: 'Every *C* is a *B*; every *B* is an *A*. Therefore every *C* is an *A*'. As in Section 3.17, the major premise is 'Every *B* is an *A*'.

The discipline of Islamic jurisprudence, *fiqh*, exists precisely because the statements that we read in the Qur'ān – in particular the commands and prohibitions – can't all be taken as self-explanatory. They need rational interpretation, and there are experts who offer this. Al-Fārābī's Part 20 can be read as a Peripatetic logician's commentary on the kind of rational interpretation that is needed.

On al-Fārābī's analysis, the reason why interpretation is needed is that when Allah tells us 'Every *D* is an *A*', Allah means us to understand 'Every *B* is an *A*', where any one of three cases can occur:

(a) *B* is *D*;
(b) *B* is a particular case of *D*;
(c) *D* is a particular case of *B*.[158]

Al-Fārābī devotes paragraphs 20.5–7 to case (b) and paragraphs 20.8–18 to case (c).[159] Case (a) is mentioned in paragraphs 20.7 and 20.10; in both places al-Fārābī remarks that we are not always told whether *D* should be understood as it stands, so that before we look for the interpretation *B*, we also need to determine whether any interpretation is needed.

The reader may be puzzled why al-Fārābī thinks that if *D* needs interpretation, it is always meant to be understood as a term either narrower or broader than *D*, as in (b) and (c).[160] Al-Fārābī's reason for mentioning the two cases (b) and (c) becomes clear at paragraph 20.10, where he comments that what he said earlier about inference to the unobserved by means of the observed (in Part 19) can be applied to case (c) with *D* as the observed and *C* as the unobserved. He discusses case (b) only briefly and to create a kind of literary symmetry. The application of Part 19 to case (c) is the real *raison d'être* of Part 20.

Al-Fārābī doesn't always mention that the speaker is Allah. In fact the example of expecting no good from one's children may be included precisely to make the point that interpretation of Allah's statements in the Qur'ān is only a special case of the interpretation of things said to us, given that Allah and humans address us in the same Arabic language. Al-Fārābī will have known of discussions by the *mutakallimūn* of the similarities between divine and human uses of language. But we don't know of any specific texts of *kalām* that he is engaging with here.

When we are addressed with a sentence 'Every *D* is an *A*', al-Fārābī considers how we can tell whether we were intended to understand *D* as *D*, and if we weren't, how we can find how we were intended to understand it. He seems to have a single method for answering both questions: namely that we look for a term *B* suitably related to *D*, such that we can prove by a syllogism that 'Every *B* is an *A*'; finding such a term *B*, we assume that we were meant to understand that we are being told 'Every *B* is an *A*'. This method is justified only if we have good reason to believe that the reading we were intended to take is in fact true. In the case where the speaker is Allah this is a rational assumption. But it is not obviously rational when the speaker is human; al-Fārābī seems to miss this point. Also al-Fārābī ignores the possibility of *asking* the speaker what they meant; this suggests that he has in mind statements that reach us from a written text or from tradition, so that there is no speaker available for us to ask.

In case (c), where the intended replacement for *D* is a term *B* that is broader than *D*, al-Fārābī's proposed method is very close to that of inference to the unobserved (i.e. cases of *B*) by means of the observed (i.e. *D*). Al-Fārābī draws attention to this similarity at 57,16f and again at 57,21f. After making this point, he repeats for case (c) a number of points that he made in Part 19 (and in Part 18d in *Syllogism*) about logical features of this form of inference. For example induction[161] can be used to verify the major premise, but the same dilemma arises as in Part 18c (cf. Section 3.20 above). In consequence the only logically watertight use of induction here is to find counterexamples so as to refute the major premise (58,13f). The method described in paragraphs 20.12 and 20.13 corresponds to what al-Fārābī called Synthesis in Part 19; i.e. the search for *B* starts with *D* and doesn't presuppose that we have a particular case to which we want to transfer the content. Also al-Fārābī repeats in paragraph 20.14 his exhortation in Part 19 to use tolerance, adding at 61,14–16 that tolerance can usefully be applied to Accepting and Rejecting.[162]

Under the head of his Fourth Principle, al-Fārābī revisits case (c) using the method of likening, which reasons from an exemplar (*mithāl*). But in one place, 63,9f, *mithāl* has to be read as meaning not an exemplar but a method; the method is one which according to Aristotle goes 'not like all to part and not like part to all, but like part to part'. Al-Fārābī is quoting *Analytica Priora* 2.24, 69a13–15, where Aristotle speaks of *parádeigma* as a method; the Baghdad Standard translates *parádeigma* here as *mithāl*.[163] This is one of the few places in his treatment of induction and likening in *Syllogism* and *Short Syllogism* where al-Fārābī refers directly to the text of Aristotle.

For al-Fārābī the method of likening, to the extent that it is a rational method at all, rests on finding a suitable universal term *B*, so as to allow the transfer from the exemplar *D* to the particular case *C* to be made by a syllogism. Al-Fārābī summarizes this point in the closing paragraph 20.19 of Part 20. But if this is so, how can Aristotle say that likening proceeds directly from the particular case *D* to the particular case *C*? Al-Fārābī's answer is that sometimes when we search for *B* and find it, we think of *B* as being connected with the exemplar *D*. For instance wheat must be exchanged fairly; so by likening, rice must also be exchanged fairly, because rice is like wheat. The analogy works only because of a concept that is true of both wheat and rice, say 'edible'. But we might think the concept as 'edible, like wheat'. If we do this then the connection to wheat makes the concept not genuinely universal (63,5). Al-Fārābī is inviting us to consider that this thought-connection is what Aristotle had in mind when he spoke of going directly from one particular case to another.

In several places this same passage refers to the concept *B* with phrases like 'the concept that makes wheat similar to rice'.[164] We have noted that al-Fārābī's method here matches Synthesis and not Analysis; so these phrases can't be read as implying that similarity to rice plays any role in the choice of the universal concept *B*. More likely al-Fārābī is preparing us for his discussion of Aristotle, roughly as follows. The prohibition on unfair exchange is transferred from wheat to rice because rice satisfies the concept *B* that makes rice like wheat. But satisfying this concept can be thought of as *being like wheat in a certain way*; by thinking of it in this way we import the concept of wheat into the concept *B* itself.

Notes

1 The first kind of example appears in al-Fārābī's *Expressions* [58] 100,3–7, and the second in his *Letters/Particles* [75] 150,13–151,8.

2 For general information on al-Fārābī and his philosophy, see also Druart [48], Fakhry [55], Janos [79] (under 'al-Fārābī, philosophy'), Netton [127] and Steinschneider [149].

3 Our chief historical sources on al-Fārābī are Ibn Zayd al-Bayhaqī (*c.* 1097–1169/70) [20], Ibn al-Qifṭī (1172–1248) [132], Ibn Abī al-Uṣaybiᶜa (*c.* 1194–1270) [158], Ibn Khallikān (1211–1282) [113].

4 On [73] and the poetic syllogism see Aouad and Schoeler [10] and Hodges and Druart [104].

5 See D'Ancona [44]; see also Hugonnard-Roche [108], particularly his Introduction, pp. 5–10.

6 See Brock [30] on Syriac studies of Aristotle and Porphyry.

7 We can date Paul's *Logic* from the fact that it carries a dedication to the Sassanid Persian emperor Khosraw I Anushirvan, who ruled from 531 to 579. Given this dedication, the work may have been written originally in Persian. The dating of Proba is looser and is based partly on style and format; see for example Brock [30] p. 7.

8 Ibn al-Muqaffaᶜ is best known for his translations from Persian, see [114]. But it's entirely possible that he translated into Arabic a Persian translation of a Syriac original.

9 There is a Syriac commentary on *Analytica Priora* which runs through both Books. It is by George Bishop of the Arabs and is dated to around 700. Since no translation is available we are unable to comment further. See Brock [30] pp. 7f.

10 See Gutas [91] on the industry of translations from Syriac to Arabic, and Hugonnard-Roche [106] on the manuscript Arabe 2346.

11 Lameer [116] pp. 3–5 identifies this Theodorus and dates the translation to the second or third quarter of the ninth century. He gives reasons for believing that the translation was made from Syriac.

12 Zimmermann [165] pp. lxviii–lxxv verified this for the *Long Commentary on De Interpretatione*, and Lameer [116] p. 8 for the *Long Commentary on Prior Analytics.*

13 The following passage illustrates this:

laysa fī l-mithāli shay'un huwa ka-juz'in ilā kullin, wa lā ka-kullin ilā juz'in, wa-ka-naḥwi mā yakūnu fī l-qiyāsi, wa lākin ka-juz'in ilā juz'in. (Baghdad Standard, Jabre [109] 402,14f.)

fa-yuzhannu bi-hādhihi al-nuqlati annahā min al-mithāli ilā shabīhihi wa-annahā min juz'ī ilā juz'ī lā min kullī ilā juz'ī ᶜalā mithāli mā ᶜalayhi al-amru fī l-qiyāsi. (*Syllogism* [66] 63,7f)

14 See Fortenbaugh [80] and Huby [105] on what is known about the logic of Theophrastus.

15 See Lee [117] pp. 66–8 or Gutas [89] pp. 261–7 for graphic examples of such trees in Greek texts.

16 Adamson [1] p. 15: '. . . as far as we can tell the Kindian tradition failed to do anything with *Analytica Priora*'.

17 The work as a whole is lost, but Uṣaybiᶜa [158] pp. 604–6 quotes several paragraphs verbatim. Fakhry [55] pp. 156–60 translates these paragraphs into English.

18 Khallikan [113] reports, some three hundred years after al-Fārābī's death, that al-Fārābī learned logic from Mattā. The story is clearly fiction, since it makes Mattā a philosopher of 'an advanced age' when al-Fārābī first arrived in Baghdad as a young man. (Al-Fārābī and Mattā were both born in around 870.) But already when the two men were alive, the educated Baghdad public may have taken Mattā to be a more senior Aristotelian than al-Fārābī; the report [54] pp. 149–163 of the confrontation between al-Sīrāfī and Mattā about the claims of Aristotelian logic in 932 contains no mention of al-Fārābī.

19 The careful study by Vallat [159] confirms that various aspects of Neoplatonic thinking had a deep effect on al-Fārābī's philosophy in general. But note that the many references to 'logique' in Vallat's book need not have much to do with *Syllogism*; al-Fārābī was apt to count as 'logic' anything mentioned in the *Organon*.

20 See Street [150] and Hodges [102]. The references to this work by other authors are almost entirely about modal logic, which at first sight is absent from *Syllogism* – though see Section 3.21 below on Tolerance.

21 The catalogue of the John Rylands Library in Manchester describes a manuscript as containing a Long Commentary by al-Fārābī on part of *Analytica Priora* 2, in fact a larger part than the Long Commentary published by Dāneshpazhūh. The manuscript can be read at <https://luna.manchester.ac.uk/luna/servlet/s/3y149g>. After looking at it we do not believe the commentary is by al-Fārābī, but we have not had a chance to do any more work on it.

22 This breakdown of the material in *Topica* is discussed by Hasnawi [98] and Mallet [120].

23 See the quotation from Averroes *Epitome in Physicorum Libros* 8.8–10 given by Gutas [90] p. 55.

24 Grignaschi [88] 93f points out that Escurial 612 contains two commentaries on al-Fārābī's abridgement of *Analytica Posteriora*, both attributed to Avempace, and its commentary on *Syllogism* is unlikely to be by Avempace since within its text it refers to him in the third person.

25 There are also back references at 50,16f; 52,10; 56,10. But we will see in Section 2.7 that these cannot have been intended to refer back into the text of *Syllogism*.

26 Rescher published a translation of *Short Syllogism* [134] in 1963, based on the edition by Türker [157]. Rescher's translation is reviewed by Sabra [138]. Sabra's critique is sounder on points of Arabic than it is on points of logic; see for example Note 98 to the translation.

27 See Note 96 to Section 3.15 below.

28 Remarks of Lameer [116] p. 194 that seem to go against this are based on his view that the account of likening in Part 17 of *Syllogism*, compared with the treatment of likening in the Tailpiece, is 'much more to the point . . . and free from repetitions'. His main criterion for being more to the point is being closer to the views of Aristotle. But is there any reason to believe that al-Fārābī came to agree more with Aristotle as he grew older?

29 The manuscript *E* of *Short Syllogism* closes its discussion of hypothetical syllogisms with a remark 'These are the bases of the hypothetical syllogisms and those are what we listed in our middle book. There remain their forms that are reducible to these.' ([67] 85,18–86,1.) Türker [157] 260 replaces this by what appears to be a piece of doggerel referring to an example just given; presumably she found this in other manuscripts. Given this state of the texts it would be unwise to build too much on the reading of manuscript *E*, not least because it is not clear what 'these', 'those' and the 'remaining' forms are intended to be – *Short Syllogism* does in fact mention all the hypothetical forms listed in *Syllogism*. But it is possible that *E* reflects a remark of al-Fārābī in which he refers back to the earlier curtailed *Syllogism* as a 'middle commentary' (i.e. an abridgement as opposed to a long *sharḥ* or a short essay.

30 For example likening is explained four times in different ways, at 36,1–37,6 in Part 17; 42,6–45,6 in Part 18d; 45,7–46,14 in Part 19; 62,1–64,12 in Part 20.

31 We have mentioned the more leisurely style of the Tailpiece compared with the two curtailed texts. The word *ḥukm* and the notion of a particular case of *A* being 'under' (*taḥta*) *A* are both noticeably commoner in the Tailpiece than in either of the two curtailed texts; in the case of *ḥukm* the word has legal overtones and could reflect an intention to address questions about the relationship of logic to Islamic legal thinking.

Some features of the language of the Tailpiece are closer to *Short Syllogism* than to *Syllogism*. To refer to entailment both the curtailed *Short Syllogism* and the Tailpiece generally use the root *lzm* rather than the root *ntj* that is favoured in the curtailed *Syllogism*. The word *ḍarb* for syllogistic mood occurs over fifty times in the curtailed *Syllogism*, but at most three times in the curtailed *Short Syllogism* and not at all in the Tailpiece.

32 At 47,11 the Tailpiece refers to the 'clear' ways in which a proposition can be known without syllogism or reflection. There is no reference back to an earlier listing of these ways, such as in Part 7 of *Syllogism* or 75,5f in *Short Syllogism*. But the manuscript *E*, which attaches the Tailpiece to a version of *Short Syllogism* referring to three such ways of knowing, emends 'clear' to 'three'. Then Rescher [134] p. 98, who is translating an Arabic text that says 'three' here but in *Short Syllogism* gives the number of ways as four, emends 'three' here to 'four'.

33 Gyekye [95] p. 135 argues that 'Al-Fārābī's main concern in this treatise [i.e. *Short Syllogism* including the Tailpiece] is to expound "the logic of the philosophical

theologians"'. This was surely not al-Fārābī's main concern in the earlier *Syllogism*. But Gyekye could be right that al-Fārābī's main reason for producing a rewritten second edition of *Syllogism* was precisely to highlight his material on the logical analysis of some Islamic arguments.

34 Zimmermann [165] p. cxx cites evidence of Sarrāj's awareness of Aristotelian logic. Al-Fārābī for his part frequently mentions questions that relate specifically to Arabic grammar. For example in his *Catalogue of the Sciences* [76] al-Fārābī includes several pages on the science of linguistics, which turns out to be Arabic linguistics rather than general linguistics. He would have been a fool to publish these pages without consulting an Arabic linguist, and Sarrāj would have been an obvious person to consult.

Moreover al-Fārābī and Sarrāj had a common theoretical interest in language as a conveyor of information between people. This accounts for the appearance of the root *fyd* in both writers in the sense of 'providing information' (as in the noun *fā'ida* and the verb *yufīdu*). For this notion in Sarrāj, see Sheyhatovitch [142]; and note that in the first half of her p. 188 she is describing Sarrāj's discussion (with his own examples) of Gottlob Frege's paradox of the Morning Star and the Evening Star.

Al-Fārābī's deepest discussion of the nature of language is in his extraordinarily original *Letters/Particles* [75] – the title is ambiguous between 'alphabetic letters' (the basis of language, and also the labels of sections of Aristotle's *Metaphysics*) and 'syncategorical words' (which al-Fārābī uses as a tool for describing the nature of metaphysical debate). In this book al-Fārābī makes a number of comparisons between Arabic and 'the other languages'. Opinions differ about whether these comparisons should be read as a contribution to comparative linguistics. Versteegh [162], himself a linguist, thinks they should. By contrast Menn [122] holds that Greek is mentioned because al-Fārābī takes for granted that Greek represents all those features of meanings that ought a priori to be represented in any natural language, and not because of any linguistic facts that al-Fārābī knows about Greek. The fact that al-Fārābī always compares the non-Arabic languages with Arabic, and never with each other, is one strong indication that Menn is right. In fact Menn's statement about Greek applies equally well to al-Fārābī's claims about Syriac, Persian and Sogdian.

35 They seem to have made a further joint decision, less happily, that they would describe pseudoconclusions as being deduced 'from the premises'. This abandoned the longstanding and very sensible convention of Alexander of Aphrodisias that pseudoconclusions, unlike logical conclusions, should be described as 'from the terms'. (A paper detailing this is in preparation.) Al-Fārābī breaks Alexander's convention at 20,2.

36 There is more about al-Fārābī and *min ḥaythu* in Hodges [102].

37 Al-Fārābī will pick up the distinction between declarative and non-declarative sentences in paragraph 20.3 of Part 20.

38 But his usage is not entirely consistent. See Note 11 to the translation.

39 See Chapter 10 Sentence Typography in Brustad [31].

40 In particular the modal sentences of Aristotle's modal syllogisms are categorical. But aren't these modal sentences different from the categorical sentences that we listed in Section 1.1? The answer is not straightforward. From the Roman Empire period up to al-Fārābī, the dividing line between modal and non-modal is surprisingly fragile; see the discussion of Tolerance in Section 3.21 and Note 152 to that section.

41 Al-Fārābī has two words for quantifier: *sūr* and *ḥaṣr* (the latter only in the passive participle *maḥṣūr*). In Arabic these words both mean 'thing that encircles', applied to anything between a city wall, a bracelet and a moral restraint (see Ibn al-Sikkīt [141] 230, 422). The word *sūr* (in the variant form *siwār*) was used already by Ibn al-Muqaffa^c [125] to mean quantifier. Via Syriac they both pick up terms used by Alexander: *diorismós* for quantifier and *adióristos* for indeterminate. On the Syriac and Arabic terms, see Hugonnard-Roche [170] p. 24, who comments that this case illustrates how the translators from Greek to Arabic via Syriac sought words that approximated the Greek concepts and would be intelligible to Arabic readers.

42 Avicenna (*Demonstration* [144] 146,2f and *Metaphysics* [145] 5.1; 195,8) will say that al-Fārābī's requirement is wrong. One can meaningfully speak of 'every sun' or 'every heptagonal house' even though there is only one sun and there may be no heptagonal houses. In his *Categories* [64] 120,14–126,19, al-Fārābī changes his view and allows that a universal can be true of nothing; see Section 3.5 on this change of opinion.

43 Ibn al-Sikkīt [141] 327,17f explains the farming idiom. The use of *muhmal* for 'indeterminate' is found already in Ibn al-Muqaffa^c for example at [125] 76,20. It is not the only 'camel' word that al-Fārābī inherited from Ibn al-Muqaffa^c; see Section 2.8 on *natīja*.

44 Al-Fārābī's word *hay'a* for the form of a sentence, covering quantity and quality, has been misread by the copyists at its few appearances in *Syllogism* – see the Textual Emendations in Chapter 4.

45 Besides having the existential quantifier 'some' (*ba^cḍ*), Arabic sometimes represents existential quantification by nunation, which is an 'n' added at the ends of nouns, often accompanied by the particle *mā*, which has a 'vague intensifying force' ([163] pp. i 277, ii 276). An example is at 15,19 'Some human is an animal', where 'Some human' is *insānun mā*. Al-Fārābī says at 15,19 that this sentence contains 'an existential quantifier', but it is not clear whether he thinks of the nunation or the particle or both together as an existential quantifier. From a linguistic point of view, existential quantification in Arabic is not straightforward; see the examples and discussion in Giolfo and Hodges [86] §§6–8.

46 Aristotle also treats opposite pairs of sentences in *Analytica Priora* 2.15, where he discusses what syllogistic deductions can be made from an opposite pair of

sentences. We have al-Fārābī's commentary on this section in his *Long Commentary on Prior Analytics* [74] 312–352.

47 There are some deathtraps connected with *laysa*. For example *laysa kull* can be read straightforwardly as 'Not every', but things can go astray if 'every' (*kull*) is replaced by 'some' (*ba*ᶜ*ḍ*). Thus *laysa* . . . *ba*ᶜ*d* in logical texts tends to mean 'For some . . . not', giving a meaning of the form (*o*). In such cases we have used roundabout translations like 'fails to' or 'is absent', so as not to violate the scoping rules of English. Also Jamal Ouhalla (personal communication) warns us to be aware that the reading of negative particles in Arabic is sensitive to questions of focus – a linguistic notion widely ignored by logicians.

48 In his *Long Commentary on De Interpretatione* [59] 221,12–222,2 al-Fārābī spells out other reasons why Aristotle was right to include in *De Interpretatione* a discussion of opposite pairs.

49 The intention behind the list seems to be that if a material sentence has all ambiguities of the listed kinds resolved, then the sentence will have a truth-value. For example some sentences change truth-value through time, so (6) ensures that the time is fixed. But we have not seen any attempt at a proof that the list is complete in this sense.

50 This classification of matters comes from Ammonius *Commentary on De Interpretatione* [8] 90,32–92,2. At [8] 88,17–19 Ammonius attributes the three-way classification of matters to unnamed 'people who care about these technical details'; but as far as we know, these people were himself.

51 This is a twentieth-century style of argument, with shades of Tarski's truth definition. But al-Fārābī does make one move in the modern direction. Ammonius [8] 91,18ff went straight to the quantified case, whereas al-Fārābī, like Tarski, takes the singular case first. Al-Fārābī differs from Tarski in that he treats the quantified case as analogous to the singular case ('and likewise', 16,10) rather than deduced from it.

52 Al-Fārābī ignores subalternation, the relations (v) and (vi) on left and right of the Square. But we can easily supply semantic readings of them as follows. Suppose a matter makes 'Every *B* is an *A*' true; then since (i) is between contraries, the matter makes 'No *B* is an *A*' false, and therefore it makes the semantic contradictory 'Some *B* is an *A*' true. A parallel reasoning shows that every matter making 'No *B* is an *A*' true also makes 'Some *B* is not an *A*' true.

53 Al-Fārābī has reinterpreted the syntactically-defined Square of Opposition as a semantically-defined square, in terms of how matters assign truth-values to the four quantified formal sentences. The same semantic definitions of the relations of the Square are also endorsed by Avicenna in his ᶜ*Ibāra* [147] and Averroes in his *Kitāb al-*ᶜ*ibāra* [13]; cf. Chatti [37].

54 To justify the three-way classification of matters, the key step is to show that (i) is a relationship between semantic contraries. So it is not sensible for Ammonius and

al-Fārābī to assume the three-way classification before showing that (i) is between semantic contraries.

55 But Ammonius counts three *matters* rather than three *kinds of matter* (e.g. at [8] 94,8). This difference of terminology makes Ammonius's notion of matter incompatible with that of Alexander, which al-Fārābī will need for example at 17,12 in Part 6. Al-Fārābī judiciously ignores Ammonius's talk of 'three matters'. This saves him from having to answer the question what kind of object a 'matter' in Ammonius's sense is.

56 Al-Fārābī's lack of awareness of these complications in *Syllogism*, compared with the much higher level of logical sophistication in *Categories*, is an indication that *Categories* was written later than *Syllogism* and may well be a relatively late work.

57 See Chatti [41] end of section 3.2.1, which analyses the question of the import of quantified categorical propositions as it is presented in al-Fārābī's *Categories*.

58 Lee [117] p. 79 comments that although Aristotle in *Analytica Priora* had no self-contained theory of conversion, such a theory was built up in the Roman Empire period, and Ammonius and Philoponus discuss conversion thoroughly and systematically. This comment needs a footnote. It is true that Philoponus gives a detailed and competent classification of kinds of conversion; but even the best classification can be wrecked by loose use of terminology. A flagrant example is Paul the Persian, a normally careful scholar with a strong sense of formalism, who tells us at [128] Latin 17, 17–19 and 29,25–30 that particular negative sentences convert because 'Some humans are not horses' and 'Some horses are not human' are both true. This is a blatant confusion of what below we call the second and third levels of conversion. Al-Fārābī does nothing so crude in his discussions of conversion.

59 The word *dā'iman* 'permanently' is used to mean that a property of formal sentences is preserved if we replace the letters by terms, or that a property of material sentences is preserved if we change the matter. This usage is not found before al-Fārābī, but on the strength of Dimashqī's translation at [7] 74,10 where a conversion is said to have *tabayyun ᶜan ashyā' dā'iman* i.e. probably 'a proof permanently from matters', we can include it among those mentioned in Section 2.8 as possible joint creations of al-Fārābī and Dimashqī.

60 By Note 52 to Section 3.5, every matter that makes 'No *A* is a *B*' true also makes 'Some *A* is not a *B*' true. It should follow that 'No *B* is an *A*' also converts to 'Some *A* is not a *B*'. But normally the Arabic logicians restrict themselves to the strongest valid converse, exactly as syllogisms are taken to have as conclusion the strongest candidate that follows logically from the premises.

61 The main use of *a*-conversion in Aristotle's syllogistic is to provide reductions of *Darapti* and *Felapton* to perfect moods in the first figure, as in Part 13 of *Syllogism*. Prima facie there are counterexamples to *a*-conversion if we allow empty terms and

don't require that universal affirmative sentences have existential import; for example 'Every eleven-legged donkey is an animal' is true but 'Some animal is an eleven-legged donkey' is almost certainly false. But examples of this kind are not mentioned either by Aristotle or by al-Fārābī.

62 Cf. *Debate* [70] 21,1f: 'There is nothing to prevent there being two sentences that are opposite and mutually contradictory or contrary but both accepted'.

63 See Black [24], e.g. 98, 141, on these two classes, particularly as they were understood later by Avicenna.

64 In *Demonstration* [71] 23,3f al-Fārābī says that there are two kinds of universal proposition that come to us with 'necessary certainty', namely those that arise through our innate nature and those that we acquire by experience. Experience here might cover knowledge by sense-perception. The issue we discuss in the text could be seen as asking whether our innate nature gives us in the first instance knowledge of propositions or recognition of the validity of inferences.

65 Al-Fārābī has removed the Arabic Aristotle's reference to the truth of the posited things, wisely since there is no reference to truth in Aristotle's Greek.

66 For example Thom [155] pp. 22 and 262.

67 Given a categorical premise-pair and its objective, the candidate conclusions for the premise-pair are the four categorical propositions whose subject and predicate are the same as those of the objective; there is one in each of the forms (*a*), (*e*), (*i*) and (*o*). Study of the semantic relationships in the Square of Opposition in Section 3.5 reveals that if a categorical premise-pair has any conclusion, then its set of conclusions is one of the following four classes: (*a*) and (*i*); (*e*) and (*o*); (*i*); (*o*). Since each of these classes has just one member that entails all other members, it follows that each productive categorical mood has one strongest candidate that it entails; this candidate is the one that al-Fārābī records as 'the conclusion'.

Like Aristotle, al-Fārābī doesn't make the dual assumption that the premises are as weak as they can be given that they entail the conclusion. The moods *Darapti* and *Felapton* are counterexamples.

68 We illustrate Aristotle's method of pseudoconclusions with one of Aristotle's own examples, from *Analytica Priora* 1.6, 29a6–10. Consider the formal premise-pair 'Some *B* is a *C*; some *B* is an *A*'. The premise-pair is in third figure, so the candidates for its conclusion are the categorical sentences with subject *C* and predicate *A*. We find two matters, namely (*A* = animal; *B* = white; *C* = human) and (*A* = animal; *B* = white; *C* = inanimate). Both matters make both premises true: some white things are human, some white things are animals, some white things are inanimate. But ignoring the premises, it is also true that 'All humans are animals' and 'No inanimate things are animals'; these are the two pseudoconclusions from the choice of terms in the matters. One of the pseudoconclusions is universal affirmative and the other is universal negative; this fact shows that none of the four candidate conclusions

follows logically from the premises, and so the premise-pair is unproductive. The book [103] will lay out the theory behind this method.

69 Aristotle's method of pseudoconclusions can be adapted to show that if the premises of a categorical premise-pair have no terms in common then the premise-pair is unproductive. If the two premises both have the same two terms, Aristotle treats the premise-pair in *Analytica Priora* 2.15, separately from his main treatment of categorical premise-pairs; we have al-Fārābī's commentary on this section of *Analytica Priora* in his [74] 312–352. This leaves the case described in paragraph 9.1.

70 There is an apparent counterexample in his proof of *Baroco* in paragraphs 12.2 and 12.3 below, which may be a sign that he is using a nonstandard form of argument.

71 Ibn al-Muqaffaᶜ used *ḍarb* to mean 'syllogistic figure', for example at [125] 70,3; Muqaffaᶜ's word for mood was *ṣanīᶜa* 'action'.

72 The earliest example of this approach that we have is Apuleius *Peri Hermeneias* xiv, [118] 104–107, who finds fourteen productive moods by using the general rules to eliminate the other moods. A better account of the general rules appears in Philoponus *Commentary on Prior Analytics* [130] 70,1–21, representing the view of the Alexandrian academy. Proba [161] 152f quotes the rules as given in Philoponus. Al-Fārābī's source for them could be either Philoponus or Proba or both.

73 According to Philoponus, the following five conditions are each sufficient for a mood to be unproductive: (**U**) Neither of the premises is universal. (**N**) Both the premises are negative. (**U'**) In first and second figures, the major premise is not universal. (**N'**) In first and third figures, the minor premise is negative. (**Q**) In second figure, both premises have the same quality. The most efficient way to apply these conditions is to use the Principle of Inclusion and Exclusion (described for example in [35] Chapter 5). Write $|X|$ for the number of moods that meet the condition X, and $|X \cap Y|$ for the number of moods that meet both the condition X and the condition Y. One must make separate calculations for each figure; we illustrate for third figure, where the conditions **U**, **N** and **N'** apply. Including the indeterminate sentences, one can calculate:

$$\begin{array}{l} |\mathbf{U}| = 16;\ |\mathbf{N}| = 9;\ |\mathbf{N'}| = 18; \\ |\mathbf{U} \cap \mathbf{N}| = 4;\ |\mathbf{U} \cap \mathbf{N'}| = 8;\ |\mathbf{N} \cap \mathbf{N'}| = 9; \\ |\mathbf{U} \cap \mathbf{N} \cap \mathbf{N'}| = 4. \end{array} \tag{3.10.1}$$

The number of unproductive moods in third figure is then calculated as

$$(16 + 9 + 18) - (4 + 8 + 9) + (4) = 43 - 21 + 4 = 26.$$

(alternating plus and minus as the conjunctions grow). Hence the number of productive moods in third figure, including indeterminates, is $36 - 26 = 10$. The reader can check that the corresponding calculation without indeterminates gives the answer 6.

Al-Fārābī begins the calculation above, using just the conditions **U** and **N** which apply in all three figures, thus:

$$(|\mathbf{U}| + |\mathbf{N}|) - (|\mathbf{U} \cap \mathbf{N}|) = (16 + 9) - (4) = 21$$

so as to eliminate all but 36 – 21 = 15 moods. But at this point he gets stuck and switches to a different calculation, namely where indeterminate sentences are ignored (22,7f). Since he gives no details of this second calculation, he is probably copying the numbers from his source.

74 Expert syllogism-watchers may find these two proofs unusual. The reason is that al-Fārābī has used the SP ordering in the premises but (in contrast to the first figure) he has put the major premise before the minor. The result is that the proof of *Cesare* needs a swap of the premises to match with the first figure *Celarent*, while the swap usually required in the proof of *Camestres* is now not needed.

75 *Prior Analytics* 1.5, 27a36–bl. He assumes the contradictory opposite of the conclusion, namely 'Every *C* is an *A*', and joins it to the premise 'Every *A* is a *B*'. This forms a premise-pair in the mood *Barbara* in the first figure, with conclusion 'Every *C* is a *B*'. This conclusion is the contradictory opposite of the other premise of *Baroco*, namely 'Some *C* is not a *B*'.

76 Thus Apuleius [118] X, 98,26; Philoponus [130] 94,16f; Proba [161] 158,26f.

77 Arguments by ecthesis can be read in two ways, according as we take *D* to stand for a subclass of *C* that is disjoint from *B*, or an individual that is a *C* but not a *B*. Al-Fārābī's phrase 'the whole of the some' (25,18; 26,16; 28,19; 29,18; 30,19, all in connection with ectheses) strongly suggests that he takes *D* as a class rather than an individual.

78 Al-Fārābī's proofs of *Baroco* show him breaking the protocols of formal logic in two ways: first by using a syntactic manipulation with no logical justification, and second by allowing an assumption not given by the formal premises to creep in via the choice of illustrative matter. Avicenna reprimands al-Fārābī for exactly these two faults, in a critique of another argument used by al-Fārābī in the missing part of his *Long Commentary on Prior Analytics* [74] and quoted by Avicenna at [146] 209,7–9 and Averroes at [137] 102,13–16. Avicenna remarks at [146] 209,9 that the argument is 'pure sophistry'. It rests on a syntactic trick, treating part of the subject as part of the predicate (as Avicenna notes at [146] 209,11–14). Moreover al-Fārābī sets out the argument using only one matter, which 'doesn't prevent there being matters' in which the argument doesn't work ([146] 210,1). Avicenna's critique of this argument of al-Fārābī is partly analysed in [102].

Avicenna himself uses ecthesis to prove *Baroco* (cf. Chatti [40] section 6 for a comparison of Avicenna's and al-Fārābī's proofs of *Baroco*). This use of ecthesis needs a justification – which could be given. But Avicenna's proof avoids the two faults mentioned above.

79 This ordering of the moods in the third figure is unusual, but it appears again in *Short Syllogism*, and in some later texts such as the twelfth century *Mulakhkhaṣ* [133] of Fakhr al-Dīn al-Rāzī.

80 Earlier logicians, whether or not they grasped the notion of existential import, were content that ecthesis works for *Bocardo* even if it doesn't work for *Baroco*. Aristotle says at *Analytica Priora* 1.6, 28b20f, that *Bocardo* has a proof by ecthesis, though he gives no details.

81 The classification into connected, complete separated and incomplete separated hypothetical sentences is found in Galen's *Institutio Logica* [83] Chapters 2 and 3.

Al-Fārābī also discusses kinds of hypothetical proposition, and the ways in which they are expressed in Arabic, at *Short Syllogism* [67] 71,11–16, at *Expressions* [58] 54,9–56,5, at *Categories* [64] 127,1–129,3 and at *Debate* [70] 102,19–104,17. In his discussions of hypothetical propositions he generally leaves it open what kinds of proposition p and q are, but when he comes to describe hypothetical syllogisms in Part 14 he requires p and q to be categorical propositions. Note that none of al-Fārābī's hypothetical propositions correspond to inclusive disjunction.

82 The ten moods are as follows:

(a) If p then q; but p. Therefore q.
(b) If p then q; but not q. Therefore not p.
(c) Either p or q (complete); but p. Therefore not q.
(d) Either p or q (complete); but q. Therefore not p.
(e) Either p or q (complete); but not p. Therefore q.
(f) Either p or q (complete); but not q. Therefore p.
(g) Either p or q (incomplete); but p. Therefore not q.
(h) Either p or q (incomplete); but q. Therefore not p.
(i) Not both p and q; but p. Therefore not q.
(j) Not both p and q; but q. Therefore not p.

Al-Fārābī adds some further refinements that we discuss later in this Section.

83 The five indemonstrables are attributed to Chrysippus. They are listed with slight variations in several places; the following list of material examples of the forms is taken from Sextus Empiricus *Outlines of Pyrrhonism* 2.157f [140].

(1) If it is day, it is light; but it is day. Therefore it is light.
(2) If it is day, it is light; but it is not light. Therefore it is not day.
(3) It is not both night and day; but it is day. Therefore it is not night.
(4) Either it is day or it is night; but it is day. Therefore it is not night.
(5) Either it is day or it is night; but it is not night. Therefore it is day.

84 There is also a short account at *Rhetoric* [60] 95,6–103,15 devoted to the question of what parts of a hypothetical syllogism can be suppressed in rhetorical applications.

From a quotation by Averroes [137] p. 197f we can infer that al-Fārābī also discussed hypothetical syllogisms in his *Long Commentary on Prior Analytics* [74], though the relevant section is now lost. The *Catalogue* of Nadīm [126] p. 424 tells us that al-Fārābī's contemporary Abū Bishr Mattā bin Yūnūs wrote an entire book on *Hypothetical Syllogisms*. We know nothing of its contents beyond the title.

85 In fact one of Hasnawi's main sources is Boethius *De Topicis Differentiis* [29], which cites Themistius; but this work of Boethius sidesteps the connection between topics and hypothetical logic.

86 The claim is widely reported, for example by Sextus Empiricus [140] 2.157. Since al-Fārābī doesn't tell us what the five indemonstrables are, he may well not know what they are; and in any case the list of hypothetical syllogisms that he gives is Peripatetic and not Stoic. But one can see how the five indemonstrables can be read as generating al-Fārābī's ten listed forms. (1) is (a) and (2) is (b). (3) is (i), and (j) can be reduced to (3) by converting the first premise to 'Not both *q* and *p*'. (4) is (c) and (g), and yields (d) by conversion of the first premise. (5) is (e) and (h), and yields (f) by conversion of the first premise. (But al-Fārābī doesn't mention conversion of hypothetical propositions.)

87 Unlike Boethius [28] 2.9.1, al-Fārābī makes no reference to the 'wholly hypothetical' syllogisms which have two hypothetical premises and a hypothetical conclusion.

88 For a Stoic example see Chrysippus's example of the reasoning dog in Sextus Empiricus *Outlines of Pyrrhonism* [140] 1.69; for Galen see *Institutio Logicae [83]* v.4. Bobzien [26] compares the views of the Stoics and Galen on the hypothetical premises in hypothetical syllogisms. Al-Fārābī in *Short Syllogism* 83,9–12 remarks that in connected hypothetical propositions the antecedent can carry a conjunction of cases, as in 'If *p* and *q* and *r* then *s*'; in the example that he gives, some of the alternatives are sentences with different subject terms.

89 The word *istithnā'* also appears in the Arabic translation of Aristotle's *De Interpretatione* by Isḥāq bin Ḥunayn (*c.* 830–*c.* 910), translating two different Greek words (cf. Gyekye [93]). These uses seem unrelated to al-Fārābī's, but the presence of the word *istithnā'* in a standard translation of Aristotle may have made it easier for al-Fārābī to adopt the term.

90 Bobzien [25] 293 notices a feature in Boethius *De Hypotheticis Syllogismis* [28] 2.2.2 [*sic* – Bobzien has 2.2.7] and in a Greek text that runs parallel to Boethius, namely that the second premise in a hypothetical syllogism is said to be a 'repeat' (i.e. of its occurrence as a clause of the first premise). She notes that the Latin translation of remarks of Averroes about al-Fārābī's hypothetical syllogisms uses *repetita* in the same sense, and she suggests that this corroborates 'the claim that there was a Greek source on hypothetical syllogisms on which both Boethius and some Arabic commentaries depend'. The many parallels between al-Fārābī's account and that of Boethius make this a safe claim anyway, but the corroboration is weak. The Arabic

word *istithnā'* derives from a root meaning 'two', and could have been read as 'duplication' if the meaning 'exception' hadn't overridden it. Averroes's Latin translator might have decided that the logical process has nothing to do with excepting, and inferred that the noun has to be read etymologically as 'duplication'.

91 Al-Fārābī knew nothing of Boethius. Their common sources include at least Porphyry and Themistius, but there is no consensus that they ran as far as Ammonius Hermiou. Cf. Marenbon [121] pp. 13, 33, 61, 126.

92 Some of the notions in this paragraph are discussed further in Chatti [39].

93 Like the English 'if', *in* in Arabic is put before p, not between p and q like $*$ in $(p * q)$.

94 Giolfo and Hodges [87] assemble some relevant material from linguistic sources and from Avicenna.

95 The credit that we give al-Fārābī for this dialogue representation of syllogism of absurdity has to depend on whether we think the representation is already implicit in Aristotle's statements about his version of the syllogism of absurdity being a kind of syllogism by hypothesis. (Striker [151] discusses these statements.) Among later Aristotelian logicians it was a commonplace that the syllogism of absurdity implies such a representation. For example Augustus De Morgan [47] p. 5 claims that a *reductio* argument in Euclid 'supposes an opponent', and proceeds to explain the argument as a debate with the opponent.

96 For example take q to be the true sentence 'The number of planets is a number less than twenty' and p to be 'The number of planets is a number greater than a hundred'. Then by *Darapti*, p and q entail r: 'Some number less than twenty is a number greater than a hundred', which is impossible. But it is certainly not true that r follows from p alone, or that it follows from q alone; nor is it true that p is impossible. Al-Fārābī seems to have been led into this error by uncritical acceptance of Aristotle's statement at *Analytica Priora* 1.15, 34a25 that what follows from a false but not impossible assumption is also not impossible.

97 The version of the syllogism of absurdity in *Short Syllogism* involves no absurdities or contradictions, leaving the name 'syllogism of absurdity' hard to explain.

98 Avicenna in his *Qiyās* [146] 8.3 will present a view of the syllogism of absurdity which removes the internal syllogism altogether, and hence the need for a division between Questioner and Responder. He does this by adding 'If p' as an antecedent to p itself and all statements below it in the internal syllogism. Thus the premise 'The world is eternal' becomes 'If the world is eternal then the world is eternal', which drops out as tautologous. The internal conclusion 'The world can't move' becomes 'If the world is eternal then the world can't move', which combines with the clearly true premise 'The world can move' to yield the required external conclusion 'The world is not eternal' by modus tollendo tollens. (See [101].) Did al-Fārābī's example help to suggest this rearrangement to Avicenna?

99 We know of no published studies of the development of a theory of procedures within Aristotelian logic. It is possible that al-Fārābī pioneered this theory. A century later Avicenna produced a sophisticated proof search procedure [100]; al-Fārābī's work on logical procedures may have been a major inspiration for this work.

100 Aristotle's use of these letters in connection with induction and paradigm is admirably consistent, except for a glitch in the use of *C*; see Note 128 to Section 3.20.

101 An equally important source may have been the 'some people' that al-Fārābī refers to at *Debate* 99,12–15 and 100,15–101,3, and at *Syllogism* 43,13–44,2, as having views on induction and likening. These people included Galen; in Section 3.21 we assemble evidence suggesting that al-Fārābī worked from a source critical of Galen, perhaps Themistius.

102 Al-Fārābī also discusses induction in the following places:

Long Commentary on Prior Analytics [74]. Al-Fārābī comments in detail on two sections of Aristotle's work: on pages 510–524 he comments on *Analytica Priora* 2.23, and on pages 529–535 he comments on *Analytica Priora* 2.25. Note that 2.23 is about induction (*epagōgḗ*) but 2.25 is about abduction (*apagōgḗ*), which is something quite different. Al-Fārābī was misled by the Baghdad Standard, which failed to distinguish between these two words and translated them both as *istiqrā'*.

Debate [70]. This work is an abridgement of parts of Aristotle's *Topica* connected with the rules and applications of debate. Pages 97,1–102,18 contain perhaps al-Fārābī's most attractive and stimulating account of induction, but it is hard to relate in detail to Aristotle's remarks about induction in *Topica*.

Analysis [68]. This work is an abridgement of parts of Aristotle's *Topica* connected with syllogism. Al-Fārābī mentions induction at 96,3–97,6 in connection with Platonic division and hypothetical syllogism, and at 123,1–125,6 in connection with the topic of similarity (*tashābuh, Topica* 2.10, 114b25–36).

Demonstration [71] 24,18–25,1 compares induction with experience (*tajriba*), possibly responding to *Analytica Posteriora* 2.19, 100a3–9. There may be a brief reference to this same passage of *Analytica Posteriora* in *Long Commentary on Prior Analytics* [74] 521,13–15. Also the passage 88,20–89,4 picks up a remark about induction at *Analytica Posteriora* 2.7, 92a34–92b2. Probably both these passages of *Analytica Posteriora* lie behind a comment on induction at *Debate* [70] 101,16–102,10.

103 In the material examples that al-Fārābī gives, the particular cases are generally subspecies, such as walking as a particular case of movement. But a discussion at *Debate* 99,17–100,6 involves a use of induction where 'things perceived by the senses' (*maḥsūs*) are examined. At *Letters/Particles* [75] 137,6–8 al-Fārābī describes how in the creation of a language, sounds are assigned to 'the perceived things

(*maḥsūsāt*) that can be pointed to, and the intellected meanings that rest on the perceived things that can be pointed to'. At least in this passage, a *maḥsūs* is an individual object in the world, not a universal.

104 This is reading between the lines. Al-Fārābī makes no explicit reference back to his discussion in Part 7 of propositions that are known without syllogism. (But see the discussion at line 47,11 below.) We remark also that al-Fārābī's name 'examination' (*taṣaffuḥ*) for induction might suggest that induction is an empirical procedure where we check real-world instances. This is not what al-Fārābī intends, as we can see from his example at 35,10–13. Clearly to check that walking takes place in time we don't need to find some animal walking and confirm that it is doing so in time; our mental concept of walking already gives the required information. So the examination can be purely conceptual.

105 In the background is a thesis of Plato, that when dividing *B* into B_1 and B_2 you should aim to make both B_1 and B_2 usable, resisting the temptation to take B_1 on its own as a class small enough to handle (Plato *Statesman* 262A-E). We thank Greg Cherlin for this reference.

106 The passage is al-Fārābī's paraphrase of *Topica* 2.2, 109b13–25 on topics of accident. At *Debate* 101,9–15 al-Fārābī makes a similar point about the application of induction to debate. Suppose the aim is not to confirm that every *B* is an *A*, but to persuade the Responder to concede that every *B* is an *A*. If the Responder is not willing to concede this straight away, he may still be willing to concede that every *C* is an *A* where *C* is some smaller class below *B* and he has a 'better understanding' of *C*. The Questioner may be able to use this fact to find several particular cases *C* where the Responder is willing to concede. Al-Fārābī then makes the very Aristotelian point (e.g. *Topica* 7.1, 156a22–26) that if the challenge to the Responder is split into several questions in this way, it increases the chances that the Questioner can extract concessions from the Responder before the Responder realizes what he is being drawn into.

107 The idea for this term comes from *Analytica Priora* 2.23, 68b20f, where Aristotle discusses how to show that bileless animals are long-lived. Aristotle writes *A* for 'long-lived', *B* for 'bileless', and he introduces a term *C* for 'the particular cases of long-lived, such as human, horse, mule'. Clearly there is a confusion somewhere, because on al-Fārābī's account of induction we should be looking for particular cases of bileless, not of long-lived. (The literature, both early and modern, sometimes tries to cover the point by invoking the fact that *B* and *A* are coextensive in this case; but the suggestion is hardly helpful, because we don't know that *B* and *A* are coextensive until we have proved that every *B* is an *A*.) This is by no means the only incoherence in al-Fārābī's attempt to make sense of *Analytica Priora* 2.23. Outside of his *Long Commentary on Prior Analytics*, he wisely abandons the attempt and proceeds without reference to any details of that passage of Aristotle.

108 When $n = 1$ the rule is simply *Barbara*. In fact Avicenna devises four forms of syllogism by cases, forming extensions of each of the four first figure moods.

109 An important technical point is that Avicenna's formulation never uses al-Fārābī's new disjunctive term. Instead it uses a new form of proposition, namely 'Every B is either a B_1 or . . . or a B_n'. One could bring Avicenna's formulation closer to al-Fārābī's by allowing it to include a definition of the new term, but this would involve further innovations.

110 In the context of hypothetical logic the sentence 'Every B is a B_1 or . . . or a B_n' is not entirely new; it is a universal quantification of the sentence form that at *Syllogism* 32,10 al-Fārābī described as 'complete' (*tāmm*) because 'there is a natural bound on the number of cases and they are listed exhaustively'. Probably this term of hypothetical logic is the source of al-Fārābī's choice of 'complete' in 'complete induction'; the connection had become clear to al-Fārābī by the time that he wrote *Short Syllogism*.

111 Avicenna's formalization (3.16.5) doesn't support the claim, even for the case $n = 1$, i.e. 'Most B_1s are As; every B is a B_1. Therefore most Bs are As'. Let A be 'flies', B_1 'bird' and B 'ostrich'.

112 The medieval dictionaries reliably find a connection to camels. Thus Jawharī (died c. 1003), *Ṣiḥāḥ* [110] sv *qra'*: 'A he-camel checks (*istaqra'a*) a she-camel by leaving her in order to see whether she is pregnant or not'.

113 In Arabic mathematics (for example Isfahānī in 1824) the term *istiqrā'* is sometimes used for a procedure in which numbers x_i are chosen in turn and each number is tested for a condition C_i; each number x_{i+1} and condition C_{i+1} depend on x_i and the result of the test of C_i. The procedure need not halt after a finite number of steps. We thank Nacéra Bensaou for this information.

114 Al-Fārābī defines 'experience' at *Demonstration* [71] 24,19–25,3 in words almost identical with those he uses to explain induction. The difference between the two is that experience, unlike induction, is required to produce in us a 'necessary certainty' of the truth of the conclusion. He adds that 'many people use one of these two names in place of the other'. These remarks are not entirely convincing, given that he tells us later in the same book that the art of carpentry can be acquired by experience alone ([71] 74,14).

115 The immediate justification for including all this material on likening in an abridgement of *Analytica Priora* is that Aristotle in *Analytica Priora* 2.24, 68b38–69a19 describes a similar form of argument under the name of *parádeigma*. Aristotle treats this form of argument again in *Rhetorica* 1.2, 1357b26–36, and it reappears in *Topica* 1.18, 108b7–19 and 2.10, 114b25–31. Al-Fārābī discusses the passage in *Analytica Priora* at 524,18–529,11 in his *Long Commentary on Prior Analytics* [74], and the passage in Aristotle's *Rhetorica* at 119,5–121,18 in his own *Rhetoric* [60]. But these passages in [74] and [60] are mostly devoted to interpreting

the text of Aristotle, and they give few clues for making sense of the treatment of likening in *Syllogism*.

116 Observed and unobserved 45,10; 46,14f; 47,2; 52,12 etc. Exemplar 62,1.2.5.9.16.17 etc. Cause 43,14–18; 47,9; 48,5 etc. Major premise and middle term 43,14; 42,17; 43,17; 47,9 etc. Content 36,5.8.11; 37,4; 43,18.19.20; 45,8 etc. Clearly 'other thing' can be used only in certain contexts, but see 45,9.12; 57,12; 62,3.16; 63,2.

117 For example at 43,13.18; 47,9; 48,9; 52,5 'cause' is short for 'cause of *A*' or 'cause of the content'. 'Up for consideration as the cause' appears at 48,5.8.11; 51,4; 52,9.13.15; 53,6f; 54,2. But at 62,20; 63,2.4.7.19 *B* is described as the cause of the similarity (i.e. between *D* and *C*); this is a different property of *B*.

118 The difference may be a matter of where the methods came from. Likening is based on Aristotle's *parádeigma*, whereas transfer from the observed to the unobserved probably owes something to Galen, and al-Fārābī himself includes under Synthesis some arguments from Islamic p jurisprudence.

119 Walter Burley discusses reduplicatives in his *Longer Treatise on the Purity of Logic* [34]. At p. 177f he takes '*C* is an *A* insofar as it is a *B*', read causally, to have five components: '*C* is an *A*', '*C* is a *B*', 'Every *B* is an *A*', 'Necessarily if a thing is a *B* then it is an *A*' and 'Being a *B* is a cause of being an *A*'. If we read al-Fārābī's (3.17.2) as a causal reduplicative, Burley's analysis makes it equivalent to the conjunction of '*C* is a *B*' and (3.17.4), and also makes (3.17.4) entail (3.17.3); these are exactly the inferences that we are ascribing to al-Fārābī. No line of transmission from *Syllogism* to Burley has been identified as yet. But it may be relevant that Avicenna's *Qiyās* [146] 4.4, 208,8–211,17 provides evidence of an attempt that al-Fārābī makes in his *Long Commentary on Prior Analytics* [74] to develop some logical properties of reduplicatives; see the analysis in Hodges [102] §2.3.

120 In the late tenth century Ibn Suwār speaks of putting an argument into 'the crafted arrangement' (or maybe 'the professional form', *al-naẓm al-ṣināʿī*, [153] 243,10). Ibn Suwār will surely have known that the example he gives is also one of the examples given by al-Fārābī in *Syllogism*, taken originally from Islamic theology.

121 The study of compound syllogisms in al-Fārābī's sense was taken up more systematically by Avicenna in the next century at *Qiyās* [146] 9.3 and 9.6.

122 The classic study of the field is Davidson [46]. Contributions came from a wide range of sources. For example Philoponus was a Christian philosopher working at the Neoplatonic academy in Alexandria; Saadia Gaon (*c.* 887–942) was an influential Jewish thinker; al-Bāqillānī i (*c.* 940–1013) was a Muslim theologian and jurist.

123 See Lameer [116] p. 212, including the remark that in his *Tamhīd* [18] al-Bāqillānī defines *muḥdath* in exactly the same way as *ḥādith*.

124 Cf. Davidson [46] p. 102.

125 E.g. *Syllogism* 38,16f. Ibn Suwār [153] p. 243 attributes the term to the *kalām* scholars. Davidson [46] pp. 136, 140 finds forms of the term in the theologians Ashᶜarī and ᶜAbd al-Jabbār.

126 Here al-Fārābī uses the two available words for 'created' to mark two ingredients of the argument.

127 'Religion, if rendered human, comes after philosophy, in general, since it aims simply to instruct the multitude in theoretical and practical matters that have been inferred in philosophy, in such a way as to enable the multitude to understand them by persuasion or imaginative representation, or both.' (Trans. Khalidi [112] p. 1.)

128 Warning: Aristotle uses the letter *C* for different purposes in induction and in paradigm. In paradigm it names what al-Fārābī calls the unobserved, i.e. the thing to which the content is transferred; in induction it stands for multiple terms such as 'horse, human, mule' (cf. Note 107 to Section 3.16 above). Al-Fārābī uses it here because in his main examples *C* plays the role of the unobserved.

129 At 42,4f al-Fārābī seems to claim that this is the only way of combining an induction with a syllogism, which is obviously false. By contrast, in *Long Commentary* [74] 529,15–17 (referring back to 520,22f) al-Fārābī says that the kind of induction he is discussing 'here' is used to justify the *minor* premise of a syllogism in the first figure. Lameer [116] pp. 153, 163 plausibly suggests that al-Fārābī has been seduced into taking this view in *Long Commentary on Prior Analytics* by the confusion between *epagōgḗ* and *apagōgḗ* in the Baghdad Standard translation. At *Analytica Priora* 2.25, 69a26f Aristotle is telling him to apply abduction to the minor premise '*C* is *B*', but he thinks he is being told to apply induction to it.

130 It is mentioned in paragraphs 18d.3, 19.6, 20.11 and 20.13, and also at *Debate* [70] 100,16. Defect is *khalal* at *Syllogism* 41,7, and *ikhtilāl* at [70] 100,16.

131 Sextus Empiricus *Outlines of Pyrrhonism* [140] ii ch. 15, 'If one examines only some particular cases, then the induction will be unreliable because a counterexample to the universal proposition could be among the cases that are omitted in the induction'. In terms of the formalization, the problem could be either that we don't know whether our man has examined all of $B_1, \ldots, B_n$, or that we do know that he has examined all of these but we don't know whether he has checked that the completeness condition is true. Under the second possibility it will not be the case, *pace* 41,9f, that there is some B_i of which we don't know whether it satisfies *A*.

132 Al-Fārābī was aware that the circularity in the argument of (3.20.2) is the result of fitting together the induction and the simple syllogism; there is no circularity in the induction itself. He considers this point in *Sophistry* [69] 152,10–18, where he declares that an inductive proof that 'knowledge of contraries is one', which

involves examining the particular cases of contrary pairs, is a legitimate induction and not a circularity.

133 We can do some preliminary sorting of these sentences, (i) and (vi) are essential parts of likening, as explained in Section 3.17 above. (i), (ii), (iii), (v) and (vi) will be discussed below under the head of the topic of Accepting and Rejecting. By al-Fārābī's own account (44,8–10), (v) says the same as (vi) but expressed differently; certainly there is a difference of emphasis. (vii) will belong with al-Fārābī's theory of logical tolerance. (iv) is problematic; *Analysis* [68] 103,6–8 suggests that it should be read here as synonymous with (v).

134 Cf. 42,2 where al-Fārābī contrasts the clearer (*aẓhar*) with the more obscure (*akhfā*). The origin of the word 'transfer' *nuqla* is almost certainly the Greek word *metábasis*, used by the medical Empiricists in the context 'transfer between similars' (*metábasis toû homoíou*). Religious sources for this terminology are less clear. Van Ess [160] 34f calls attention to Qur'ānic texts contrasting the worldly *shāhid* with the divine *ghā'ib*, adding that the use of these notions in Islamic *kalām* predates the translation of Galen. But note that not a single one of al-Fārābī's examples in *Syllogism* makes the unobserved object divine. (A solitary example at *Short Syllogism* 93,7f has Allah as the unobserved, and even in this case al-Fārābī dismisses the suggested application of likening.)

135 In Part 18d he doesn't suggest that there are two ways of organizing the search in likening; in fact the procedure for likening in Part 17 fits Analysis and not Synthesis. A likely reason for this difference between Part 18d and Part 19 is that after writing Part 18d al-Fārābī became aware of the point he makes in paragraphs 20.15 to 20.17, that some of the best-known applications of the method of analogy (*qiyās*) in Islamic jurisprudence can be formalized as transfer from observed to unobserved in the form of Synthesis.

136 Gyekye [94] misses this point and is sidetracked into looking for a connection with Pappus's distinction between analysis and synthesis in geometrical proofs. But Gyekye does observe ([94] 37) that al-Fārābī's Synthesis makes no use of the notion of similarity; this is true and important, in the sense that the middle term *B* is found purely on the basis of the exemplar *D* and the content *A*, ignoring other things similar to *D*. Of course similarity reappears when we apply the major premise to a particular case *C*, because *C* has to fall under *B*, and the things that fall under *B* are precisely the things that are relevantly similar to the exemplar.

137 It could happen that the syllogism fails to be self-sufficient because it has a premise that needs proof. In this case al-Fārābī allows us to include with the syllogism any syllogisms needed to prove its premise, any syllogisms needed to prove the premises of these syllogisms, and so on (44,12).

138 At 62,18–63,2 al-Fārābī gives another formulation of the self-sufficiency of syllogism.

139 12,5.8; 24,19; 25,4; 35,14; 37,3; 46,13; 47,3.8; 63,16; 64,11.

140 *wujūd* and *irtifāᶜ*, *wujūd* is barely translatable; it could mean 'finding', 'existence' or 'truth' among other things. *Irtifāᶜ* translates Aristotle's *anaireîn*, with the difference that Aristotle normally applies it to propositions while al-Fārābī (like Porphyry, cf. Barnes [19] p. 245) nearly always applies it to terms. Al-Fārābī's idiom is 'we reject the content *C* from *D*', meaning that we say *D* is not a *C*. See al-Fārābī's brief definition of *irtifāᶜ* at 50,17f.

141 See Hasnawi [98] on al-Fārābī's view of topics in general. This description of topics as a means for finding premises is strongly reminiscent of Alexander's incorporation of Stoic indemonstrables into the Aristotelian theory of topics, as discussed by Bobzien [27]. Hasnawi divides this section of *Analysis* into two parts, the first ([68] 102,4–19) for finding hypothetical propositions and the second ([68] 102,19–107) for finding categorical propositions.

142 There is an obvious similarity between Accepting and the natural deduction rule of →-introduction. But al-Fārābī doesn't require that the inference should be formal; it could depend on material properties of the sentences put for *p* and *q*.

143 This use of the topics disagrees with the semantics that al-Fārābī gives for universal affirmative sentences in his *Categories* [64] 124,10–19, since the validity of the inference doesn't entail that at least one thing is a *B*; cf. Section 3.5 above.

144 In terms of Note 140 above, al-Fārābī often suppresses the oblique phrase 'from *C*' when he rejects *A* or *B* from *C*. From the point of view of style, compare *Syllogism* 33,7 'This number is either greater or smaller or equal', where the implied oblique phrase 'than or to that number' is suppressed.

145 Al-Fārābī puts a strange amount of emphasis on this mistake, considering how elementary it is. We can account for this in two ways. First, al-Fārābī believes that there are real-life arguments where the direction of inference is unclear; see below on Galen and proving causes. Second, and more disturbing for a modern reader, al-Fārābī apparently thinks that the inference in the wrong direction is not entirely wrong; it is merely 'very weak' (50,6). For al-Fārābī a rhetorical argument is good if it persuades audiences, and a dialectical argument is good if it leads to resolution of a dispute. Even arguments with no logical validity at all can serve these purposes.

146 Al-Fārābī claims at [68] 107,3f that a sentence proved by Accepting and Rejecting need not express a primary predication or signify a substance. This is one of the very few hints that al-Fārābī sees any connection between the notion of a cause (*ᶜilla*) and the notions on which he builds his theory of demonstration (cf. Strobino [152]).

147 See Tieleman [156] and the passages he cites from Galen's *De Placitis Hippocratis et Platonis* [81].

148 'The cause' 43,14; 44,2; 'a cause' 43,17f; 48,5; 52,4.9.14. Some references to 'the cause' may be references to 'the cause we are considering' without any implication of uniqueness; but 'the cause' at *Analysis* [68] 123, 10 reads as implying uniqueness.

149 Galen himself confirms that he rejects induction; for example at *Thrasybulus* [82] 37,20–22 'We showed in our *De Demonstratione* that induction is useless for scientific demonstration'. But to say that Galen replaced induction by likening is an oversimplification. We know that he distinguished two kinds of inference by analogy. The first, which he calls analogism, is where *C* is taken to be an *A* because it is similar to *D* which is known to be an *A*, but *C* may be 'invisible' in the sense that we have no way of testing whether *C* is in fact an *A*. The second kind of analogy – known as epilogism – is where, even if we have no means of testing that *C* is an *A* at the time when we make the inference, we can in principle test it. Galen accepts epilogism but not analogism. (See *On Medical Experience* [85] 88–94.) This is an issue about sound general strategies in medical reasoning, not about the cogency of a particular inference; in this sense it is rather sideways from al-Fārābī's concerns.

150 An obvious candidate is the work of Themistius that Hasnawi [97] identified through references in Averroes and Boethius. Hasnawi argues for there being two works by Themistius on topics: a commentary which Averroes knew, and a more free-standing 'personal essay' which Boethius knew and in which Themistius 'classified and ranked the topics according to their epistemic value' ([97] 215, 232). Chiaradonna [42] calls attention to passages of Themistius's *Commentary on Physics* where he leaves the text of Aristotle in order to criticize views of Galen; if he did the same in this 'personal essay', the work could account for a large part of al-Fārābī's material in Parts 18d and 19 of *Syllogism*.

151 A quotation by Maimonides [139] 81,7–10 from al-Fārābī's *Long Commentary on Prior Analytics* almost certainly shows al-Fārābī drawing exactly this conclusion. Also at *Demonstration* [71] 44,16f al-Fārābī takes 'most' as a variant of 'possibly'.

152 There is evidence of this looseness in the Roman period. Compare for example Ammonius's use of modal names for his three 'matters', cf. Section 3.5. Also the Hebrew paraphrase of Themistius *Analytica Priora* [136], after listing three different kinds of sentence that count as 'necessary', says disconcertingly on p. 95 that 'The *de inesse* is said in the same ways in which the necessary is said'.

153 Avicenna does twice claim to be using tolerance towards al-Fārābī and other logicians with similar attitudes (*Qiyās* [146] 91,9; 210,13). This is surely irony.

154 Introducing Part 20 at 54,6, al-Fārābī claims that in his *Analytica Priora* Aristotle speaks of 'jurisprudential syllogisms' (*al-maqāyīs al-fiqhīya*). There is no such reference in the Greek text of *Analytica Priora*. But at *Analytica Priora* 2.23, 68b11 Aristotle speaks of 'rhetorical syllogisms', and Theodorus in the Baghdad Standard ([109] 399,5) translates Aristotle as referring to 'syllogisms that are *khuṭubīya* and [syllogisms that are] *fiqhīya* and [syllogisms that are] *mushwarīya*'. Al-Fārābī has picked up the second of these adjectives and taken it as the word of Aristotle himself. He must be assuming that Aristotle could point to Greek counterparts of

Islamic jurisprudence. He seems not to have responded to Theodorus's mention of *khuṭubīya* and *mushwarīya* syllogisms. Probably Theodorus meant *khuṭubīya* to refer to 'public speeches' and *mushwarīya* to 'consultations'; see the discussion in Lameer [116] pp. 234–9. Although in al-Fārābī's time the root *kh ṭ b* could be used to refer to Aristotelian rhetoric, Lameer shows that this usage is probably later than Theodorus.

155 The Qur'ānic references are given in the Notes to the translation of Part 20 below: (1) 'Every [kind of] wine is forbidden', Note 21; (2) 'Abstain from false statement', Note 124; (3) 'Be sure to wash your faces and your hands', Note 125; (4) 'When you speak, be just', Note 126; (5) 'Honour your commitments', Note 127; (6) 'The thief must have his hand cut off', Note 133; (7) We are forbidden to say "Uff" to our parents, Note 137; (8) Usury is forbidden, Note 144; (9) 'There is not a grain's weight of injustice in Allah', Note 146. The exceptional example (10) is a popular saying 'No good is to be expected from [one's] friends and [one's] children', Note 130.

156 At 54,18–55,1 al-Fārābī gives a list of six types of sentence that need to be paraphrased in this way so as to be made declarative, but it is not clear how his list correlates with the types just described. He discusses the replacement of nondeclarative forms by declarative forms more fully at *Short Interpretation* [65] 45,13–48,2. There he lists the nondeclarative types as 'imperative, entreaty, request and vocative', adding that entreaty and request are both expressed in Arabic as imperatives. This list may be based on Ammonius [8] 2, 9–15, which lists the nondeclarative sentence types as vocative, imperative, interrogative and optative.

157 Al-Fārābī distinguishes between ambiguous (*bi-ishtirāk*, literally 'shared') and unambiguous (*bi-tawāṭu'*, see Note 128 to the translation) at *Short Interpretation* [65] 141,9–15 (= [165] p. 228). Aristotle defined the related notions of homonymy and synonymy at the beginning of his *Categories*, but seemingly taking them as properties of things rather than of words or concepts. It may be dissatisfaction with Aristotle's explanations that caused al-Fārābī to move the explanation of ambiguity from *Categories* (it is not mentioned in his *Categories* [64]) to his *Short Interpretation*.

158 At the beginning of Part 20 al-Fārābī tells us that this Part will discuss four 'principles'. The second principle turns out to be case (b), and the third and fourth principles are case (c) considered from slightly different viewpoints. Al-Fārābī has a rather loose notion of 'principles'.

159 Al-Fārābī arranges his examples so that in case (b) the explicit statement is stronger than the intended one (e.g. it is not intended that *all* thieves should have their hands cut off), whereas in case (c) the explicit statement is weaker than the intended one (e.g. the prohibition on unfair exchange is intended to apply to other commodities besides wheat). This shows that the term that is intended differently from how it is

spoken is the subject term (i.e. *B* or *D*) and not the predicate term. Al-Fārābī doesn't make this point explicitly, and it is not obvious from the wording of some of his examples. For example at 56,15 'So-and-so doesn't have a grain's weight of injustice in him' has to be paraphrased along the lines 'Every grain is such that so-and-so's level of injustice is less than the weight of it', making 'grain' the subject term.

160 Al-Fārābī could have found in the *fiqh* literature plenty of examples where a word has to be interpreted by another word, and neither of the two words expresses a particular case of the other. For example in his *Risāla* [111] 78 al-Shāfiᶜī, the great scholar of *fiqh*, cites Qur'ān *Sūrat Yūsuf* 12,82 'Ask the town in which we have been', and interprets 'the town' as 'the people of the town'.

161 Here and at 61,11 al-Fārābī speaks of the method of 'examination' (*taṣaffuḥ*); at 35,2 he identified this method with that of induction.

162 How would one apply tolerance in the method of Rejecting, when the aim is to verify 'Every *B* is an *A*'? Perhaps by being content to check just a few things that are not *A*s, and confirm that none of them is a *B*. This is interesting because of an asymmetry that Hempel [99] famously pointed out. We can confirm that ravens are black by looking at a few ravens and seeing that they are black. But can we confirm this same claim by looking at a few things that are not black (grass, chalk, lemonade, the moon . . .) and seeing that they are not ravens? If al-Fārābī had paid closer attention to details, and made tighter distinctions such as that between proving and confirming, Hempel's paradox could have become al-Fārābī's paradox.

163 This is the passage quoted in Note 13 to Section 2.3 above. Al-Fārābī slightly rearranges the Baghdad Standard text.

164 For example *bihi shābaha al-aruzzu al-burra* at 62,11. See also 62,1f; 62,4; 62,6; 62,15f; 63,2; 63,4; 63,7.

Textual Emendations

See Section 2.5 for a list of the manuscripts. In these emendations we have used a transcription which respects spoken rather than written Arabic, as is normal among Arabic scholars. Elsewhere in the book we have erred on the side of transcribing the written Arabic, which may be easier for readers not fluent in Arabic.

13,8	For *ḍammana* read *taḍammana.*
17,17	For *kammīyatuhā* read *ka-hay'atihā,* cf. 18,7.
18,1	For *kammīyatuhā* read *ka-hay'atihā,* cf. 18,7.
18,7	For *kammīyatuhā* read *ka-hay'atihā,* as ms *H.*
26,12	For the final *b* read *a,* as mss *K, M.*
41,10	For *b ā* read *b.*
42,3	For *faṣlun* read *faḍlun,* as [45].
44,1f	Delete *fa-idhan ... al-*^{c}*illa,* as mss *K, M.*
46,16	After *at-taḥlīl* add *mabda'u l-ta'ammuli mina l-ghā'ibi wa-l-tarkībi,* as ms *E.*
47,8f	Delete *wa-l-amru alladhī ... al-ḥaddu l-'awsaṭ* and add it between lines 48,7 and 48,8; see Note 99 of the translation.
47,14	For *juz'ī* read *jazmī,* as ms *E.*
48,1	For *lil-ghā'ib* read *lil-amr,* as ms *E.*
48,6	For *wujūd* read *ibṭāl,* as ms *E.*
51,6	After *jisman* add *wa kadhālika in kāna l-fā*^{c}*ilu idhā irtafa*^{c}*a min ḥaythu kāna irtafa*^{c}*a al-jismu lam yalzam an yakūna kullu fā*^{c}*ilin jisman,* as ms *E.*
51,7	After *fā*^{c}*ilan* add *wa in lam yaṣiḥḥ lā hādhā wa lā dhālika lam yalzam lā an yakūna kullu fā*^{c}*ilin jisman wa lā an yakūna kullu jismin fā*^{c}*ilan,* as ms *E.*
53,4	For *fī-mā* read *fī-hā,* as [157].

53,17–54,1	For *fī n-natījati* ... *jismī* read *fī n-natījati wa-sti*ᶜ*mālu l-alif wa-l-lām anna kulla fā*ᶜ*ilin jismī,* as [157] but retaining ᶜAjam's *jismī.*
55,10	For *muqaddamatāhu* read *muqaddamātun.*
55,11	Omit *asmā'* (last occurrence).
57,9	For *wa innamā* read *aw anna mā.*
62,2	After *al-ākharu* add *wa yaskutu* ᶜ*an dhālika-l-ākhari,* as ms *E.*
62,4	After *tashābahā* add *idhā tabayyana lanā ṣiḥḥatu dhālika l-ḥukmi* ᶜ*alā kulli dhālika sh-shay'i alladhī bihi tashābahā,* as mss *E, H.*
64,1	For *bi-itlāfihi* read *bi-'tilāfihi,* as [157].
64,13	For *al-juz'īyyati* read *al-jazmīyyati,* as ms *E.*

Al-Fārābī

Syllogism: *An Abridgement of Aristotle's Prior Analytics*

Translation

Saloua Chatti and Wilfrid Hodges

The Book of Syllogism

5.0 Part 0 [Contents]

[0.1] Our aim is to enumerate the discourses which seek to verify the objectives 11,1
in all reflective arts, and which are used in general to prove or refute an opinion. We show from what, for what purpose and how they are fitted together. These discourses are what are called syllogisms, and some people call them inferences.[1] Throughout this we try as much as possible to make our discussion brief, easy and close to the understanding.

[0.2] There are eighteen parts in the book. Part 1 is about propositions without qualification, what they are composed of, how many kinds [they comprise] and the difference between the hypothetical and the categorical ones. Part 2 is a discussion of the kinds of categorical proposition without qualification. Part 3 is a discussion of the distinction between the propositions that are in opposition and those that are not, and what the conditions are for [two] propositions to be opposites. Part 4 [is about] how many kinds of opposite propositions there are. Part 5 [is about] the way in which each kind of opposite pair [of propositions] is distinguished by truth and falsehood. Part 6 is about the convertible and non-convertible propositions and the meaning of conversion. Part 7 is about the kinds of proposition that are known without any syllogism. Part 8 is about the definition of the syllogism without qualification, what the syllogism is for, what it is composed of, and the distinction between the categorical and the hypothetical syllogism. Part 9 is about categorical premise-pairs, how many premise-pairs [of 12,1
them] there are, and how many syllogistic figures. Part 10 is about the premise-pairs of each figure, how many there are and how many of them are productive. Part 11 is about enumerating the moods of the categorical syllogisms in the first figure. Part 12 is about enumerating the syllogistic moods in the second figure. Part 13 is about enumerating the syllogistic moods in the third figure. Part 14 is about enumerating the moods of the hypothetical syllogisms. Part 15 is about the syllogism of absurdity. Part 16 is about the syllogism of induction and how it is reducible to the syllogisms of the categorical figures, and how it can be viewed as potentially a syllogism. Part 17 is about likening, [the method of] example,

and the likening discourse, what is the nature of each of these, how they can be viewed as potentially syllogisms, and how they can be reduced to the syllogisms of the categorical figures. Part 18 is a general discussion of how one can use the syllogism in dialogues and books.

5.1 Part 1 [The proposition]

[1.1] A proposition, or declarative[2] sentence, is a sentence in which one thing is used to make a judgement about another thing, or to give a piece of information about the other thing, as when we say 'Zayd is going away' or 'ᶜAmr is walking' or 'Humans are animals'. The piece of information is called the predicate, while the thing that the information is about is called the subject. The predicate may be a noun as when we say 'Humans are animals'; and it may be a verb, i.e. what the Arabic grammarians call 'act'[3], as when we say 'Humans walk'.[4]

[1.2] Among the verbs, some signify past time, as when we say 'Zayd has walked', some [others] signify the future, as when we say 'Zayd will walk', and some signify the present, as when we say 'Zayd is walking'. A proposition whose predicate is a noun does not signify that its predicate is satisfied by its subject in one of the three times, by itself and without there being adjoined to it a verb of the kind called copular[5], such as 'was', 'is', 'became', 'becomes', 'existed', 'exists', 'will exist', 'is now' and equivalent expressions. Thus the [Arabic] sentence 'Zayd (is) white' does not indicate by itself at what time he is white, as opposed to 'Zayd was white' which signifies the past, or '[Zayd] will be white' which signifies the future, or
13,1 '[Zayd] is now [white]' which signifies the present. A proposition which indicates by itself that its predicate is true of its subject in one of the three times, without making use of any copular verb, is called two-fold. One which wouldn't signify any of the three times if it didn't include a copular verb is called three-fold.

[1.3] Every proposition either affirms something of something, as when we say 'Humans are white', or denies something of something, as when we say 'Humans are not white'. Each of these two [kinds] is either categorical or hypothetical. The categorical is the one that expresses a categorical judgement, as when we say 'Humans are animals', 'The sun is up', 'It is daytime', 'This number is even' and 'This time is at night.' The hypothetical [proposition] is where the judgement is made under a condition. It takes two forms, the connected and the separated. The connected is where the condition is that the [second] sentence is connected to the [first] sentence so as to follow from it, as when we say 'If the sun is up then it is daytime'. The separated [proposition] is where the condition is that the [second] sentence is separated from the [first] sentence so as to be incompatible with it, as when we say 'This number is either even or odd', and 'This time is either in the night or in the day'.

5.2 Part 2 [The categorical proposition]

[2.1] In some categorical propositions the subject is a universal meaning, as in the sentence 'Humans are animals', while some [others] have individuals as the subjects, as when we say 'Zayd is an animal'. A universal meaning is one that expresses a way in which many things are similar, and an individual [meaning] is one that can't express a way in which two things are similar. Of the propositions whose subjects are universal meanings, some of them are quantified, while some others are indeterminate, i.e. without quantifiers. The quantified ones are all those where a quantifier is adjoined to their subject; this quantifier is an expression which signifies 14,1
that what is asserted by the predicate applies to part of the subject, or to the whole of it. There are four quantifiers: 'Every', 'None', 'Some' and 'Not every'. And there are four [propositions] delimited by quantifiers: affirmative universal, negative universal, affirmative particular and negative particular. The affirmative universal [proposition] is one whose quantifier signifies that the predicate is affirmed of the whole of the subject, as when we say 'Every human is an animal'. The negative universal [proposition] is one whose quantifier signifies that the predicate is denied of the whole of the subject, as when we say 'No human is a stone'.

[2.2] The affirmative particular [proposition] is one whose quantifier signifies that the predicate is affirmed of some of the subject, as when we say 'Some animals are human'. The negative particular [proposition] is one whose quantifier signifies that the predicate is denied of some of the subject, or denied [by saying] 'not all of it', as when we say 'Some humans are not white' or 'Not all humans are white'. Denial and affirmation are both called the quality of the proposition. What the quantifier signifies by 'Some' or 'Every' is called the quantity of the proposition.

5.3 Part 3 [Opposites]

[3.1] An affirmative [sentence] and a negative [sentence] sometimes form a pair of opposites, and sometimes they do not. They form a pair of opposites just when (i) the meaning of the subject in one of the two is the same as the meaning of the subject in the other, and (ii) the meaning of the predicate in one of the two is the same as the meaning of the predicate in the other, and (iii) if a condition is stated – or ought to be stated – in one of the two, either explicitly or implicitly, in terms of time or place or part or aspect or situation or anything else, then the same condition is stated also in the other [sentence]. So when the two have different subjects, as when we say 'The human is an animal' and 'The wall is not an animal', they are not a pair of opposites. Likewise if their predicates are different, as when we say 'The human is an animal' and 'The human is not a stone'.

[3.2] And if the condition in one of the two is a time,[6] but the other [sentence] either has no condition of time, or has a condition involving a different time, then the two [sentences] are not a pair of opposites. An example is when we say 'Zayd was sick yesterday', and 'Zayd [is] not sick', or '[Zayd] is not sick today'. Likewise if one of the [sentences] contains a condition in terms of place, but the other one contains no such condition or a condition involving some other place. An example is when we say 'Zayd is generous at home' [as against] 'Zayd is not generous' or 'Zayd is not generous in the market'. Likewise if one of the two [sentences] contains a condition involving a part[7], but the other [sentence] contains no such condition, or a condition involving some other part. An example is the sentence 'Zayd is sick in his eye' [as against] 'Zayd is not sick', or '[Zayd] is not sick in his hand'. Likewise if some aspect or situation[8] is a condition in one of the two but not in the other, like the sentence 'Zayd is skilful in writing' [as against] 'Zayd is not skilful' or 'Zayd is not skilful in medicine'. The same applies if one of the two sentences contains any other condition, either explicit or implicit[9], that is not present in the other sentence.[10] And likewise, if the two sentences are such that there is a condition that should have been stated in [at least] one of them but is not stated as a condition, then the two are not opposites. For example when we talk about an anklet made of a mixture of gold and silver, the condition that should be applied to it is that a part of this anklet, or such-and-such a part of it, is gold, and a part of it, or such-and-such a part of it, is not of gold. If the two [sentences] were taken absolutely and not restricted by any condition, either explicit or implicit, so that what was said was that this anklet is gold and that this anklet is not gold, then the two would not be opposites.[11]

5.4 Part 4 [Opposite pairs]

[4.1] In each pair of opposite sentences, either the two sentences are both singular, or they are a contrary pair or a subcontrary pair or a contradictory pair, or they are both indeterminate. A pair of [opposite] singular [propositions] is

one where their [shared] subject is an individual, as when we say 'Zayd is white' and 'Zayd is not white'. A contrary pair is one where the [shared] subject has a universal quantifier adjoined to it in both sentences, as when we say 'Every human is an animal' and 'No human is an animal'. A subcontrary pair is one where the [shared] subject has a particular quantifier adjoined to it in both sentences, as when we say 'Some human[12] is an animal' and 'Not every human is 16,1
an animal.' A contradictory pair is one where the [shared] subject has a universal quantifier adjoined to it in one sentence and a particular quantifier in the other sentence.

[4.2] There are two kinds [of contradictory pair]. In one kind, the subject of the affirmative [proposition] has a universal quantifier adjoined to it, and [the subject] of the negative [proposition] has a particular quantifier, as when we say: 'Every human is an animal' and 'Not every human is an animal.' In the other kind, the subject of the affirmative [proposition] has a particular quantifier adjoined to it, and [the subject] of the negative [proposition] has a universal quantifier, as when we say 'Some human is an animal' and 'No human is an animal.'

[4.3] The indeterminate pairs [of opposites] are those where neither sentence has any quantifier at all, either universal or particular, as when we say 'Human is an animal' and 'Human is not an animal'.[13]

5.5 Part 5 [Matters]

[5.1] A pair of [opposite] singular propositions are always distinguished by truth and falsehood – [in other words] there is no situation where they are both true and no situation where they are both false. Rather, when one of the two is true the other is false, and when one of the two is false the other is true. Likewise in a contradictory pair, propositions are always distinguished by truth and falsehood. There is no situation in which they are both true or both false; rather when one of the two is true the other is false, and when one of the two, whichever it happens to be, is false, the other is true.[14] Moreover this holds in all things[15] and matters, regardless of whether [the matters] are necessary or prevented or possible;[16] and it holds for both kinds of contradictory pair. Using necessary [matter] in the first of the two kinds of contradictory pair is like saying 'Every human is an animal' and 'Not every human is an animal.' Using prevented [matter] is like saying 'Every human is a stone' and 'Not every human is a stone.' Using possible [matter] is like saying 'Every human is white' and 'Not every human is white.' With the second kind [of contradictory pair], using necessary [matter] is like saying 'Some human is an animal' and 'No human is an animal'; using prevented [matter] is like saying 'Some human is a stone' and 'No human is a stone'; and using possible [matter] is like saying 'Some human is white' and 'No human is white.'

[5.2] In the case of a contrary pair, the two [propositions] are distinguished
17,1 by truth and falsehood in necessary things[17] and in prevented things, and both are false together in possible [matters]. In necessary [matter] this is like saying 'Every human is an animal' and 'No human is an animal.' In prevented [matter] it is like saying 'Every human is a stone' and 'No human is a stone.' In possible [matter] it is like saying 'Every human is white' and 'No human is white.' Subcontrary pairs are distinguished by truth and falsehood in necessary [matter] and prevented [matter], and they are both true in possible [matter]. In necessary [matter], this is like saying 'Some human is an animal' and 'Not every human is an animal.' In prevented [matter] it is like saying 'Some human is a stone' and 'Not every human is a stone.' In possible [matter] it is like saying 'Some human is white' and 'Not every human is white'. The behaviour of a pair of indeterminate [opposite propositions] in relation to truth and falsehood is the same as that of a pair of subcontraries.

5.6 Part 6 [Conversion]

[6.1] Some quantified propositions convert and some don't convert. Converting a proposition is reversing the order of its parts, so that its subject becomes the predicate and its predicate becomes the subject, [in such a way that] its quality remains the same and its truth is preserved permanently in whatever matter it is, and [likewise] with a modality.[18] When the order of its two parts is reversed and its quality remains as it was, but its truth is not preserved in all those matters, this is called reversal of the proposition, not conversion of it. One [kind of proposition] that doesn't convert is the negative particular, because [conversion] doesn't preserve its truth in all matters. Thus when we say 'Some animal is not a human', its truth is not preserved when it is reversed, either when its quantity is preserved or when it is changed. For neither of the two sentences 'Some human is not an animal' and 'No human is an animal' is true alongside [the initial proposition]. Among the [propositions] that convert, there are some where the quantity is converted so that their quantity, their quality and their truth are preserved, while in some others the quantity is changed. There are two
18,1 [propositions] that convert maintaining their form. The first of the two is the negative universal [proposition], as when we say 'No human is a stone'. This

converts to become 'No stone is a human', and this [conversion] is permanently the case in all things and matters. The second one is the affirmative particular, as when we say 'Some animal is white'. This converts and becomes 'Some white thing is an animal'. This is permanently the case in all things and matters. [A proposition] that changes its quantity when it converts is the affirmative universal [proposition], as when we say 'Every human is an animal'. For the sentence which has its truth preserved permanently in all matters is the sentence 'Some animal is a human' and not the sentence 'Every animal is a human.'

[6.2] The negative universal [proposition] converts as itself, because when it is true, its two parts are totally disjoint, so that they are not both true in any individual at all, nor at any time. So if either one of its two parts is true of some individual, the other part cannot be true of that individual. This is because if the two are both true of some individual, then the predicate will be true of an individual of which the subject is also true. But this is impossible, because it contradicts what was posited as true at the beginning, to the effect that its predicate is not true in any of the individuals of which its subject is true. And the affirmative particular too, its two parts are not separated at all, [since they overlap] in the 'some' which is common to them, so that that 'some' is some of both together. Because of that some, they preserve the truth under conversion in all matters permanently. As for the affirmative universal [proposition], the facts about its conversion are clear.

5.7 Part 7 [Known without syllogism]

[7.1] Propositions differ in how they are known [to be true]: for some of them the knowledge becomes available[19] without [being deduced by] a syllogism, while for others the knowledge becomes available through a syllogism. Those for which the knowledge becomes available without a syllogism are of four kinds: the accepted, the standard, the sense-perceived and the intellected universal primary [propositions]. The accepted [propositions] are those which are received either from one person who agrees to them or from a community who agrees to 19,1 them. The standard [propositions] are the opinions that are favoured by everybody or most people or the scholars or the intellectuals or most of these, without any one of them or anybody else disagreeing. The sense-perceived propositions are those singular propositions of [whose truth] we are made aware by one of the five senses. The intellected universal primary propositions are sentences like 'Every three is an odd number' and 'Every five is half of ten' and

'Every part of a whole is smaller than that whole', and the like. For everything that goes beyond these four kinds of known thing, knowledge of it becomes available just from a syllogism.

5.8 Part 8 [Syllogism]

[8.1] A syllogism is a discourse in which more than one thing is posited, such that when [these things] are composed, something other than them follows from them, by themselves, and not by accident but necessarily. What follows from the syllogism is called the conclusion; it is also called the consequence. The syllogism is composed with a view to a previously given objective, which is first adopted and then verified by the syllogism. The objective consists of the two parts of a contradictory [pair of sentences], joined together by a disjunctive particle, and with an interrogative particle linked to them both so as to ask which [of the alternative parts] is the case. The disjunctive particle is the particle 'or', or something equivalent, and the interrogative particle about what is the case is the particle 'Is it?' or something equivalent, as in the sentence 'Is it [the case] that every body is mobile, or is it [the case] that not every body is mobile?' The objective is also sometimes called the question. For each objective, one of its two parts is true, though we [may] not be able to specify which of the two it is. [The true part] is either the affirmative one or the negative one, though we [may] not be able to specify which of the two it is. The syllogism related to this objective tells us that a specific one of the two [is true], and it does so through the fact that it follows necessarily either that the truth lies in the affirmative of the pair alone and not the negative, or that it lies in the negative of the pair alone and not the affirmative.

[8.2] It is clear that when the composition of the discourse is one from which there follows sometimes an affirmative universal sentence and sometimes its contrary or its contradictory, we don't know – when we compose things in that way – which of the two parts of the contradiction the composition will yield [as conclusion], since the affirmative part is no more appropriate than the negative. Discourse like that doesn't provide us with any knowledge about the objective, apart from what we already knew before composing [the premise-pair]; therefore it is not a syllogism.[20]

[8.3] Some syllogisms are categorical and some are hypothetical; the categorical is composed of categorical propositions, and the hypothetical is composed of hypothetical propositions.[21] Every proposition that is taken to be a component of a syllogism, or is prepared[22] for being taken as a component of a syllogism, is for this reason called a premise; a component of the premise is called a term, either a predicate or a subject.

[8.4] There can be [configurations in which] several propositions follow [as conclusions] from syllogisms, and these same propositions are component [premises] of other syllogisms, or are prepared for being taken as components of other syllogisms.[23] These propositions are called conclusions because they follow from syllogisms, and they are called premises because they are components of other syllogisms.

5.9 Part 9 [Categorical syllogisms]

[9.1] A categorical syllogism is composed of at least two premises linked together, and [at least] three terms [altogether], where any two linked premises share a single component [i.e. term], and differ in their two other terms. This is as when we say 'The human is an animal; and every animal is sentient'. These two linked premises share a single component, namely 'animal', and they differ with regard to the two other components, namely 'human' and 'is sentient'. Thus the two [propositions] that share a component and differ in [the other] two components contain [altogether] three terms. The component that is shared between the two linked premises is called the middle term, while the two parts that are different in these [premises] are called the extremes.

[9.2] Of the two extremes, the one that is the predicate in the objective is called the first or great extreme,[24] and the one that is the subject in the objective is called the last or minor extreme. The premise in which one of the terms is the predicate of the objective (i.e. the great extreme) is the major premise, while the [premise] in which one of the terms is the subject of the objective is called the minor [premise]. The middle term can be arranged in the two linked premises in three ways. Namely, either it is a predicate in both [premises], or it is a subject in both of them, or it is a predicate in one of them and a subject in the other. The arrangement of the middle term in the two linked premises is called the figure. Accordingly there are three figures of categorical syllogisms. The first figure is the one where the middle term is the predicate in one of the [premises] and the subject in the other. The second figure is the one where the middle term is the predicate in both premises. The third figure is the one where the middle term is the subject in both [premises].

5.10 Part 10 [The figures]

[10.1] In each figure, the two linked premises are either [1] both universal, or [2] both particular, or [3] both unquantified, or [4] the major premise is universal and the minor premise is particular, or [5] the major premise is particular and the minor premise is universal, or [6] the major premise is universal and the minor is indeterminate, or [7] the major premise is indeterminate and the minor premise is universal, or [8] the major premise is particular and the minor premise is indeterminate, or [9] the major premise is indeterminate and the minor premise is particular. In each of these nine [premise-pairs], [the premises] are either both affirmative, or both negative, or the major premise is affirmative and
22,1 the minor is negative, or the major premise is negative and the minor premise is affirmative. The former nine cases are multiplied by the latter four, giving rise to thirty-six premise-pairs in each figure.

[10.2] A premise-pair consisting of two negative [premises] is not productive, in any figure and regardless of the quantities of the premises. Nor is a premise-pair consisting of two particular premises, or of two indeterminate premises, or one where the major premise is particular and the minor premise is indeterminate, or one where the major premise is indeterminate and the minor premise is particular. Thus there are twenty-one unproductive premise-pairs in each figure.[25] It is a property of the first figure that of the remaining fifteen premise-pairs, those where the minor premise is negative are unproductive, and so are those where the major premise is particular or indeterminate. A property of the second figure is that those of its premise-pairs whose premises are both affirmative are unproductive, and so are those whose major premise is particular or indeterminate. A property of the third figure is that those of its premise-pairs where the minor premise is negative are unproductive. Furthermore, we count the indeterminate [premises] in productive syllogisms as having the same force as particular premises, so the particular premises make the indeterminate premises redundant. This gives four productive premise-pairs in the first figure, four in the second figure and six in the third. So there are in total fourteen productive categorical moods in the three figures.

[10.3] Each of [these moods] is from two premises that are linked as major [premise] and minor [premise]. [Altogether] they have three terms: first, middle and last. Aristotle wrote *A* in place of the first term, *B* in place of the middle term and *C* in place of the last term. So these letters of the alphabet are symbols which
23,1 embrace all the things that happen to be taken as components of the premises in the various arts. But he didn't use meaningful expressions as replacements for

these letters, because he wanted to avoid people thinking that [the consequences] that followed from the [resulting] compositions [followed] because of the matters that the expressions signified.

5.11 Part 11 [First figure]

[11.1] The first mood of the first figure is ‘*A* is true of everything that is a *B*; and *B* is true of everything that is a *C*’. It produces the conclusion ‘*A* is true of everything that is a *C*’. The second [mood] is ‘*A* is true of everything that is a *B*; and *B* is true of some *C*’. It produces the conclusion ‘*A* is true of some *C*’. The third [mood] is ‘*A* is in nothing that is a *B*; and *B* is true of everything that is a *C*’. It produces the conclusion ‘*A* is not in anything that is a *C*’. The fourth [mood] is ‘*A* is not in anything that is a *B*; and *B* is true of some *C*’. It produces the conclusion ‘*A* is absent from some *C*’ or ‘*A* is not in every *C*’. This is how [things] are ordered if you go from the first extreme to the last.

[11.2] But if you go from the last to the first, following the most usual custom, then in the case of the first mood you say: ‘Everything that is a *C* is a *B*; and everything that is a *B* is an *A*’. It produces the conclusion ‘Everything that is a *C* is an *A*’. The second [mood] is ‘Something that is a *C* is a *B*; and everything that is a *B* is an *A*’. It produces the conclusion ‘Something that is a *C* is an *A*’. The third [mood] is ‘Everything that is a *C* is a *B*; and nothing that is a *B* is an *A*’. It produces the conclusion ‘Nothing that is a *C* is an *A*’. The fourth [mood] is ‘Something that is a *C* is a *B*; and nothing that is a *B* is an *A*’. It produces the conclusion ‘Something that is a *C* is not an *A*’, or ‘Not everything that is a *C* is an *A*’. Either of these two orderings is permissible and serves the purpose.

[11.3] An example of the first mood using material things is ‘Every human is an animal; and every animal is sentient’. It produces the conclusion ‘Every human is sentient’. The second [mood is illustrated by] ‘Some body is an animal; and every animal is sentient’. It produces the conclusion ‘Some body is sentient’. The third [mood is illustrated by] ‘Every human is an animal; and no animal is a stone’. It produces the conclusion ‘No human is a stone’. The fourth [mood is illustrated by] ‘Some body is an animal; and no animal is a stone’. It produces the conclusion ‘Some body is not a stone’, or ‘Not every body is a stone’.

[11.4] It is possible to order these [syllogisms] in the first way by saying them as follows. [For the example of the first mood:] ‘Sentient holds of every animal; and animal holds of every human’. This produces the conclusion ‘Sentient holds of every human’. The second [mood would be] ‘Sentient holds of every animal;

and animal holds of something that is a body'. This produces the conclusion 'Sentient holds of something that is a body'. The third [mood would be] 'Stone holds of no animal; and animal holds of every human'. It produces the conclusion 'Stone holds of no human'. The fourth [mood would be] 'Stone holds of no animal; and animal holds of some bodies'. It produces the conclusion 'Stone fails to hold of some bodies'.

[11.5] Thus the middle term is the reason and the cause, because it is the reason why the two extremes come together and the reason for our knowledge of the conclusion; [the two extremes *C* and *A*] are linked to the middle term because it is found in answer to the question 'Why is [*C*] an [*A*]?'.[26] The first [mood consists] of two affirmative universal premises and produces an affirmative universal conclusion. The second [mood] has its major premise affirmative universal and its minor premise affirmative particular, and it produces an affirmative particular conclusion. The third mood has its major premise negative universal and its minor premise affirmative universal, and it produces a negative universal conclusion. The fourth [mood] has its major premise negative and its minor premise affirmative particular, and it produces a negative particular conclusion.

[11.6] These four moods are self-evidently syllogisms and productive without needing a proof through other things to show that they are productive. Now just as some propositions are self-evidently true while others need to be proved true by other means, the same applies to syllogisms. The syllogisms that are self-evident are called perfect, while those which need something else to prove that they are syllogisms and that they are productive are called imperfect. The imperfect syllogisms are shown to be productive by being reduced to perfect syllogisms.

5.12 Part 12 [Second figure]

25,1 [12.1] As to the moods of the second figure, the first one is '*B* is in no *A*; and *B* is in every *C*'. This produces the conclusion '*A* is in no *C*', because the negative universal premise converts to become '*A* is in no *B*', and *B* was in every *C*; so [the premises] reduce to the third mood of the first figure[27], listing [the moods] as we do in this book. Thus it is proved that [the premise-pair] is a syllogism and that it produces the conclusion '*A* is in no *C*'. The second mood is the following: '*B* is in every *A*; and *B* is in no *C*'. This produces the conclusion '*A* is in no *C*', because the negative universal premise, if it is converted, becomes ‘*C* is in no *B*’, and [we had] ‘*B* is in every *A*’, so [the premises] reduce to that same mood of the first figure.[28] So it is proved that it produces the conclusion ‘*C* is in no *A*’. This conclusion in turn converts so as to become ‘*A* is in no *C*’. Thus this mood is proved by two conversions: the conversion of the minor premise and the conversion of the conclusion of the first figure mood to which [this mood] is reduced. The third mood is ‘*B* is in no *A*; and *B* is in some *C*’. It produces the conclusion ‘*A* is absent from some *C*’, or ‘*A* is not in every *C*’, because the negative universal [premise] converts so as to become ‘*A* is in some *B*’; and we had ‘*B* is in some *C*’, which reduces to the fourth mood of the first figure. The fourth mood of the second figure is ‘*B* is in every *A*; and *B* is absent from some *C*’. It produces the conclusion ‘*A* is absent from some *C*’, or ‘*A* is not in every *C*’. This is not proved by conversion. But there was assumed ‘*B* is absent from some *C*’, and this shows that *B* is denied of the whole of that some. Let us take out that some on its own and call it *D*, so [the premise-pair] becomes ‘*B* is in every *A*; and *B* is in no *D*’, which is reduced to the second mood of this same figure. But it has already been shown that this reduces to the first figure by converting the negative universal [premise] so that it becomes ‘*D* is in no *B*’, while [we had] ‘*B* is in every *A*’. This produces the conclusion ‘*D* is in no *A*’. Then this conclusion is converted so that it becomes ‘*A* is in no *D*’. But *D* is some *C*, so the conclusion has been produced that ‘*A* is absent from some *C*’. This ordering begins at the middle term and finishes at the two extremes, so that the first extreme is the starting point in the ordering of the discourse.

[12.2] But in the ordering that is most commonly used, one says in the first [mood] ‘No *A* is a *B*; and every *C* is a *B*’. This produces the conclusion ‘No *C* is an *A*’, because the negative universal [premise] is converted so that [the premise-pair] becomes ‘Every *C* is a *B*; and no *B* is an *A*’. The second mood is as follows: ‘Every *A* is a *B*; and no *C* is a *B*’. This produces the conclusion ‘No *C* is an *A*’, because the negative universal [premise] is converted so that [the premise-pair] becomes ‘Every *A* is a *B*; and no *B* is a *C*’. This produces the conclusion ‘No *A* is a *C*’, and then this conclusion is converted so as to become ‘No *C* is an *A*’. The third mood is as follows: ‘No *A* is a *B*; and some *C* is a *B*’. This produces the conclusion ‘Some *C* is not an *A*’, or ‘Not every *C* is an *A*’, because the negative universal [premise] converts so that [the premises] become ‘Some *C* is a *B*; and no *B* is an *A*’. The fourth mood is as follows: ‘Every *A* is a *B*; some *C* is not a *B*’. It produces the conclusion ‘Some *C* is not an *A*’, or ‘Not every *C* is an *A*’, because *B* is denied of the whole of that part of *C*. Let this part [of *C*] be *D*. Then we have ‘Every *A* is

a *B*; and no *D* is a *B*', which is the composition of the second mood of this same figure. Now it was already shown that this reduces to the first figure by converting the negative universal [premise] so that [the premises] become 'Every *A* is a *B*; and no *B* is a *D*', which produces the conclusion 'No *A* is a *D*'. Then this conclusion
27,1 converts so that it becomes 'No *D* is an *A*'. But *D* is some *C*, so therefore some *C* is not an *A*.

[12.3] An example of the first mood in [material] things is 'No stone is an animal; and every human is an animal'. It produces the conclusion 'No human is a stone', because the negative universal [premise] converts so that [the premises] become 'Every human is an animal; and no animal is a stone'. The second [mood is illustrated by] 'Every horse is an animal; and no plant is an animal'. It produces the conclusion 'No plant is a horse', because the negative universal [premise] converts so that [the premises] become 'Every horse is an animal; and no animal is a plant'. This produces the conclusion 'No horse is a plant'. Then this conclusion converts so as to become 'No plant is a horse'. The third [mood] is [illustrated by] 'No stone is an animal; and some body is an animal'. It produces the conclusion 'Some body is not a stone' or 'Not every body is a stone', because if the negative universal [premise] is converted [the premises] become 'Some bodies are animals; and no animal is a stone'. The fourth [mood] is [illustrated by] 'Every horse neighs; and not every animal neighs'. It produces the conclusion 'Some animal is not a horse', or 'Not every animal is a horse', because if we take some animal which we have denied neighing of, human for example, [the premise-pair] becomes 'Every horse neighs; and no human neighs'.[29] It produces the conclusion 'No human is a horse' as we have already shown. But then human is some animal, so therefore some animal is not a horse. One can also arrange these examples in the first ordering.

[12.4] The first mood has its major premise negative universal and its minor premise affirmative universal, and it produces a negative universal conclusion. The second [mood] has its major premise affirmative universal and its minor premise negative universal; it produces a negative universal conclusion. The third mood has its major premise negative universal and its minor premise affirmative particular; it produces a negative particular conclusion. The fourth mood has its major premise affirmative universal and its minor premise negative particular; it produces a negative particular conclusion. These are the only productive premise-pairs of the second figure. It is not possible for a premise-pair [in this figure] to be productive unless the premises differ in quality; [a premise-pair with] two affirmative premises is never productive in this figure.

5.13 Part 13 [Third figure]

[13.1] As for the moods of the third figure, the first is as follows: '*A* is in every *B*; and *C* is in every *B*'. It produces the conclusion '*A* is in some *C*', because the minor [premise], namely '*C* is in every *B*', converts to an affirmative particular [premise], so that [the premises] become '*A* is in every *B* and *B* is in some *C*', which reduces to the second mood of the first figure in the listing that we use in this book.[30] The second mood is '*A* is in no *B*; *C* is in every *B*'. It produces the conclusion '*A* is absent from some *C*', because the affirmative minor premise converts to a particular [premise] so that [the premise-pair] becomes '*A* is in no *B*; and *B* is in some *C*', so it reduces to the fourth mood of the first figure. The third mood is as follows: '*A* is in every *B*; *C* is in some *B*'. It produces the conclusion '*A* is in some *C*', because if the affirmative particular minor premise is converted to a particular, [the premise-pair] becomes '*A* is in every *B*; and *B* is in some *C*', so it reduces to the second mood of the first figure in terms of our listing.[30] The fourth mood is as follows: '*A* is in some *B*; *C* is in every *B*'. It produces the conclusion '*A* is in some *C*', because if the particular major premise is converted, [the premise-pair] becomes '*C* is in every *B*; and *B* is in some *A*', which produces the conclusion '*C* is in some *A*'. Then this conclusion converts, becoming '*A* is in some *C*'. The fifth [mood] is as follows: '*A* is in no *B*; *C* is in some *B*'. It produces the conclusion '*A* is absent from some *C*', because the affirmative particular minor premise converts so that [the premise-pair] becomes '*A* is in no *B*; and *B* is in some *C*', which reduces to the fourth mood of the first figure. The sixth [mood] is as follows: '*A* is absent from some *B*; *C* is in every *B*'. It produces the conclusion '*A* is absent from some *C*'. [The premise-pair] is reduced to the first figure, not by conversion but by the fact that when *A* is denied of some *B*, [*A*] is denied of the whole of that some. Let us suppose that this some is *D*. Then if *C* is in every *B*, it is in every *D*, so that [the premise-pair] becomes '*A* is in no *D*; and *C* is in every *D*', which reduces to the second mood of this same figure.

[13.2] Now if the ordering is taken as in the most usual custom, the meaning of the first [mood] is as follows: 'Every *B* is an *A*; every *B* is a *C*'. It produces the conclusion 'Some *C* is an *A*' because if the minor premise is converted [the premise-pair] becomes 'Some *C* is a *B*; and every *B* is an *A*'. This reduces to the second mood of the first figure as we listed them.[30] The second [mood] is 'No *B* is an *A*, and every *B* is a *C*'. It produces the conclusion 'Some *C* is not an *A*', because if the affirmative universal minor premise is converted [the premise-pair] becomes 'Some *C* is a *B*; and no *B* is an *A*', which reduces to the fourth mood of the first figure. The third [mood] is 'Every *B* is an *A*; some *B* is a *C*'. It produces the conclusion 'Some *C* is an *A*', because if the minor affirmative particular is converted [the premise-pair] becomes 'Some *C* is a *B*; and every *B* is an *A*'. It reduces to the second mood of the first figure as we listed them.[30] The fourth [mood] is as follows: 'Some *B* is an *A*; every *B* is a *C*'. It produces the conclusion 'Some *C* is an *A*', because if the major premise is converted [the premise-pair] becomes 'Some *A* is a *B*; and some *B* is a *C*'. It produces the conclusion 'Some *A* is a *C*'. Then this conclusion converts so as to become 'Some *C* is an *A*'. The fifth [mood] is 'No *B* is an *A*; and some *B* is a *C*'. It produces the conclusion 'Some *C* is not an *A*', because if the affirmative minor [premise] is converted, [the premise-pair] becomes 'Some *C* is a *B*; and no *B* is an *A*', which reduces to the fourth mood of the first figure. The sixth [mood] is 'Some *B* is not an *A*; and every *B* is a *C*'. It produces the conclusion 'Some *C* is not an *A*', because if *A* is denied of the whole of the 'some *B*', and we take that some [*B*] to be *D*, [the premise-pair] becomes: 'No *D* is an *A*; and every *D* is a *C*', which reduces to the second mood of this [same] figure. It has been shown that this mood reduces to the fourth mood of the first figure.

[13.3] An example of the first mood in [material] things is 'Every theoretical science is learned; and every theoretical science is good'. It produces the conclusion 'Some good things are learned', or 'Some good thing is learned', because the minor premise converts so that [the premises] become 'Some good thing is a theoretical science; and every theoretical science is learned', which reduces to the second mood of the first figure as we have listed them.[30] An example of the second [mood] is 'No theoretical science is natural; and every theoretical science is good'. It produces the conclusion 'Some good things are not natural', or 'Some good thing is not natural', or 'Not every good thing is natural', because the minor [premise] converts so that [the premise-pair] becomes 'Some good thing is a theoretical science; and no theoretical science is natural', which reduces to the fourth mood of the first figure. The third [mood] is [illustrated by] 'Every human is an animal; something that is a human is white'. It produces the conclusion 'Something that is white is an animal', because the minor premise converts so that [the premise-pair] becomes 'Something that is white is human; and every human is an animal', which reduces to the second mood of the first figure as we have listed them.[30] The fourth [mood] is [illustrated by] 'Some animal is white; every animal is a body'. It produces the conclusion 'Some bodies are white', or 'Some body is white', because the particular major premise converts so that [the premises] become 'Some white thing is an animal; and every animal is a body'. This produces the conclusion 'Some white thing is a body'. Then this conclusion converts so as to become 'Some bodies are white', so that the conclusion of this syllogism is proved by two conversions. The fifth [mood] is [illustrated by] 'No animal is a stone; some animal is white'. It produces the conclusion 'Some of what is white is not a stone', or 'Not every white thing is a stone', because the minor premise converts so that [the premises] become 'Some white thing is an animal; and no animal is a stone', which reduces to the fourth mood of the first figure. The sixth [mood] is [illustrated by] 'Some animal is not white; and every animal is a body'. It produces the conclusion 'Some bodies are not white', or 'Some body is not white', or 'Not every body is white', because when whiteness is denied of the whole of the 'some animal', let us take it to be the crow for instance, [the premise-pair] becomes 'No crow is white; and every crow is a body', which reduces to the second mood of this same figure. It has been proved that that [mood] reduces, by conversion of the minor [premise], to the fourth mood of the first figure.

[13.4] The first mood of this figure produces an affirmative particular conclusion 31,1
from two affirmative [premises]. The second [mood] has a negative universal major [premise] and an affirmative universal minor [premise], and it produces a negative particular conclusion. The third [mood] has an affirmative universal major [premise] and an affirmative particular minor [premise], and it produces an affirmative particular [conclusion]. The fourth [mood] has an affirmative particular major [premise] and an affirmative universal minor [premise], and it produces an affirmative particular conclusion. The fifth [mood] has a negative universal major [premise] and an affirmative particular minor [premise], and it produces a negative particular conclusion. The sixth [mood] has a negative particular major [premise] and an affirmative universal minor [premise], and it produces a negative particular conclusion. These are all the categorical syllogisms.

5.14 Part 14 [Hypothetical syllogisms]

[14.1] Now we have to speak about the hypothetical syllogisms. The hypothetical syllogism is also composed of two premises, a major [premise] which is a hypothetical [sentence] and a minor [premise] which is a categorical [sentence], and adjoined to the pair of them is a particle of detachment such as 'nevertheless', 'however', 'but' or an equivalent expression. The hypothetical syllogism is of two kinds: connected and separated; the connected [syllogism] is where the major [premise] is a connected hypothetical [sentence], while the separated is where the major [premise] is a separated hypothetical [sentence]. The connected [syllogism] has two primary[31] moods, while the separated has three primary moods; so there are five primary hypothetical moods in total.

[14.2] Thus the first mood of the connected hypothetical [syllogism] is [the following]: 'If this visible thing is a human, then it is an animal; but it is a human'. This produces the conclusion that 'It is therefore an animal'. The major premise in this mood is the sentence 'If this visible thing is a human, then it is an animal'. This is a single hypothetical [sentence] compounded from two sentences which are its parts, the first [part] being 'This visible thing is a human' and the second being 'it is an animal'. A condition is adjoined to the first part, namely 'if it is' which comprises[32] the connecting of the second part, i.e. 'it is an animal', to the first part, i.e. 'If this visible thing is a human'. Thus the first part of the hypothetical [sentence] is called 'antecedent' and the second part is called 'consequent'. This condition, namely 'if it is' and similar expressions such as 'when', 'when it is' and 'if it were', and phrases of this kind, comprises the connecting of the consequent to the antecedent.

[14.3] The separated [sentence] has a condition which comprises separating the consequent from the antecedent, as when we say 'This number is either even
32,1 or odd'; this condition, which is 'or' or something similar, comprises separating the consequent from the antecedent.

[14.4] In both kinds of syllogism, the minor [premise] is a categorical premise to which the particle of detachment is added, and it is called 'the detached [sentence]'. It is always one of the parts of the hypothetical [premise], either its antecedent or its consequent.[33]

[14.5] The first mood of the connected hypothetical [syllogism], in which the unaltered antecedent is detached, produces the unaltered consequent, as when we say 'If this visible thing is a human, then it is an animal; but it is a human; therefore it is an animal'. The second mood of the connected hypothetical [syllogism], in which the opposite of the consequent is detached, produces the opposite of the antecedent, as when we say 'If this visible thing is a human, then it is an animal; but it is not an animal'. This produces: 'it is therefore not a human'. But in this and similar cases, if we were to detach the opposite of the antecedent, or the unaltered consequent, then there would be no conclusion that this premise-pair necessarily produces.

[14.6] As to the separated [hypothetical syllogism], its major [premise] is a separated hypothetical [sentence] while its minor [premise] is a detached categorical [sentence]. The hypothetical [premise] is composed of two or more conflicting parts, as when we say 'This number is either even or odd'. The conflict [in these premises] can be complete, namely where there is a natural bound on the number [of cases] and they are all listed exhaustively; while when the conflict is incomplete, either we do not have a natural bound on the number [of cases], or we do have such a bound but the speaker fails to list all [the cases] exhaustively. When the conflict is complete, there can be two [cases] or more than two. As an instance of only two conflicting [cases], we say 'This number is either even or odd'. An instance of more than two conflicting cases would be 'This water is either cold or hot or middling'. An example where the conflict is not complete is 'This colour is either white or red or dusty'. In cases where the conflict is not complete, the conflict can be natural, as when we say 'This colour is either white or black'; or it can express a posit, as when we say 'It is not the case that Zayd is present and ᶜAmr is speaking'.[34]

[14.7] In all the separated hypothetical [sentences] containing only two conflicting [parts], where the conflict is complete, if either one of the parts is detached, this produces the opposite of the other one; and if the opposite of either one of them is detached, this produces the other one unaltered. For instance: 'This number is either even or odd; but it is even; therefore it is not odd' or 'but it is odd; therefore it is not even' or 'but it is not even; therefore it is odd' or 'but it is not odd; therefore it is even'. If there are more than two [parts] and their conflict is complete, then if we detach any one of them, this produces the opposites of the remaining ones. Thus when we say 'This water is either cold or hot or middling' and we make a detachment by saying 'But it is cold', this produces that 'it is neither hot nor middling'. Then when we detach the opposite of either of these two, this produces the remaining one of the conflicting [parts].[35] So whenever we detach the opposite of one of the remaining conflicting [parts], then this produces the rest of the conflicting [parts], until only two conflicting [parts] remain. At that point, when the opposite of one of the remaining [parts] is detached, this produces the other [part]. Thus when we say 'This number is either greater [than] or smaller [than] or equal [to another one]; but it is not smaller', this produces that 'it is therefore either equal or greater'. When after that one detaches 'it is not greater', then this produces that 'therefore it is equal'. The same applies however many conflicting [parts] there are in it.

[14.8] If the conflict is not complete, then traditionally the particle 'or' is not used; rather something is adjoined to the sentence to signify that the two conflicting [parts] cannot be true together, as when we say 'This colour cannot be [both] white and black', or 'Zayd is not in both Shām[36] and Iraq'. Likewise in those cases where the conflict expresses a posit, as when we say 'It is not the case that Zayd is walking and ᶜAmr is talking'. In this mood, one or other of the two [parts] is detached, and this produces the opposite of the other [part] – as when we say 'Zayd is not both in Shām and in Iraq; but he is in Iraq'; this produces that 'he is therefore not in Shām'. [Or] 'but he is in Shām', and this produces that 'he is therefore not in Irāq'. In this mood there is no conclusion that it would necessarily produce if what was detached was the opposite of one of [the parts]. This mood was called by the Ancients the mood that starts with a negative and leads to a negative, since it always produces a negative [conclusion].[37]

5.15 Part 15 [On the syllogism of absurdity]

[15.1] A categorical syllogism whose premises are both clearly true is called a direct syllogism. It necessarily produces a true conclusion. An example is: 'Every human is an animal, and every animal is sentient; therefore every human is sentient'. But if either one of its two premises is clearly true, and the other is doubtful and not known to be true or to be false, and [the premises] produce a conclusion that is clearly false and impossible, this syllogism is called a syllogism of absurdity. This syllogism is used to prove the truth of the contradictory opposite of the doubtful premise. Thus when the conclusion is clearly false it is known that a falsehood is involved in the syllogism, because if no falsehood was involved in it at all, then the conclusion would have to be true. So if [the conclusion] is false, then the syllogism contains a falsehood. The falsehood is either in both premises or in one of them. But one of the two premises is clearly true, and the conclusion cannot possibly owe its falsity to the true premise; rather [its falsity] comes from the other premise, the one that is doubted. A sentence from which a falsehood follows is [itself] false, so the doubted premise is false, and so its contradictory opposite is true. And this is what we wanted to prove from the beginning. That is why, if we want to prove the truth of some proposition, we take the contradictory opposite of it and we add to it a premise whose truth is not doubted. Then if this composition is a syllogism that produces a conclusion that is clearly both false and impossible, we have thereby proved the truth of the first proposition, namely the one which we were aiming to prove.

[15.2] As an example of this, when we want to prove for instance that 'Every human is sentient', we say that the sentence 'Every human is sentient' is true. If this was not conceded to us [by the Responder], then he must have conceded its contradictory opposite, which is 'Not every human is sentient'. We take this contradictory opposite as the doubted [premise], and we add to it a premise whose truth is not doubted, namely the sentence 'Every human is an animal'. This composes [a premise-pair] in the sixth mood of the third figure:[38] 'Not every human is sentient, and every human is an animal'. [The composition] produces 'Not every animal is sentient'; but this is false, prevented and impossible. This impossible [sentence] can't follow from the sentence 'Every human is an animal' since this sentence is true. Therefore the impossible [sentence] follows from the sentence 'Not every human is sentient', and so this sentence is [also] impossible. Therefore its contradictory opposite, namely the sentence 'Every human is sentient' that was put up for consideration[39] at the outset, is true. This is the sentence that we wanted to prove true.

5.16 Part 16 On induction

[16.1] Induction is an examination of the various particular cases which are 35,2
included under some universal concept [*B*],[40] in order to verify whether a content [*A*] is true or false of that concept [*B*].[41] Thus, if we want to prove or refute that a universal content [*B*] satisfies a content [*A*], we examine the known[42] particular cases that are included in that universal concept [*B*]. If we find the content [*A*] true of all or most[43] of the particular cases of the universal concept [*B*], this shows that the content [*A*] is true of the universal concept [*B*], either of all of it or of most of it. If we examine [the particular cases] and we don't find the content [*A*] to be true of any of them, or we find that it is false of all or most of them, we will have proved that the content [*A*] is false of the universal [concept *B*]. Then our examination of each one of its particular cases, to see whether the content is true of it, is induction, and the conclusion of the induction is that the content [*A*] is affirmed or denied[44] of the universal concept [*B*].

[16.2] An example of this is that when we want to prove that every movement [*B*] is in a time [*A*], we examine the forms of movement; these are the particular [cases of] movement such as walking and flying and swimming, and other things that we can take to be particular cases [of the concept *B*]. We pursue them so that we find that each of the particular cases [of *B*] which we examine is in a time. This makes available to us the fact that each movement is in a time. Induction is a piece of discourse which has the potential[45] of a syllogism in the first figure. Its middle term is the particular cases that are examined, namely walking, flying and swimming and so on, its major term is the expression 'in a time', and its minor term is the expression 'movement'. They are composed as follows: 'Every movement is either walking or swimming or flying or etc.; and every walking and swimming and flying etc. is in a time'. By composing the first mood of the first figure,[46] this yields the conclusion that every movement is in a time.

5.17 Part 17 [On likening]

36,1 [17.1] Likening is when some [content *A*] is taken or known at the outset to be true of some particular entity [*D*],[47] and then a person transfers that [content] from that entity to some other particular [entity *C*] that is similar to the first one, asserting that the content [*A*] is true of [the second entity *C*], when [the following hold. First] the two particular entities [*C*, *D*] are particular cases of the[48] universal concept [*B*] because of which the content [*A*] is true of the first particular [entity *D*]. [And second,] the fact that the content [*A*] is true of the first entity [*D*], is clearer and better known, while it is more hidden in the case of the second [entity *C*]. The first [entity] is said to be like[49] the second, and the second is [said to be] comparable to the first. When we take the content [*A*] that was true of the first [particular entity *D*], and assert it of the second particular [entity *C*] because of its similarity to [the first], this is called likening the second to the first. The discourse verifying that the content which is true of the first [entity] is true also of the second, because of the similarity between the two [entities], is called the likening discourse. Likening is the transfer of the content from a particular [entity] to another particular [entity] that is similar to it, when the content's being true of [the first] is better known than its being true of [the second]. The two [particular entities] both fall under the universal concept because of which and in view of which the content is true of the better known [entity].

[17.2] For example we already knew by observation that a wall starts by having a maker.[50] Then we find that the sky is similar to the wall in being a body. Let [body] be the universal concept [*B*] because of which there is something that brings the wall into existence. Then we assert that the same content [*A*] is true of the sky, viz. that because [it is a body] it was brought into existence and has a maker. So the likening discourse, because it is likening, [is composed] in the following way: 'The wall was brought into existence; the wall is a body; and the sky is a body. Therefore the sky was brought into existence'. This discourse, taken as a whole, is equivalent to a compound syllogism made from two syllogisms in the first figure. The first [syllogism] says that our finding by observation that the wall was brought into existence verifies for us that bodies are brought into existence. The reason is that because the wall is a particular case of body, and [body] so to say forms the object of examination, something is found to be true of [body], namely a content that is true of [body] universally. So the likening discourse is composed as follows: 'Body is the wall or the other particular
37,1 [entities] that are similar to it; and the wall was brought into existence. Therefore bodies are brought into existence.'[51] Then we take the conclusion of this syllogism,

and we pair it with [the premise] that the sky is a body, thus reaching the composition: 'The sky is a body; and bodies are brought into existence. Therefore the sky was brought into existence'. In this way the likening discourse is reduced to a syllogism as a result of a syllogistic potential in it that makes it persuasive.[52]

[17.3] [The resulting discourse] is close to being an inductive discourse. But induction works by the content being true of all or most of the particular cases of the universal, while the likening discourse [rests on] just one particular [entity]. In [likening, i.e. the method of] exemplar,[53] this single particular [entity] takes the place of the 'all or most particular cases' [that appear in] induction.[54]

5.18 Part 18a [A general observation]

[18a.1] These syllogisms that we have enumerated[55] are not always used in the [kind of] composition that we mentioned first [in this book], nor are the premises and conclusion of every syllogism spelled out without omitting any of them. Rather, it often happens that their compositions are changed, many of the syllogistic premises are removed[56], and other pieces of discourse are added in among the syllogistic premises, [and these additions] may not all be helpful for producing the syllogistic conclusion. This is common both in spoken discourse and in books. In the cases where the discourse is not composed in any of the ways that we have mentioned [earlier in this book], and then[57] things have been added or left out, and the ordering is changed so that its composition is turned into the [kind of] composition that we [have just] mentioned, but the sense of the original discourse is retained as it was before the change, [in these cases] the discourse is [still] a syllogism. But in the cases where the discourse is put in place of any of the syllogistic compositions that we mentioned [earlier] in such a way as to change the sense of the original discourse into something different, this discourse is not a syllogism.

5.19 Part 18b [Compound syllogisms]

[18b.1] Next, it doesn't always happen that the two premises of the syllogism used are known in one of the four ways[58] that we mentioned. Rather [the syllogism] is sometimes composed of two premises, one or both of which are known by means of [another] syllogism; and in that other syllogism too, one or both of the premises are not things known from the outset; in many cases one or 38,1 both of [these premises] also needs to be proved by a syllogism. The same applies to this syllogism, just like the previous one, and so on and so on[59] until we arrive at syllogisms composed of premises known in one of the four ways. When we want to prove something by a syllogism whose premises are such that they are also known by means of syllogisms, and the premises of the latter [syllogisms] also need to be proved by other syllogisms, and so on until we reach syllogisms whose premises were known from the outset and not derived by a syllogism at all, then the way to do it is to start with the syllogisms whose premises are known from the outset, and to take their conclusions and pair them with other [propositions] to form premise-pairs [with further conclusions, and so on] until we reach the two premises that were combined as a syllogism so as to produce the conclusion that we aimed at from the outset.

[18b.2] However, if we spell out the components of all these syllogisms exhaustively, the discourse becomes lengthy. For this reason we should restrict ourselves to just some of the plethora of premises, leaving out those that are implied by [other premises] that have [already] been spelled out, if it is clear and obvious [that they are implied] and if they are needed in the discourse. The resulting syllogism will form a compound of several syllogisms in which some of the premises have been removed and others have been retained.

[18b.3] To take an example, suppose we want for instance to prove that the world is created, by means of the [following] syllogisms: 'Every body is composed, and every composed thing is attached to an irremovable accident;[60] therefore every body is attached to an irremovable accident'. Then we take this conclusion and we pair it with [the premise] 'Everything that is attached to an irremovable accident is attached irremovably to a created thing'. From this there follows 'Every body is attached irremovably to a created thing'. Taking this conclusion, we pair it with [the premise] 'Nothing that is irremovably attached to a created thing existed before the created thing'. From this there follows 'For every body there is some created thing which the body does not precede in time'. We take the conclusion of this third syllogism and we pair with it 'Everything for which there is some created thing that it doesn't precede exists at the same time as that created thing', from which there follows 'Every body exists at the same time as a created thing'. Then we take this conclusion and we pair it with 'Everything that exists at the same time as a created thing exists after having been nonexistent'. There follows from this 'Every body exists after having been nonexistent'. We pair the conclusion of this fifth syllogism with 'Everything that exists after having been nonexistent has a created existence'. From this there follows 'Every body has a created existence'. We pair the conclusion of this sixth syllogism with 'The world is a body' so that there follows from [this] seventh syllogism 'The world is created'. However, if we present in full all the components of these [syllogisms], the discourse will be lengthy. So we should remove those premises of these syllogisms that were conclusions of other earlier syllogisms, and restrict ourselves to those [premises] that are not [also] conclusions, given that the conclusions are implied by [the premises] that produce them. Then at the end of the whole [array] there comes the final conclusion.

[18b.4] [Thus] an example of [such a compound syllogism] would be: 'Every body is composed', 'Every composed thing is attached to an accident that is irremovable from it', 'Everything that is attached to an accident that is irremovable from it is attached to a created thing that is irremovable from it', 'Nothing that is attached to a created thing that is irremovable from it precedes the created thing', 'Everything that doesn't precede a created thing exists at the same time as the created thing', 'Everything that exists at the same time as a created thing exists after having been nonexistent', 'Everything that exists after having been nonexistent is created', 'The world is a body'. Therefore 'The world is created'. Things like this are compound syllogisms.

[18b.5] Compound [syllogisms] can be formed from syllogisms of different kinds, for example some of them hypothetical and others categorical, or some of them by absurdity and others direct.[61] Also they can be formed from different kinds of direct syllogisms.

[18b.6] An example is [the following]: 'The world is either eternal or created. 40,1
If [the world] is eternal, it is not attached [to created things]. But it is attached to created things, because it is a body, and if a body is not attached to created things then it is free of them, and what is free of created things is not composed and can't move; but this[62] is impossible. Therefore the world is created.' This syllogism is a compound of a separated hypothetical syllogism, a connected hypothetical [syllogism], a categorical syllogism of absurdity and a direct categorical syllogism.

5.20 Part 18c [Induction and syllogism]

[18c.1] A discourse can be a compound of an induction and a syllogism.[63] This happens when someone tries to prove an objective by a syllogism in the first figure, where the minor premise of the syllogism is clearly true but it is not clear that the major premise, which should always be universal in order for the conclusion to follow necessarily [from the premises],[64] is universally true.[65] So he wants to verify that it is universally true by applying induction to the particular cases of the subject [of the major premise], i.e. [the particular cases of] the middle term, after which he will pair [the verified major premise] with the minor premise so that it produces the conclusion whose proof was sought at the outset. For instance, when the objective is 'Is *A* true of every *C* or not?',[66] then he will seek to prove it by [the syllogism] 'Every *C* is a *B*; and every *B* is an *A*'. Suppose we find that the sentence 'Every *C* is a *B*' is clearly true, but the sentence 'Every *B* is an *A*' is not clearly true, so that we want to verify [the latter sentence] by applying induction to the things that are described by the term *B*. For instance let them be *D*, *H*, *Z*, *T*, *Y*. When we find that *A* is true of each of these [things], we see that *A* is true of every *B*. We pair with this [the premise] 'Every *C* is a *B*', so as to produce 'Every *C* is an *A*'.

41,1 [18c.2] As an example, [consider] the objective 'Is the bee procreated by a male and a female parent, or not?' We aim to prove this by finding that the bee is an animal and every animal is procreated by a male and a female parent. [In fact] we find that the sentence 'Every bee is an animal' is clearly true, but the sentence 'Every animal is procreated by a male and a female parent' is not clearly true. So we perform an induction on the kinds of animal, such as humans, horses, cows, sheep, donkeys and dogs, and we find that each of them is procreated by a male and a female parent. So for that reason we judge that 'Every animal is procreated by its male and female parents'. We pair this with 'Every bee is an animal', and that produces the conclusion 'Every bee is procreated by its male and female parents'. Thus this discourse is a compound of an induction and a syllogism.

[18c.3] But there is a defect in [this discourse]. [Suppose first that] when someone tries to verify the universal major premise by an induction on what falls under its subject term, he fails to examine everything below [the term], so that something remains which is described as a *B* but we don't know whether or not it is an *A*, because we haven't made certain that he included everything that is described by the term *B*.[67] Then it has not been verified that *A* is true of whatever is a *B*, and consequently it is not yet known that the proposition ['Every *B* is an *A*'] is universally true. If [supposedly] everything described by the term *B* was examined, was *C* included among the things that were examined, or was it not? If it was not included, then there is something that is described as a *B*, and we don't know whether or not it is described as an *A*. [In that case] it is not verified that everything that is a *B* is an *A*, since *C* is a *B* but we don't know whether or not it is described as an *A*.

[18c.4] [On the other hand] suppose he did make the examination and knew as a result that *C* is an *A*. Then [we grant] he would know that every *C* is an *A*

because of the correctness of the syllogism by which we sought to verify precisely that objective. But there was no need for us to use this syllogism. In fact, given [the verification of] 'Every *B* is an *A*', if we went on to take that premise and pair it with 'Every *C* is a *B*' so as to produce 'Every *C* is an *A*', then we would have used 42,1
the sentence '*C* is *A*' to verify some other sentence, and then used that other sentence to verify '*C* is *A*', [in which case] we would have verified the clearer through the more obscure.[68] No previously unknown fact can be verified in that way. Also we used a thing in a proof of that same thing, making the proof circular. That is something off limits and prevented,[69] and we can do without it. It is not a possible way to prove something that was hidden.

[18c.5] To sum up, a discourse that is a compound of a syllogism and an induction asks for the verification of the universal truth of the major premise [of the syllogism].[70] This premise provides the information to show that the conclusion of the syllogism follows with necessity. If the discourse is deficient then the universal truth of the major premise doesn't follow from it, and so nothing follows necessarily from that discourse.

5.21 Part 18d [Likening and syllogism]

[18d.1] Sometimes in such places[71] likening can be used in place of induction, so that the discourse becomes a compound of a likening and a syllogism. Namely, we use a single one of the entities that fall under *B*, such as *D* on its own. Then if *A* is true of every [thing that is a] *D*, it appears that it is correct that *A* is true of every [thing that is a] *B*. If this is not verified by induction then it is even less likely to be verified by likening. But likening can be used to verify an objective, including the objective 'Is it the case that every *C* is an *A*, or not?' Thus we aim to verify [this objective] using the fact that we already knew from the outset that *A* is true of every *D*. We find that the term *C* is of the same kind as, and similar to, the term *D*, where [the similarity consists of] a universal concept [*B*][72] that they both fall under. But there is nothing to be gained from this if the similarity [*B*] between the term *C* and the term *D* is [just] whatever concept it may be among those that [*D* and *C*] both happen to fall under. Suppose it happens that the term *C* is similar to the term *D* through falling under many of the same concepts, and it is not just any of these concepts that is helpful for verifying that *A* is true of *C*, but rather [just one of them will be helpful] by being the[73] universal concept [*B*] that makes *A* true of *C*;[74] then we have to verify which of these concepts this is. When we have found it, it becomes the middle term that is put between *A* and *C*.

So *A* is true of the universal concept [*B*], and the universal concept is true of *C*. But if it is just proved that *A* is true of that concept [*B*] indeterminately[75], [i.e.] without a universal quantifier, there is no guarantee against *A* being true just of 43,1 some of that concept and not of all of it. So there is no guarantee against *C* falling under some part of the concept [*B*] that *A* is not true of. If that is a possibility, it won't follow with necessity that *A* is true of *C*. So therefore, if what is intended is that with necessity *A* is true of *C*,[76] then it has to be that *A* is true of all of the concept [*B*], so that if *C* fell under the concept [*B*], it would follow necessarily that *A* was true of *C*. Hence we have to verify that *A* is true of all of that concept.

[18d.2] Let the concept be *B*.[77] It is clear that [the sentence '*A* is true of all of *B*'] is not verified by the knowledge that *A* is true of *D*, since *D* is [only] a particular part of the concept [*B*]. And as we said,[78] it is also not enough if we show by induction that 'things similar to *D*' also fall below the concept [*A*]. Therefore likening cannot verify that *A* is true of *C*, either on its own or supported by induction. In fact if it was supported by induction, the verification by likening would lapse, and the induction on its own would be what did the verifying. So [induction] would not be supporting [likening], but rather the speaker[79] and the interlocutor would have discarded likening and transferred [their efforts] from it to induction. And if [the sentence] was verified by one of the aforementioned syllogisms,[80] then both the likening and the induction would lapse, since the syllogism on its own would do the verifying. The thing that verified that *A* is true of *C* would be a syllogism, and so neither likening nor induction would serve any purpose.[81]

[18d.3] When induction is used to support the major premise ['Every B is an A'] of the likening discourse by verifying that it holds universally, there is a gap concerned with considering the middle term as the cause. Some of these people[82], when they became aware of this gap, rejected [this use of] induction, and [instead] gave their support to the likening discourse. They did this by looking at what it is that makes the second entity similar to the first. Suppose that when *B* is not true of a thing, *A* is not true of it either; they counted this as [showing that *B*] is the cause of the content [*A*] being true [of all *B*].[83] So they took the major premise to be the universal sentence ['Every *B* is an *A*'], and as a result, when they found an entity that fell under [*B*] – which they took to be a cause – they asserted that the same content [*A*] was true of this entity. But there was a [logical] gap here too, namely that [by showing that] if [*B*] is not true of an entity then the content [*A*] is not true of that entity, we don't show that it follows that if [*B*] is true of an entity then the content [*A*] is true of it too. [Take] for instance animals and humans. If 'animal' is not true of this visible thing, then being human is not true of [this visible thing]. 44,1 But if some animal exists, it doesn't follow necessarily that some human exists.[84]

And if a person wants to verify that *A* is true of the concept [*B*], by [citing] the fact that if the concept [*B*] is true of *D* then *A* is also true of it, this is no use for showing that it follows necessarily that *A* is true of *C*.[85] One would also need to show that wherever and whenever [*B*] is true of something, then *A* is also true of that thing – so that when *C* falls under the concept [*B*] it follows necessarily that *A* is true of [*C*]. Without this, the fact that [*B*] is true of *D* gives no assurance that *A* is true of the concept [*B*]; *A* might be true of [just] some of what is described by the concept [*B*], not all of it, so (as we said) it wouldn't follow necessarily that [*A*] is true of *C*. The difference between saying 'Wherever and whenever the content [*B*] is true of something, *A* is also true of it' and saying 'Everything that is described by the concept [*B*] is an *A*' is purely a difference of expression. If [these sentences] are known to be true, they form a universal premise that came to be known without a syllogism; neither induction nor likening gave any help at all [for knowing it]. If [the premise] had become known through another syllogism, it would be sufficient to use that [other] syllogism alone.

'[18d.4][86] If [a person] wanted to verify [the premise] from the fact that when that concept [*B*] is true of *D* then *A* is true [of *D*], and when [*B*] is not true of *D* then *A* is not true [of *D*], that [fact on its own] wouldn't help; he would also need the fact that wherever and whenever [the concept *B*] is true of some entity, *A* is also true of that entity, and also (as we said)[87] the fact that wherever and whenever [*B*] is not true of an entity, *A* is not true of it either. For if this was the case, then *A* would be true of all of the concept [*B*]. The two universals [*A* and *B*] would be true of the same things, and substitutable for each other. Everything described as a *B* would be an *A*, and every *A* would be described as a *B*. So it would follow necessarily that *A* is true of every *C*. We would have a syllogism with two premises, and the major premise would be affirmative universal ['Every *B* is an *A*']. Its [universal affirmative] converse ['Every *A* is a *B*'] would also be true, but this conversion of the major premise would be superfluous and not needed for the conclusion to follow necessarily [from the premises]. Even without converting, [the premise] suffices for showing that *A* is true of all of the concept 45,1
B. The conversion of the premise adds nothing to the necessity of the entailment. This is the state of affairs about *A* being true of the concept [*B*], since it [has to have been] already known either without any syllogism at all, or by some other syllogism, [given that] likening and induction are no help in verifying [the premise]. Thus it has been proved that likening and induction are not helpful in such places, and that one shouldn't use either of them when the purpose of investigating the objectives is to acquire certainty about [the objectives]. If [such a method] is used then it should be used for what it is suitable for, in verifying

beliefs and persuasive points that don't involve certainty.[88] Likening by itself is persuasive,[89] but induction applies in more cases.

5.22 Part 19: Transfer

[Transfer from observed to unobserved]

[19.1] We must now speak about how, when some content [*A*] is perceived by the senses to be true of something [*D*], or is known by some other means to be true of it, the content is transferred to something [else, *C*] which is not [known] by sense-perception to satisfy the content, in cases where the second thing [*C*] doesn't fall under the first thing [*D*]. People nowadays refer to this as 'inference to the unobserved by means of the observed'. The way in which this transfer is made is that we know by sense-perception that something [*D*] has some property [*A*], [or] that some concept [*A*] is true of the thing [*D*], and the mind transfers that property or concept [*A*] from that thing [*D*] to another thing [*C*] that is similar to it, thereby judging that [*A*] is true of [*C*].[90]

[19.2] For instance we [know] by sense-perception that some bodies, such as animals or plants, are created; the mind transfers 'created' from animals or plants, and judges that the sky and the planets were created. The transfer of this content from animal to sky, which ascribes to the sky the createdness that was perceived in the animals by sensation, is possible only when there is a certain kind of similarity between animal and sky. [It must be] not just any similarity; rather it must be a similarity because of which animals are described as created. More precisely, animal and sky [have to be] similar to each other in the sense that there is a concept [*B*] that is true of both of them, and 'created' is true of the whole of [*B*]. An example is that [*B* could be] 'attached to created things',[91] for instance. But [even] if it is known by sense-perception that animals are created, and animals are similar to the sky in being attached to created things, and the content 'created'
46,1 can correctly be applied to something attached to created things, and the sky is attached to created things, this is not [yet enough to make it] possible to perform the transfer from animal to sky. The reason is the possibility that a thing that is attached to created things satisfies 'created' only [if it satisfies] a [further] restricting condition that is not met by the sky. This would make the sky dissimilar to animals in the respect that makes creation true of animals, since in this case 'created' is true of animals because they are attached to created things by a [special] form of linking that is not true of the sky. If this is so, the transfer can't

be made at all. If it is not shown that everything attached to created things [is created], or indeed if the transfer itself is the source of our belief that a thing attached to created things is created, then the content has been transferred from animal to sky, and [this] transfer has been made to what could be [counted as] similar to animal, but not using a concept [*B*] that makes 'created' true of it; so the transfer is not really correct even if it seems to be obviously correct. So therefore, if one is resolved to verify the transfer, it is still required that the concept [*B*] which makes the two similar to each other is such that the content 'created' is true of the whole of [*B*], so that everything attached to created things is created. If the sky is similar to the animal in how it is attached [to created things], it follows necessarily that the sky is created. This [method] is potentially[92] a syllogism composed in the first figure, namely: 'The sky is attached to created things, and everything attached to created things is created. Therefore the sky is created.'

Analysis and Synthesis

[19.3] Transfer from the observed to the unobserved is of two kinds: one is by the method of Synthesis and the other is by the method of Analysis. With Analysis the reasoning starts with the unobserved, while with Synthesis it starts with the observed.[93] If we want to use the method of Analysis to infer to the unobserved by means of the observed, we have to know the content that we are seeking [to transfer to] the unobserved thing, and then we study the question which are the sense-perceived things that satisfy that content. Then when we know something sense-perceived that satisfies that content, we use it to take those concepts that make the unobserved thing similar to the sense-perceived thing. Then we study the question which of those concepts is such that the whole of it satisfies the content that is observed in the sense-perceived thing. When we find such a concept, the content transfers necessarily from the thing observed by the senses to the unobserved thing. So therefore the inference to the unobserved by means of the observed, using this method, is in potential a question, i.e. an objective, which a syllogism in the first figure is able to resolve.

[19.4] If we want to use the method of Synthesis to infer to the unobserved by means of the observed, we [first] examine the sense-perceived thing *D*, which is observed to satisfy a certain content [*A*]. We take the other concepts that are true of this sense-perceived thing, and we study the question which of these concepts is such that the whole of it satisfies the content [*A*]. If such a concept [*B*] becomes available to us, and then we find a thing [*C*] that falls under [*B*] but it is not [yet] known whether the content is true of it, it follows necessarily that the content which we could verify in the sense-perceived thing transfers to [*C*]. This method too is in potential a syllogism in the first figure.

[Proving or refuting the major premise]

[19.5] The fact that the content is true of one of the concepts that make the unobserved similar to the observed is something that can be known in many cases [directly from the concepts] themselves, not by a syllogism or by thinking or reflection at all, in one of those clear ways in which we know the primary premises[94]. If it is not self-evidently true it needs something else to prove it. There are several ways of showing that it is true. One way is to verify it by a syllogism composed in one of the ways that we mentioned earlier, either categorical[95] or hypothetical. Another way is to examine[96] the subspecies of that concept [*B*]; if the content [*A*] is found to be true of all [the species that] fall under it, the content is true of the whole of that concept [*B*]. If [the content] is not found to be true of any of them, this verifies that it is not true of any of that concept. And if it was just proved for some subspecies of [*B*] that the content is not true of them, this refutes that [the content] is true of the whole of the concept [*B*], and the resulting [proposition][97] is particular.

[19.6] Now when this method is being used just to verify that a content which is true of the whole of the concept transfers to some particular thing that falls under [that attribute], this method ceases to be helpful for inference to the unobserved by means of the observed. This is because, if one has examined the thing to which the content is transferred, and has found that the content is true of it, then the thing was known by itself to satisfy the content, without making any transfer. Because you know that [the content] is true of the concept [*B*] that makes the unobserved thing similar to the sense-perceived thing, there is no need to make a transfer. [On the other hand] if [the unobserved thing] has not been examined, or if it has been examined but we don't know whether that content is predicated of it or not, then it is not known that the content is true of the whole of that concept – but if it is not true [of the whole of the concept], then the transfer to the unobserved is not sound, as we said in the case of induction. Thus it has been shown that this method can't be used to verify that the content is true of the whole of what is under consideration as a cause. But when the [objective] up for consideration is that the content is true of all of that concept, it is possible by this method to show that the content is not true of all [of it].

[19.7] This method is what people of our time call 'drawing out the content of the cause with regard to its effects'.[98] The concept [*B*] such that the content is true of the whole of it is what people nowadays call the cause, and this is the middle term.[99] By the effects they mean the things that fall under the concept that is up for consideration as a cause. And the content which the cause necessarily satisfies is the one for which we seek to verify that it is true of the whole of the [cause], or [at least] the objective is that it is true of the whole of it. 'Driving out'[100] the content, or its particular cases, with respect to the effects consists of examining, taking them one by one, whether it is true in the things that fall under the concept that is up for consideration as a cause. So it has been shown that 'driving out' whatever content is necessarily satisfied by the cause with regard to the effects is of no use for verifying that the content is true of the concept up for consideration as the cause; it is only helpful for refuting that.

[19.8] An example of this is where a person wants to show that the world was created from pre-existing matter. To show that, he sees that a wall is created from matter and that an animal is created from matter. Also [he sees that] the sky is similar to the animal in being a body. If he wants to verify that this content ['created from pre-existing matter'] is true of the sky because of this similarity, viz. that both are bodies, then he should show first that the bodiliness that makes 49,1
the sky similar to the animal is the concept that causes the animal to be created from matter. This [will tell him] that every body is created from pre-existing matter. If he wants to verify [that every body is created from pre-existing matter] by examining the kinds of bodies so as to come to each of them, he will not be able to do that without examining the sky too. If he can't do that, he will not verify that every body is created from matter. And if he doesn't verify that, then he can't show that the sky is created from matter because it is a body.

[19.9] But this method on its own is sufficient for refutation. Thus suppose someone believes that every change is from one thing to another thing, so he examines kinds of change and finds that generation is change from nothing to thing, and corruption is change from thing to nothing. [By doing this] he refutes [the belief] that every change is from a thing to a thing, because generation is change but it is not from a thing to a thing. [This refutation] can be composed in the third figure,[101] as follows: 'Every generation is a change; and no generation is from a thing to a thing. Therefore not every change is from a thing to a thing.'

[The methods of Accepting and Rejecting]

[19.10] It is possible to verify [the major premise] in another way.[102] Namely one studies those concepts [*B*] – it could be either the concepts that express a similarity that make the sense-perceived thing similar to the unobserved thing, or else the concepts by which the sense-perceived thing is described, not including the content [*A* itself] – which are such that whenever and wherever[103] [*B*] is true [of a thing] the content [*A*] is also true [of that thing]. An example of this is that one studies the things that are attached to created things, to see whether in every possible situation where a thing is attached to created things, that thing is created. If that is the case, then everything attached to created things is created. There is no difference between saying 'wherever a thing is attached [to created things] it is created' and saying 'whatever thing is described as attached to created things is also described as created'. In both cases it is being said that everything attached to created things is created. When this method of verification is used, the inference [by means] of the observed to the unobserved is sound, and it would not be possible to oppose it at all. But if it was restricted so as to say that when [*B*] is found to be true just of that sense-perceived thing, the content [*A*] is found to be true of it too, it wouldn't follow necessarily that when [*B*] is found to be true of the unobserved thing, the content [*A*] is [also] true of it – because that would mean we verified that the [transfer of the] content just follows if [the content] is found to be true of that one sense-perceived thing alone, and not in anything else. The same applies if one just verifies that when [*B*] is found to be true of the sense-perceived thing the content [*A*] is [also] found to be true of it, but doesn't know that the content is true [of a thing] wherever [*B*] is true [of that thing], since in that case it is possible that [the content] is specific to the sense-perceived thing without us being aware of that, or that it is tied to a condition that is satisfied [only] by some things that don't include the unobserved thing, so that the transfer is not verified. We have shown how this method can be used to verify [the major premise], and how it can not.

[19.11] [One might hope] to verify ['Every *B* is an *A*'] by examining whether, if [*B*] is false [of something] then the content [*A*] is also false [of that thing]. [This proposed method] is very weak, because if [*B*] being false [of the thing] makes the content [*A*] false [of the thing] too, it doesn't follow necessarily that when *B* is true [of a thing] then the content [*A*] is true [of that thing]. What does follow is the converse of this, i.e. that when the content is true [of a thing] then [*B*] is also true [of that thing]. An example of this [is the following]: if something is not an animal then this thing is not a human. It doesn't follow that when [something] is an animal then it is a human. Rather the converse holds, namely that if [something] is a human, it follows necessarily that [the thing] is an animal. For this reason, [the rule] 'When [*B*] is false [of a thing] then the content [*A*] is false [of that thing]' doesn't make it necessarily the case that the content [*A*] is true of all of [*B*]. If we want to verify ['Every *B* is an *A*'] by the method of Rejecting, then we must examine whether or not [*B*] is false [of a thing] when the content [*A*] is false [of that thing], i.e. if the content [*A*] being false of a thing makes [*B*] false of it; [in which case] it follows necessarily that when [*B*] is true [of a thing], the content [*A*] is true [of the thing], [The method of Rejecting] is not restricted to this alone [(namely that [*B*] being false of something makes [*A*] false of it too)]. It also includes the case that when the content [*A*] is false [of something], [*B*] is false [of that thing too], and in this case it follows necessarily that whenever [*B*] is true [of a thing], the content [*A*] is true [of it too]. It is clear that this is an example of the kind of hypothetical syllogism that we spoke about,[104] in which the contradictory opposite of the consequent is detached. 'Rejecting' the content [*A* from a thing] is the same as denying that the content is true of that thing; the same holds for rejecting [*B*]. Let us take the antecedent to be that the content [*A*] is false [of a thing] and the consequent to be that *B* is false [of that thing].[105] Then we detach the contradictory opposite of rejecting [*B*], which is the same as detaching the contradictory opposite of the consequent. What follows necessarily is the contradictory opposite of what was put for the antecedent, namely that the content is true [of the given thing]. This is why, if we want to verify 'Every agent is a body', we [have to] see whether when body is false [of something] then agent is false [of that thing]. When that is the case, it is necessary that every agent is a body, because [if] the thing up for consideration is not a body then it is not an agent; then when we detach the contradictory opposite of the consequent, which is that [the thing up for consideration] is an agent, it follows necessarily that [the thing up for consideration] is a body. So therefore if it is an agent then it is a body. This is how we must use this method for verifying that the content [*A*] is true of the term [*B*] that is up for consideration as a cause.[106] Namely, we investigate whether if the content [*A*] is false [of the thing up for consideration], then [*B*] is false [of that thing]. If it is not the case that 'body' is false of whatever 'agent' is false of, it doesn't follow necessarily that every agent is a body. Likewise if it is the case that 'agent' is false [of a thing] when 'body' is false [of the thing], it doesn't follow that every agent is a body,[107] but it does follow that every body is an agent. And if neither of these two things is the case, it doesn't follow either that every agent is a body or that every body is an agent.[108]

[19.12] It is redundant to use the method[s] of Accepting and Rejecting together for verification. This is because [by Rejecting,] if [*B*] is false [of something] then the content [*A*] is false [of that thing], and [by Accepting, if *B*] is true [of something] then the content [*A*] is true [of that thing]. It follows from the first that if the content [*A*] is true [of something] then [*B*] is true [of that thing], and it follows from the second that if the content [*A*] is false [of something] then [*B*] is false [of that thing]. So it follows [from the two together] that [*B*] and

the content [*A*] are true of each other. For example if something doesn't neigh then it is not a horse, and if something does neigh then it is a horse. So each of the two, [i.e. 'neighs' and 'horse',] is true of the same things as the other[109], and each is a proprium of the other. But in the [relevant] syllogism there is no need for this kind of predication. For if the premise is universally true, then [even] if its two terms are not true of the same things as each other, the syllogism fits together just as well as it would if its two terms were true of the same things as each other. Thus if we want to show that the world is created because it is a body, then we must just verify that 'created' is true of every body, because what we want [to show] is that 'created' is true of a certain thing that falls under 'body'[, namely the sky]. We wouldn't need to verify [the converse, i.e.] that bodiliness is true of every created thing, unless we wanted to establish that 'body' is true of something that falls under 'created'. The only case where we need to verify [both] that every body is created and that every created thing is a body is when we want to verify [(for example)] both that creation is true of a certain thing that falls under 'body', and that 'body' is true of a certain thing that falls under 'created'. If we only wanted to
52,1 establish that 'created' is true of a certain thing that falls under 'body', we would just need to verify that every body is created. [Even] if it turned out, in the course of our verifying that every body is created, that it was also true that every created thing is a body, we would [still] not verify that every body is created by verifying the converse statement. This is so because it has been shown that the truth of a universal affirmative proposition doesn't make its universal converse true – though it does make its converse particular proposition true.[110] Having 'body' and 'created' true of the same things is not the only way that 'body' can become a cause with 'created' true of it. In fact the reason why we needed to have 'body' as the cause is that this allows us to verify that a certain thing that falls under 'body' is created. For this purpose it suffices to verify that every body is created. This is why it is redundant to use the method[s] of Accepting and Rejecting together to verify the universal premise that enables the transfer of the content [true] of the observed to the unobserved. In fact for verifying [that a certain body is created] it is enough to confirm that the content ['created'] is true [of this particular body] through the fact that the concept up for consideration as a cause, wherever it is and whatever it is about, is true [of this body].[111] This is as we said.

Arguments that are useful through tolerance

[19.13] We must scrutinize and study the thing [*D*] perceived by the senses, [to see] if we observe that it satisfies a concept [*A*] which is true of the whole of

some other concept [*B*] which makes the sense-perceived thing [*D*] similar to the unobserved thing [*C*]. [If we do observe such a concept *B*,] this will make it possible to transfer [*A*] from the thing [*D*] observed by the senses to the unobserved thing [*C*]. Is it the case that the sense-perceived thing [*D*] has some use or utility for giving us the knowledge that [*A*] being true of the thing observed by the senses makes *A* true also of the concept [*B*] that is up for consideration as the cause? Or is there another way of verifying that the content [*A*] is true of the whole of the concept [*B*] that is up for consideration as a cause, so that the fact that the sense-perceived thing satisfies the content [*A*] would not be used for verifying that the concept [*A*] is true of the concept [*B*] that is up for consideration as a cause? If there is something to be said on both sides of the question, our own view is that if [the sense-perceived thing] is useful then it is so in one of two ways: either[112] the sense-perceived thing itself is taken as middle term [for a syllogism] composed in the third figure. For instance: 'This mason is an agent; and he is a body. So it follows from this that the agent is a body.'[113] 53,1
But what follows with necessity is not that every agent is a body, but that some agent is a body.

[19.14] Indeterminate [premises] are sometimes treated with tolerance, being treated as if they had universal quantifiers, [and then] the [resulting] unquantified conclusions are thought of as having universal quantifiers. This is particularly so when the indeterminate sentences are expressed using the definite article, as when we say 'The agent is a body'. In this [proposition] the definite article creates a misleading impression that [we are being told that] every agent is a body, since the definite article is often used in place of the word 'every'. So in this way of approaching things and to this extent, the sense-perceived thing can be useful for verifying that the content [*A*] is true of the concept [*B*] which is up for consideration as a cause. It does this by yielding a conclusion that is in fact particular and specific. But we take the conclusion as an indefinite proposition expressed with the definite article, and treat it with tolerance, so that in practice it will give a false impression that the content [*A*] is true of all of the concept that is up for consideration as a cause.

[19.15] And the other way [in which the sense-perceived object can be useful] is that the sense-perceived thing is taken as middle term [for a syllogism] in the first figure. An example of that is [the following]: if we want to verify that 'Every agent is a body', we consider the things that fall under agent, [taking] tailor and mason, and we find that both of them are bodies. Then we convince ourselves that it follows that every agent is a body, by using the middle term 'tailor and mason' in the induction.[114] [The syllogism] is composed as follows: 'The agent is

a mason and the mason is a body'. Here the mason stands in place of what would be all the kinds of agent, if all of them or most of them were examined. It is as if just one or two cases were given as meeting the requirement to examine agents, so that these one or two stand in place of the whole or most of it. This is exercizing tolerance about generality, but it is done by omitting the quantification. So one says: 'The agent is the tailor and the mason and the cobbler and the carpenter; and every [tailor and mason and cobbler and carpenter] is a body. Therefore the agent is a body.' Then this indeterminacy in the conclusion, together with the use of the definite article, gave a misleading impression that [the conclusion was
54,1 that] every agent is bodily – for this is how [the definite article] was used. So these are two ways in which the sense-perceived object can be useful for verifying that the content is true of the thing that is up for consideration as a cause. These are the ways that have traditionally been used for verifying the [major] premise that enables the inference to the unobserved by means of the observed.

5.23 Part 20: Jurisprudential syllogisms

[20.1] Let us speak now about the specific principles of those arts which are pieced together from the primary accepted propositions. These principles are what go to compose the discourses that Aristotle[115] calls jurisprudential syllogisms, and which he mentions at the end of his book known as *Analytica Priora*. He says that they can be reduced to the syllogisms which he listed at the beginning of that book. In his own words: 'And it is not just the dialectical and the demonstrative syllogisms that are in the figures that were spoken of, but also the rhetorical and the jurisprudential syllogisms.'[116] There are four such principles. One of them is the universal [proposition] that is up for consideration[117] as being universally true; the next is the universal [statement] being put in place of an intended particular case; the next is the particular case being put in place of an intended universal [statement]; and [the fourth] is [the method of] example.

[Universal as universal]

[20.2] As for the universal [proposition] that is up for consideration as universally true: an example of this is the universal premise that is accepted[118] as universally true,[119] and which has its content[120] transferred to something that verifiably falls under the subject of that premise. An example is 'Every [kind of] wine is forbidden',[121] which is a universal and accepted premise. So when it is verified that something is wine, the prohibition is applied to that thing. This transfer [of 'forbidden'] takes place through a syllogism composed in the first figure,[122] thus: 'Every wine is forbidden; and this in the vessel is wine. Therefore what is in the vessel is forbidden.'

[20.3] Some of these accepted principles are expressed by a declarative[123] sentence, such as 'Every intoxicant is forbidden'. Others are expressed by other [kinds of] sentence that have the same effect as declarative ones, such as permissive, prohibitive, hortative, renunciative, imperative and proscriptive [sentences], as when the Almighty says 'Abstain from false statement',[124] and when the Almighty says 'Be sure to wash your faces and your hands'[125] and 'When you speak, be just'[126], and 'Honour your commitments'.[127] Then when we are faced with other accepted [propositions] that are not expressed in declarative sentences, and we want to use these [propositions] as premises in syllogisms, we have to replace [the sentences] by sentences that are declarative. For example when we are told 'Avoid wine', and we want to use this sentence as part of a syllogism, then we have to replace it by the sentence 'All wine is to be avoided' or '[All wine] should be avoided'.

[20.4] The subjects and predicates of these premises can be expressed by nouns that are said ambiguously, and also by nouns that are said unambiguously. A noun said unambiguously[128] is one which covers many things but signifies a single meaning that covers [all of] them. An ambiguous noun is one that covers many things and doesn't signify one single meaning that covers them [all]. Accepted [propositions] will just count as universal premises when their subjects and predicates are expressed using nouns that are said unambiguously. As for the [propositions] that are expressed using nouns that are said ambiguously, these might be thought to be universal [propositions] but they are not really [single] universal [propositions].[129]

[Universal for particular]

[20.5] As for the universal [statement] that is used in place of an intended particular case: this is where an accepted universal premise is put in place of a premise with a more specific [subject]. It can happen that the thing intended by the speaker is a particular case, but he makes a universal [statement] that is a generalization of the particular case that he intends. For instance a person can say 'No good is to be expected from [one's] friends and [one's] children', just meaning certain [friends and children].[130] When we happen to have an accepted universal [proposition] and we know that what is intended by it is one of its

particular cases, and we know which particular case was intended, then we take
56,1 [it to mean] that particular case. If [in turn] that particular case covers some further things[131] then we use it in the same way as we said that universal [premises] are used.[132] In other words, whenever a thing verifiably falls under this narrower universal, the content which was true of the narrower [universal] transfers to the thing.

[20.6] An example of this is a proposition that we take as accepted, namely 'The thief must have his hand cut off'.[133] This is put in place of 'Some thieves [must have their hand cut off]', for example any person who steals [at least] a quarter of a dinar. Then we take it that when a thief satisfies this description, we judge of him that his hand must be cut off. This gives us a universal premise, and accordingly when it is verified that Zayd is a thief who satisfies this description, it follows that his hand should be cut off. This [inference] is another syllogism composed in the first figure.[134]

[20.7] Many universals that are used in place of a particular case can be brought down to the particular case that was intended, as long as the particular case was [known] from the outset and needed no reflection [to find it]. But often [the intended meaning] is present from the outset but hidden, so that it is not known whether [the universal statement] is being used in place of a particular case or not. Where it is known that it is being used in place of a particular case, often the particular case is hidden and one doesn't know which [particular case] it is. When it is hidden one should seek to identify it by means of a syllogism that is composed in the ways we have said. If this particular case is made clear to us through a syllogism that gives us a universal premise, the result is that we [can] use [the universal premise] in the same way as we use any other universal [premise].

[Particular for universal]

[20.8] As for putting a particular case in place of a universal [proposition]: this [occurs] when a phrase means a concept [that we intend to express], but [we express] a particular case of that concept instead of the concept that we intended.[135] Then [the particular case] is used on the basis that what is true of that particular case is also true of all of the [intended] concept. This is as when we say 'So-and-so doesn't have a grain's weight of injustice in him', meaning that he doesn't have even an insignificant degree [of injustice]; some particular insignificant degree, namely the weight of a grain, is put in place of the unqualified word 'insignificant'. We could also discuss movement but speak in terms of

walking, which is a [particular] kind of movement, on the basis that something that is true of the particular case – walking – is true of all movement. And likewise when some accepted proposition happens to express that a content is true of some [subject], if [the subject] is stated in place of some universal and we know what that universal is, then regardless of what the universal is, we count that content as being true of that universal [rather than the stated concept]. This 57,1
gives us a general premise, which can be used in the same way as the premises that were accepted in the first place as generally true, like the two kinds that we mentioned at the outset.[136]

[20.9] An example of this is a proposition that we accept, namely that 'It is forbidden for us to say "Uff" to our parents'.[137] This [proposition] is not intended to forbid just this expression; what it is intended to forbid is all of this kind of talk, namely speaking disrespectfully to one's parents. When we know that what is intended is this universal [concept], it provides us with a universal premise, namely that speaking disrespectfully to one's parents is forbidden. Then when it is shown that something is a case of speaking disrespectfully to one's parents, we judge that the thing is forbidden, [using] a syllogism composed in the first figure.[138]

[20.10] Suppose we are presented with a concept that is judged to satisfy some content, but we don't know at all whether the concept was put in place of an [intended] universal, or that the thing intended by the concept was that thing itself; or else we do know that the concept was put in place of some [intended] universal, but it [falls under] many universals and we don't know which of them it was put in place of. [In either case] we are not in a position to transfer the content from that concept to anything except what falls under it. Rather we can transfer the content only to the particular cases that fall under the concept. When we know that the concept was put in place of a universal and we know which universal that is, then we [can] transfer that content to some other concept that shares with the first concept the property of falling under that universal. As for how we can know whether the concept was put in place of a universal or not, and if it was, which was the universal that it was put in place of: sometimes this is self-evident without needing any reflection. If it is not self-evident, one should seek to identify it by means of a syllogism that is composed in one of the ways that we mentioned earlier,[139] or by using the methods that we mentioned in connection with inference to the unobserved by means of the observed. It becomes clear to us what is the universal that had a particular case put in place of it when the content is [seen to be] true of the whole of the universal, and it is a universal that has that particular case, as in inference to the unobserved by means of the observed. The most reliable way to verify that this universal [is the one we are looking for] is for us to verify it by one of the syllogisms in the forms that we mentioned.

[20.11] As for verifying it by the method of Examination,[140] the situation here is similar to that of inference to the unobserved by means of the observed,[141] which is that we resort to an [exemplar *D*] that is judged to satisfy the [given] content [*A*]. We consider the universals [*B*] that are true of that [exemplar], and then we examine the particular cases of each of these universals. Whatever universal [*B*] we find, if all of its particular cases satisfy that content *A*, we know that this universal is what was intended when that [exemplar *D* was stated], and that that [exemplar] has been used in place of this universal. But it is clear that if we proceed in this way, we will have known that the [given] content [*A*] is true of the things that fall under that universal [*B*] before we know that the content is true of the universal [*B* itself]. So if our reason for verifying that this universal satisfies the content was just so as to know that the content is true of some particular cases falling under the universal, then it is clear that if we proceed in this way, then there would be no need after that for us to transfer the content from that universal to something that falls under it, since we already knew that the content [*A*] is true of each [particular case] falling under that universal [*B*] before we knew that it was true of the universal [*B*] itself. [On the other hand] if, [for any of the universals] whatever, when we examine the particular cases one by one, there is one particular case of this universal such that the examination fails either to verify for us that the case satisfies the content, or to make clear to us that the content is false of the case,[142] then evidently we are not able to judge how the content applies to any of these universals, either that they satisfy it or that they don't. And if when we examined them we found that some of the particular cases of a particular universal couldn't satisfy that content, this would show that the content [*A*] fails to be true of the whole of that universal [*B*]. So clearly this method is not helpful for verifying that the universal [is the one intended], but it is very helpful for refuting this. In fact suppose that someone thinks that some universal [*B*] is the one that has had put in place of it a particular case [*D*] that satisfies some content [*A*], and then when we examine what falls under that universal, we find one of its particular cases that can't satisfy that content [*A*], then this sort of case can be used to compose a syllogism in the third figure, and it follows from the syllogism that the content fails to be true of the whole of this universal [*B*]. We have already explained this in the section on inference to the unobserved by means of the observed.[143] This method is the same one that is used in drawing out the content of the cause with regard to its effects. As for the other ways in which one can verify that a universal [is the intended one], like [the methods of] Accepting and Rejecting and so on, we have already explained the facts about them in that section too.

[20.12] An example of that is [the following]. One of the [propositions] accepted by us is that 'Exchanging wheat for wheat in unequal quantities is forbidden'.[144] So we have to know if what is intended by that judgement is just 59,1
wheat, or whether 'wheat' has been put in place of a universal, namely the edible or the measurable or some other universal that is true of wheat. Then 'wheat' was said in place of the universal, but what was intended [by 'wheat'] was the edible or the measurable or some other universal true of wheat. So what was said was a particular case, but what was meant by saying it was the universal. Let us take it as[145] known that [the particular case] was put in place of a universal. But while there are many universals that are true of wheat, including the edible and the measurable, and so long as it is not known which of these has 'wheat' put in place of it – is it the measurable or the edible or something else? – we can't transfer the prohibition to anything except things that fall under wheat. As for how we know whether wheat has been put in place of one of the universals that are true of it, or which universal it has been put in place of, in many such cases this is self-evident and needs no reflection; there just is a universal intended by the particular case. We know this for the statement of Allah, the Great and Almighty: 'There is not a grain's weight of injustice in Allah'.[146] In those cases where it is not self-evident what [concept] is [intended] by 'wheat', one should seek to identify [the concept] by means of a syllogism that is composed in one of the ways that we mentioned. We succeed in showing what was the universal that had wheat put in place of it, when we verify that one of the universals true of wheat, such as the edible or the measurable, satisfies the content, viz. that the prohibition applies to all of it. Then when it is verified that everything edible is forbidden [to be exchanged] in unequal quantities (or the same for every measurable thing), then it is verified that the universal that had wheat put in place of it is the edible (or the measurable).

[20.13] When the verification is made by the method of Examination,[147] we proceed as follows. We take the universals true of wheat, such as the edible and the measurable. Then we inspect the subspecies of the measurable and the subspecies of the edible. Whichever of these two is such that the prohibition applies to all of its subspecies, that one is the universal which had the wheat put in place of it. Let us take it that it is verified for the subspecies of the measurable. 60,1
Then in that case we knew that the prohibition was true of every subspecies of the measurable before we knew that the prohibition applies to the measurable.

So now we have that we already knew that the prohibition applies to rice before we knew that it applies to everything measurable. That is the situation when we used Examination. If our reason for wanting to verify that the prohibition applies to the measurable was just so as to know that this content is true of something that falls under the measurable, such as rice for example, then there was no need for us to transfer the prohibition from the measurable to rice, since we already knew that the prohibition was true of the rice before we knew that it applies to the measurable. [On the other hand] if we hadn't already examined the rice while we were examining the subspecies of the measurable, then we would still not know whether the content applied to rice, and so it would not be possible for us to say that the prohibition applies to everything measurable, since something measurable has not been examined so as to know whether prohibition applies to it or not. And if when we examined it we didn't know whether certain subspecies of it are subject to the prohibition or not, it would not have been possible for us to judge either that the prohibition applies to everything measurable, or that it applies to nothing measurable. So we suspend judgement until things become clear to us. But if someone were to posit that the prohibition applies to everything measurable, and then we inspected the subspecies of the measurable and we found among its subspecies one that the prohibition doesn't apply to, say plaster,[148] then it would be false that the prohibition applies to everything measurable. A syllogism for this is composed in the third figure,[149] namely: 'Plaster is measurable; and the prohibition doesn't apply to plaster. Therefore the prohibition doesn't apply to everything measurable.' So it has been shown that this method is not helpful for verification but it is helpful for refutation.

[Tolerance]

[20.14] However, one must take into account in these things what Aristotle said,[150] that it is not appropriate to seek the same kind of exact investigation in all matters; but each thing should be investigated as is appropriate for its subject-matter. One should investigate each matter to a degree of exactness that is adequate for it; what [counts as] adequate for each subject is not [necessarily] to arrive at complete certainty about it. Rather [we can investigate] many matters far enough while restricting our knowledge of them to something less than
61,1 certainty. Aristotle himself said: 'If one asks for the same degree of exactness in every investigation, this shows some lack of experience in giving demonstrations about things in general.'[151] The same holds here as in the investigation of what people do in commercial and social relationships, namely that, as the saying

goes, 'to probe is to create discord'. The result of close inspection in the present case can be what we intended; but equally the result of close inspection in the case of the syllogism can be the contrary of what we intended to achieve through the syllogism. The aim of the syllogism is to give a proof and remove doubt and confusion; but in some circumstances when we want to achieve something by a syllogism, and we carry out a closer inspection than was needed, the result is that the thing [that we wanted to prove] is not proved at all. So as for those [situations] in which one can exercise tolerance about what is known, setting aside precise inspection: [this practice] is very helpful in the art of jurisprudence and many other arts, where it is natural to make much use of tolerance about what is known. But this [practice] should not extend beyond these arts. In fact it is highly beneficial within these arts, but when it is extended beyond them to other [arts], then either one doesn't reach what was intended at all, or it would bring one to the contrary of what was intended. For this reason the method of Examination is something that could be sufficient for verification of universal [propositions] in such arts, in a situation where one examines most of the things that fall under [the subject term of] the universal [proposition]. This is not the only situation [where Examination can be applied tolerantly]. Another is where one examines the things that fall under the [subject term of the] universal [proposition] and finds no case where the content could not be true. So one can be content [to use tolerance] even within the [method of] Examination. The same applies when only a few things are examined, or just one or two. The same applies also to the other approaches to [the method of Examination] for a universal proposition, such as the method of Accepting and Rejecting and some other methods. This approach is extremely helpful in such arts, even though it involves accepting that they are not investigated in detail. Perhaps it has to be accepted that they are not investigated in the thorough way that is necessary in many sciences.

[The exemplar]

[20.15] The exemplar is one of two similar things, where [we have two things 62,1
and] one of them [*D*] satisfies a content [*A*] because of its being described by the concept that makes the two things similar; nothing is said about the other thing.[152] The one [of the two] that is known to satisfy the content is [called] an exemplar for the one that is not known to satisfy the content. Then the content [*A*] that is true of [the exemplar *D*] transfers to the other thing [*C*] that was similar to it. The knowledge that the content that was true of [the exemplar *D*] is

true of that thing [*C*] comes from the concept [*B*] that makes the two things similar, since we have succeeded in verifying that the content is true of all of that concept [*B*] that makes the two things similar. The effect is that the thing [*D*] which explicitly satisfied the content has been put in place of the concept [*B*] that made the two things similar. So the exemplar is very like a particular thing that has been used in place of a universal. The content [*A*] is known to be true of the concept [*B*] that makes the two things similar, in the same way in which it was known to be true of the universal that was used in place of the particular. And when we know that the content [*A*] is true [of that concept], the result is a universal premise.[153] Then when something is shown to fall under the subject term of this premise, the content that was true of the exemplar transfers to this thing, leading to a syllogism composed in the first figure.

[20.16] The same example that we mentioned in the preceding section can appropriately be used here too. Thus wheat is [treated as] resembling rice when it is verified that the prohibition [on unequal exchange] applies to [rice] because of a concept that makes wheat resemble rice; this concept is either 'edible' or 'measurable'. And when it is verified that the prohibition applies to every eaten thing, or to every measurable thing, this [can be seen as] making clear to us the concept because of which [the prohibition] applies to [rice]. The verification takes place by working out what is the universal that was replaced by the particular; the route followed is the same [in both methods]. We should exercise some tolerance in verifying the universal in these arts;[154] otherwise we won't achieve [our] aim.

[20.17] The concept that makes the exemplar similar to the other thing can be conceptualized by the mind, alone and independent of the exemplar, so that a universal premise becomes available, based on that [concept] and the content that was true of the exemplar. Then when something is found to fall under the subject term of that premise, the content which is true of the exemplar transfers to that thing. Since this is how it works, one [should] not think that the transfer goes just from the exemplar to the thing that is similar to it, or that the exemplar [on its own] is sufficient [to justify] the transfer to whatever is similar to it. Rather we [should] ascribe the sufficiency just to the universal premise that was composed from the content and the concept which caused the similarity. And one should not think that the content's being true of the exemplar [*D*] is sufficient to verify that this content is true of the concept [*B*] that made the exemplar similar to the other thing [*C*]. But it can happen that the thing which is found to be the cause of the similarity is not extracted from or separated from the exemplar; rather it is just conceptualized in the mind as linked to the exemplar, so that when one verifies that the content is true of the concept that causes the similarity to occur, that [concept] is [conceived as] linked to the exemplar. When this happens, the universal premise that becomes available is not genuinely universal but is tied to the exemplar, which is a particular case. Nevertheless this premise will have the force of a universal [premise]. Hence it is correct to transfer [the content] to the things that fall under the concept that causes the similarity to occur, but one thinks of this transfer as being from the exemplar to what is similar to it, going from particular to particular, and not from universal to particular as in a syllogism. This is why [people] think that likening doesn't proceed by a syllogism. This is also why Aristotle said about [the method of] Example that it is something that goes, not like all to part and not like part to all, but like part to part.[155] The transfer in [the method of] Example is not a transfer from a pure particular without a universal, nor is it from a pure universal without a particular. Rather it is from a particular linked to a universal, or from a universal linked to a particular. For this reason the particular becomes like a universal that is like a particular.

[20.18] This being so, it is clear that Aristotle doesn't think that when the universal premise is separated from the exemplar and a transfer is made from it to what falls under the subject term of the premise, the transfer is being made by [the method of] Example. Rather he just thinks of likening and transfer by [the method of] Example as being of the second kind that we have sketched.[156] In our view the first [kind of argument] is a pure syllogism; the second is not a syllogism, but it is potentially a syllogism. This second kind is that in which the exemplar is found to be useful for making the transfer, because the first step is to use the exemplar to show that the content is true of the concept which makes the exemplar similar to another thing, so that the concept becomes an intermediate between the content and the thing that is similar to the exemplar. And as for how the examplar is useful for verifying that the content is true of the concept that causes the similarity: this can take place in either of the two ways that we mentioned in connection with inference to the unobserved by means of the observed, namely by composing a syllogism in the third figure or by composing a syllogism in the first figure.[157] Aristotle seems to have considered that [the method] is useful when composed in the first figure. In many cases[158] the transfer from the exemplar to what is similar to it through the intermediary of a similarity is not mentioned, and one just mentions the exemplar and the target of the transfer. But there are also many cases where all three are spoken of. In the case of induction and the other methods that we listed after it, Aristotle says that one shouldn't press so hard with the detailed investigation of the universal propositions that are at the heart of the matter. Rather in both cases[159] one should restrict oneself to an investigation commensurate with the pieces of knowledge that [the reasoning] gives us, because the arts in which these sentences are used are of a nature to be highly tolerant in their treatment of the pieces of knowledge that they provide. So if we made a thorough investigation of the things involved, going beyond the amount that is sufficient for them, we would lose the benefit that they provide.

[20.19] Thus it has been shown that the starting point in these [syllogistic] arts is the universal [proposition], and that the other starting points can serve for investigating the objective and for providing the content of something that at the outset is not known to satisfy the content, when you reduce things to a starting point that is universal; these [other starting points] are potentially universal. So it has become clear how what Aristotle called the jurisprudential syllogisms are reduced to syllogisms of the declarative[160] figures.

This reaches the limit of what we wanted to say here, and is the final topic of our book, God willing. The book *Syllogism* is completed. True praise be to Allah!

Notes

1 'Inferences': *dalā'il*. The word doesn't appear again in *Syllogism*, but in Part 19 we will meet its close relative *istidlāl* with a similar meaning.

2 'Declarative': *jāzim*. This word appears in the Baghdad Standard translation of *De Interpretatione* 17a2 as a translation of *apophantikós*, explained there by Aristotle as a sentence containing truth or falsehood. In Part 20 al-Fārābī will call sentences *jāzim* to distinguish them from sentences with an imperative verb (like 'Wash your faces' 55,2).

Unlike Aristotle, al-Fārābī has plenty to say about hypothetical statements, as in paragraph 1.3. He seems content to assume that hypothetical statements are declarative, i.e. true or false; so he needs another word to distinguish those declarative statements that are not hypothetical. For this he uses the word 'categorical' (*ḥamlī*) in *Syllogism*, as at 13.6. This word became common in this meaning after al-Fārābī, but it has not been found before him; it may be his own coinage. (Perhaps al-Fārābī had some hesitance about introducing the word. In *Short Syllogism* categorical sentences are not called *ḥamlī*; they are called *jazmī*, on which see Note 95 to the translation.)

3 *fiᶜl*, the normal Arabic word for 'action', is the linguists' word for verb.

4 The predicate can also be an adjective, as 'white' in the next paragraph; Arabic makes little distinction between nouns and adjectives. In logical examples the predicate is often a participle (as for example 'going away' in 12,12), which for Arabic linguists is a 'noun of the verb' (*ism al-fiᶜl*). Participles are not mentioned in *Syllogism*, but in his *Long Commentary on De Interpretatione* al-Fārābī discusses them at length under the description 'derived noun' (*ism mushtaqq*).

5 'Copular': *wujūdī*. The name 'copular' is used by modern linguists for verbs like 'is', 'was', 'becomes' (e.g. Moro [124]). Arabic linguists spoke of this or a closely related set of verbs as 'sisters of *kāna*', from *kāna* 'was'. See Zimmermann [165] p. lx Note 1 on al-Fārābī's choice of *wujūdī* to name copular verbs, and Hasnawi [96] p. 30f on al-Fārābī's view that copular verbs can serve as pure representations of tenses. Al-Fārābī's notion of *wujūdī verbs* should not be confused with his notion of *wujūdī sentences*, i.e. sentences without modality; he doesn't refer to this class in *Syllogism*, but see for example *Short Interpretation* [65] 158,4f (Zimmermann [165] pp. 243f).

6 'Time' appears at (6) in Ebbesen's reconstruction of Porphyry's list; cf. Section 3.3 above.

7 'Part' appears at (3) in Ebbesen's reconstruction of Porphyry's list.

8 Medicine and writing are two aspects (*jiha*) of skill. The example of the 'skilled doctor' whose skills lie elsewhere than in medicine is from the Arabic version of *De Interpretatione* 11, 20b35 (Aristotle and his Greek successors had a cobbler rather than a doctor). But note that on Ebbesen's reconstruction of Porphyry's list, item (5) is a condition expressing a modality; since *jiha* can also mean modality, al-Fārābī's source may have mentioned modality at this point.

9 Implicit is *fī al-ḍamīr;* see Section 3.3 on this word.

10 At first sight this clause is misplaced, because al-Fārābī still has one kind of opposition to mention. But comparing with Ebbesen's reconstruction of Porphyry's list, specifically his item (4), it seems possible that al-Fārābī's source mentioned not 'another condition' but 'a condition about some other individual'.

11 Somebody has lost concentration here and added a wrong 'not'. If the two sentences carry exactly the same condition, viz. none, they should by definition be opposites – and this is exactly why a condition should have been stated.

12 On 'some human' here, see Note 45 to Section 3.2.

13 By the rules of Arabic syntax, every noun has to carry either an indication that it is definite (e.g. a definite article) or that it is indefinite. As a result, Aristotle's examples of sentences with no quantifier don't translate convincingly into Arabic, causing Avicenna to wonder aloud whether Arabic really has any indeterminate sentences (*ᶜIbāra* [147] 21.16). In the present example al-Fārābī writes 'the human' (*al-insān*), but 'the' is there purely because the syntax says it must be, and not to express any meaning. But in paragraphs 19.14 and 19.15 below al-Fārābī will suggest a logical use for indeterminate sentences written with the definite article.

14 Literally: they are never both true together (*maᶜan*). This is a common phrase in Arabic logic, normally meaning that if both sentences are interpreted in the same context, for example at the same time and with all ambiguities resolved in the same way, then they are not both true. Similarly for the phrase about 'both false'.

15 Al-Fārābī is using 'things' (i.e. concepts) as an alternative name for matter or matters. See Sections 3.2 and 3.5 for the definition of 'matter'.

16 The names 'necessary', 'prevented' and 'possible' are taken from Ammonius *Commentary on De Interpretatione* [8] 88,19, except that for 'prevented' (*mumtaniᶜ*) Ammonius has 'impossible' (*adúnaton,* for which the normal Arabic is *muḥāl*). The reason for the choice of *mumtaniᶜ* to translate *adúnaton* is unknown, but the choice goes back as far as Muqaffaᶜ.

As to why Ammonius and al-Fārābī use modal terms for a distinction involving only categorical sentences: this illustrates how fragile the distinction between modal and non-modal was through the Roman Empire period and up to al-Fārābī. For an example in Themistius see Note 152 to Section 3.21 above.

17 'Things' here means matters, as in Note 15 above.

18 'With a modality': *fī jiha.* If al-Fārābī wrote this phrase, he presumably meant that the rules of conversion carry over to modalized sentences, so that for example 'Contingently some *B* is an *A*' entails 'Contingently some *A* is a *B*'. But the phrase sits oddly and is very likely a marginal gloss.

19 'Becomes available': *yaḥṣulu.* The root *ḥṣl* occurs so often in both al-Fārābī and Avicenna that it clearly means something important to both of them. But the precise meaning is hard to pin down, since it varies from context to context. There are two main candidates here: (1) To become actual or available, to exist in a strong sense. (2) To be made specific and well-defined (noting that the passive participle *muḥaṣṣal* was used for Greek *hōrisménos,* cf. Kutsch [115]). In case (2) the verb would be *yuḥaṣṣalu;* in Arabic script both forms of the verb are written the same way. Evidence for (1) as against (2) is that (2) tends to imply that we have worked on the knowledge ('validated' it, in Gutas's phrase [92] p. 617), whereas al-Fārābī emphasizes in *Burhān* 23,4–9 that universal primary knowledge forces itself on us without our seeking it in any way.

20 See Note 68 to Section 3.8 for the method of Aristotle that al-Fārābī is trying to describe. Al-Fārābī mistakenly believes that the relevant requirement on 'Every *C* is an *A*' and 'No *C* is an *A*' is that one is affirmative and the other is negative. But Alexander [5] 89,31–91,33 showed that the requirement is that these two sentences have the forms (*a*) and (*e*); nothing less will suffice.

21 This definition of 'hypothetical syllogism' is incorrect; see 31,9 below for the correct definition.

22 In *Debate* [70] 63,3–8 and *Long Commentary on De Interpretatione* [59] 182,1–10 al-Fārābī explains that being 'prepared for' something is close to 'having a potential for' the thing.

23 This refers to compound syllogisms, which al-Fārābī will explain in more detail in Part 18b below.

24 The first or great extreme is usually called the major (*akbar*) extreme (even by al-Fārābī).

25 At this point the manuscripts *M* and *N* include a full list of the twenty-one moods that are excluded in all figures.

26 This sentence has nothing to do with the enumeration of syllogisms, so that it breaks the flow of al-Fārābī's text. Probably it is a marginal gloss that has been copied into the text. But its contents fit with al-Fārābī's views in the book. The phrase about 'the reason why the extremes come together' might pick up al-Fārābī's notion that the two premises have to be 'composed' in order to produce the conclusion (cf. (3.8.1) and (3.8.2)). The emphasis on the middle term matches that in Part 17 and later Parts, cf. Section 3.17.

27 The reduction is to *Celarent,* which is usually the second mood of the first figure, though al-Fārābī has listed it third.

28 Again *Celarent,* the normal second mood of the first figure.

29 The fact that some animals are humans is a piece of real-world information not contained in the premises, so that al-Fārābī is not entitled to use it to justify a formal syllogism.

30 I.e. *Darii,* not *Celarent.*

31 The reference to the 'five primary hypothetical moods' is presumably to the Stoic indemonstrables, of which there were five. For the separated case with two premises he describes four moods; he may have been working from a Peripatetic source that didn't tell him what the corresponding three Stoic indemonstrables were. Cf. Section 3.14.

32 More precisely, when X is a phrase, 'X *taḍammana(t)* Y' means that Y is included in what is being said when one utters X. For example at *Letters/Particles* [75] 127,5–10 al-Fārābī uses it to explain that when we say 'Human is animal', we are using 'is' to express a certain relation between the mental idea 'human' and the mental idea 'animal', and not to assert either that there are humans or that there are animals in the world outside the mind. Al-Fārābī may have taken this usage from the linguists; for example we find *ḍamāna* used in a similar way by Al-Sīrāfī [143] 299,12.

33 Strictly it is either one of the parts of the hypothetical premise, or the contradictory opposite of one of these parts. Al-Fārābī has slipped into thinking of a sentence and its contradictory opposite as being the same proposition seen from opposite sides.

34 The sentence begins with 'It is not the case that' (*lā*). But there is nothing in the sentence to indicate the scope of this negation. Since al-Fārābī is discussing the separated incomplete case, which expresses that the two clauses are not both true, probably the scope is the whole sentence and the intended sense is equivalent to 'If Zayd is present then ᶜAmr is not speaking'. Avicenna may have read al-Fārābī that way, hence his example 'Either Abdullah doesn't speak, or ᶜAmr allows him to', [146] 405.15f; Avicenna describes this as an *ittifāq,* presumably an 'agreement' corresponding to al-Fārābī's 'posit'.

35 Al-Fārābī has confused himself. 'It is neither hot nor middling' is not a hypothetical sentence by his definitions; and even if it were, adding a premise 'But it is hot' would give no sensible argument. From the paragraph as a whole we can see that al-Fārābī meant to write '. . . by saying "But it is not cold", this produces that "it is either hot or middling"'.

36 Shām was a region of the Islamic Empire with similar boundaries to the modern state of Syria.

37 The mood 'starts with a negative' because the first premise is the negation of a conjunction, as in the Stoic third indemonstrable. There is no connection with *modus tollendo tollens.* (We thank Susanne Bobzien for this observation.)

38 *Bocardo,* cf. Section 1.3.

39 'Put up for consideration': *furiḍa.* This term is used of an objective set up at the beginning of a logical enquiry, with a view to showing which side of it is true and

which is false; or more generally a statement put up to be proved or refuted. Cf. Section 1.2. Distinguish this from a posited statement (*waḍ*ᶜ), which is agreed to be available to use as a premise.

40 As explained in Section 3.16, our translation attaches letters to some of the main components in al-Fārābī's more complex arguments, extending the use of these same letters by Aristotle and al-Fārābī.

41 In other words the aim is to verify whether or not every *B* is an *A*, by checking it for particular cases of *B*.

42 The role of this restriction to 'known' particular cases of *B* is not clear. The best interpretation is that we begin by assembling, from among those particular cases that we know, a list that exhausts *B*; though the reader will hardly see this. The word 'known' is missing in the parallel passage in *Short Syllogism*.

43 See the remark on 'most' in Section 3.16.

44 Does denying *A* of *B* mean asserting that no *B* is an *A* or that not every *B* is an *A*? It could mean either; at 47,15–17 al-Fārābī will consider these two different kinds of denial as different outcomes.

45 On potential see Section 3.21, the final paragraph under '2. Search'.

46 I.e. *Barbara*, cf. Section 1.3.

47 'Particular' in this passage is sometimes *juz'* 'part' and sometimes *juz'ī* 'particular'. Since these particulars need not be individuals (see Section 3.17) and nothing has been given that they are parts of, both expressions should be read loosely as meaning things that fall under some universal not yet specified.

48 The definite article suggests that al-Fārābī thinks there is a unique such *B*. Later passages using 'the concept' or 'that concept' seem to confirm this suggestion. But in the first place al-Fārābī never gives a hint of any reason why *B* should be unique. And second, he speaks for example about 'the concept that makes the exemplar similar to the other thing' (62,16), and elsewhere (e.g. 42,14; 46,19) he has made it clear that he thinks that in general there are many concepts by which two similar things *C* and *D* are similar. Probably his use of the definite article is just an idiom – a poor idiom but by no means peculiar to al-Fārābī.

49 'Like' (*mithl*) and 'comparable with' (*mumaththal*): These look like a proposed pair of terms to distinguish the two directions of similarity between *C* and *D*. If that is what they are, then probably *mithl* is a miscopying of *mithāl* 'exemplar', which al-Fārābī assigns to *D* at 20.15. (*mithl* is stubbornly symmetric.)

50 Within this paragraph al-Fārābī treats as equivalent the contents 'came into existence', 'has something that brings it into existence' and 'has a maker'. His concern is only with the logical structure of the argument, not with the philosophical niceties of the terms.

51 Al-Fārābī calls this argument a syllogism, though it is not a syllogism in any of the senses that he has defined.

52 Taken with Note 89 to the translation, it seems that al-Fārābī's point here is that you can persuade people to believe something by stating it as the conclusion of a syllogism, regardless of whether there is any good reason to believe the premises.
53 Normally al-Fārābī distinguishes between likening (the method) and exemplar (the concept *C* in likening).
54 This paragraph is trying too hard to give some sense to the remark of Aristotle quoted at 63,8f below. The relationship that al-Fārābī describes between likening and induction in Part 18d is more illuminating.
55 Presumably 'we have enumerated' refers to the listing under figures in Parts 10–12 and 14 above. Then 'mentioned first' means how al-Fārābī first described syllogisms, i.e. formally as opposed to the later discussion of how they are used in practice.
56 *yuḥdhafu*; this can simply mean 'is missing' or 'is omitted'. But al-Fārābī tends to use the word where the speaker intends a certain meaning but says nothing to express it explicitly. That is probably what he means here, since in lines 37,14 and 37,16 he refers to the 'original discourse', i.e. what the speaker originally had in mind.
57 The force of 'then' here is obscure, but there is no obvious emendation.
58 For the four ways in which a proposition can be known without a syllogism, see Part 7 above.
59 Al-Fārābī is describing a procedure that needs to be repeated over and over until it comes to a halt, and in advance we have no means of knowing whether or when that will happen. It is important to distinguish the case where it does eventually come to a halt from the case where it doesn't. Unfortunately al-Fārābī blurs the distinction by saying that the procedure goes on 'for ever' (*abadan*) even in the case where it halts.
60 'Irremovable accident' (*ᶜaraḍ lā yanfakku minhu*) recalls the Peripatetic notion of an inseparable accident. But the expression that al-Fārābī uses comes from Islamic theology, not from Peripatetic philosophy. See Section 3.19 for this and other terminology in the proof.
61 Compare *Analytica Priora* 1.42, 50a5–7: 'We must not overlook the fact that not all conclusions in the same syllogism come through a single figure, but one through this and one through another' ([11] p. 59).
62 In *Syllogism* we are not told what 'this' is. But the version at *Short Syllogism* 90,8 adds that what is impossible is 'that it is not possible for it to move'.
63 Aristotle says at *Analytica Priora* 1.25, 42a3f that an argument can include both a syllogism and an induction.
64 By 22,4–6.
65 Here and elsewhere (e.g. 40,8; 51,13; 54,12), al-Fārābī writes 'universal' for 'universally true'.
66 I.e. 'Is every *C* an *A* or not?'
67 In Section 3.20 it is suggested that the splitting of the action between 'we' and 'he' may be a device used by al-Fārābī to objectify the procedure followed by 'him'.

68 Though it is hard to find a precise statement, the Peripatetic assumption about more and less known seems to be that after performing the syllogism we should know something that we didn't already know before it. This is impossible if the conclusion is also one of the premises. The issue is separate from the validity of the syllogism.

69 *mumtaniᶜ*: this is the word used to translate Aristotle's *adúnaton*, but here al-Fārābī uses it in a way closer to its everyday sense; cf. Note 16 to the translation.

70 Al-Fārābī has said nothing to justify this claim. If the minor premise of the original syllogism is universal then this premise might be proved by induction. Cf. Note 129 to Section 3.20.

71 I.e. in arguments that are compounds of a syllogism and an induction, cf. 42,4 above.

72 Al-Fārābī will introduce the label *B* for this concept at 43,5 below.

73 'The' implies uniqueness, but al-Fārābī is not saying that there is a unique *B* meeting all the requirements. There could be several, but we would still need to verify that whichever one we choose does meet the requirements.

74 In Section 3.17 we read between the lines to conclude that al-Fārābī derives '*C* is an *A* because it is a *B*' from '*C* is a *B*' and (3.17.4) 'Every *B* is an *A* because it is a *B*', which in turn is true because *B* was chosen to make it true that '*D* is an *A* because it is a *B*'.

75 From here to the end of the paragraph, al-Fārābī is discussing the form that the major premise might take. He has already introduced reasons for reading it as 'Every *B* is an *A*' (e.g. at 40,11) or as 'Every *B* is an *A* because it is a *B*' or as 'Most *B*s are *A*s' (35,5). Here he suggests that it might be taken to be the indeterminate proposition 'The *B* is an *A*' (as defined at 13,17). This is a variant of 'Most *B*s are *A*s'; we have seen in Section 3.21 the role that these two sentence forms play in al-Fārābī's theory of logical tolerance.

76 There is an implied modal syllogism here: '*C* is a *B*; and necessarily every *B* is an *A*. Therefore necessarily *C* is an *A*.' This is the modal mood that *Harmony* [77] 87,3–6 and Avicenna in *Qiyās* [146] 148,9 both say that al-Fārābī endorsed. Al-Fārābī doesn't mention the implication that the second premise must be read as necessary, but he will make this point explicit in paragraph 18d.3.

77 The argument of this paragraph is as follows. Suppose (as at the beginning of the previous paragraph) that we have an inductive proof of 'Every *B* is an *A*' which is being used as a premise for '*C* is an *A*' (as in paragraph 18b.3), but we are trying to remove the need for induction by invoking likening instead. So we have used an exemplar *D* that is an *A* in order to find an appropriate middle term *B*. We will still need to find a verification of 'Every *B* is an *A*'. Likening on its own is no help for this. Induction is a possibility, but we are trying to remove it. Another possibility is that 'Every *B* is an *A*' can simply be derived as the conclusion of another syllogism; but in that case the syllogistic part of the argument is self-sufficient (cf. Section 3.21 under '2. Search') and again there was no need for likening. So the stage is set to find

another way of justifying 'Every *B* is an *A*' that does make proper use of the choice of *B*. Paragraph 18d.3 (44,10f) will propose that there is such a way.

78 Cf. 42,13–16.

79 Speaker and interlocutor: like 34,14 above, this is a place where al-Fārābī unexpectedly slips into the terminology of debate. See Sections 1.2 and 3.15 on this move.

80 I.e. the categorical and hypothetical moods; cf. 47,13 below and the note on it.

81 I.e. they would serve no purpose for verifying the major premise 'Every *B* is an *A*'. The syllogism being used to verify it will have its own premises, and they in turn will need to be verified.

82 Al-Fārābī has not explicitly identified any people, but he could be assuming that his readers will have picked up an implied reference at 42,7 to people who rejected induction in favour of likening. See Section 3.21 for the evidence that the people in question include Galen.

83 In other words they proposed to use the topic of Accepting and Rejecting as a means of proving 'Necessarily (or causally) every *B* is an *A*'; see the description of this topic in Section 3.21.

84 At this point the manuscripts have a sentence 'So therefore inevitably what is verified by this approach is the major premise and not the cause.' This makes no sense in its present position, but it would be a reasonable comment on the lines that follow it at 44,2–8. Since there is no place where it would naturally fit, we assume it is a reader's gloss.

85 Here al-Fārābī addresses the question how we have to understand the sentence 'Every *B* is an *A*' in order to be able to use it as major premise for concluding that *C* is an *A*. We expect the answer to be that 'Every *B* is an *A*' has to be shown to be necessarily true. Al-Fārābī's answer is that 'Every *B* is an *A*' needs to be true at all times and places (44,8, repeated at 44,14); this fits with the Peripatetic habit of blurring the difference between alethic modalities ('necessarily') and temporal ones ('always'). So far so good; but now al-Fārābī bewilders us by claiming that to show 'Necessarily every *B* is an *A*' it is sufficient to show 'Every *B* is an *A*'. At 44,9f he adds an equally bewildering reason, namely that these are the same proposition though differently expressed.

86 This paragraph conflates two points that common sense suggests should have been kept separate; the second of them is dubious anyway. The first point is sound but trivial: that proving 'Every *A* is a *B*' is no help for proving 'Every *B* is an *A*'. The second is that if we don't prove that every *B* at any time or place is an *A*, we leave open the possibility that some *B* is not an *A*. What makes this point dubious is that al-Fārābī implies here and elsewhere that proving 'for every *B* at any time or place' is something different from and stronger than simply proving 'for every *B*'. If it really is stronger, then it is not a necessary condition for proving 'for every *B*'. The conflation of the two points would be explained if al-Fārābī was reading from a source in which somebody did make the two mistakes that al-Fārābī criticizes.

87 The reference is unclear. In fact it is clearer that al-Fārābī contradicted this statement, for example at 43,19f.

88 It is not clear what al-Fārābī thinks he has said to suggest that likening and induction yield results that are less than certain. Likening proves nothing; it merely produces middle terms *B*, and another method would be needed to prove the major premise 'Every *B* is an *A*'. Complete induction leaves no logical gap in the proof of 'Every *B* is an *A*'. Is al-Fārābī suggesting that a proof of 'Every *B* is an *A*', as opposed to 'Every *B* at any time or place is an *A*', leaves it in doubt whether every *B* is an *A*?

89 In this context 'persuasive' can only mean that people are liable to be persuaded, not that they are right to be persuaded. Al-Fārābī sees it as the task of the orator to persuade people, so an orator can use likening as one of his tools. 'The things whose nature is to persuade are two: enthymemes and likenings. The enthymemes play the same role in rhetoric as demonstrations do in the sciences and syllogisms do in debate. And the enthymeme is like a rhetorical syllogism, while a likening is like a rhetorical induction.' (Al-Fārābī *Rhetoric* [60] 69,7–9).

90 The letters are as in the explanation in Section 3.17; *A* is the content, *D* is the exemplar, and *B* (to be introduced below) is the middle term.

91 'Being attached to created things', *muqārana lil-ḥawādith*, is not known to be a standard phrase in any medieval branch of study, though it occurs (with slight variants) seventeen times in Parts 18b and 19 of *Syllogism*. Rescher in [134] translates it as 'being contingent'. Lameer [116] p. 214 suggests 'coeval with contingent entities', and notes that Türker [157] 230 translates the phrase into Turkish with the meaning 'open to contingency'. In fact al-Fārābī is taking into account only what he considers to be the logical and epistemological structure of the argument, and for this the meaning of *muqārana lil-ḥawādith* is irrelevant. So we translate it word-for-word. For the religious and philosophical sources of arguments of this kind, see Lameer [116] ch. 7 and Adamson [2].

92 See Section 3.21, the last paragraph of '2. Search', on the meaning of 'potentially a syllogism'. The syllogism that al-Fārābī sets out is in the mood *Barbara*.

93 The manuscripts *B* and *H* omit the words 'starts with ... Synthesis it'. Given that the chief distinction between the two methods is that al-Fārābī's Synthesis makes no use at all of the unobserved *C* until after the middle term *B* has been chosen, the reading of manuscripts *B* and *H* can hardly be what al-Fārābī intended. We have followed the text of *E*, though it may be a late attempt to correct the error.

94 In its present context in *Syllogism* this must be a reference back to Part 7 on propositions known without syllogism. But the fit is not good. Al-Fārābī will go on to describe in Parts 19.6, 19.9 and 19.11 three ways of verifying a universal proposition without making it the conclusion of a syllogism, and none of these three ways appear in Part 7. This misfit is discussed in Section 3.7.

95 The word for 'categorical' here is not the word *ḥamlī* that al-Fārābī uses for 'categorical' in Parts 1–18 of *Syllogism*. In fact the bulk of the manuscripts, both here at 47,14 and

in a parallel passage at 64,13, read *juz'ī* 'particular', which makes no sense in this context. We have followed manuscript *E* in its plausible reading *jazmī* in both passages.

The word *jazmī* is used several times in the Baghdad Standard translation of *Analytica Priora* to represent Aristotle's *deiktikós* 'demonstrative' as a description of those *syllogisms* (not propositions) that are direct rather than by *reductio ad absurdum* (e.g. at 29a31, 45a28, 45b7). The reason why we have translated it as 'categorical' rather than 'demonstrative' is that al-Fārābī in *Short Syllogism* uses *jazmī* rather than *ḥamlī* to mean 'categorical' (proposition), as at 71,9f. He understands Aristotle's distinction between *deiktikós* and absurdity syllogisms as a distinction between those syllogisms that don't contain hypothetical premises and those that do; thus *Short Syllogism* 76,3; 82,9; 90,9. This allows him to read *jazmī* as 'categorical as opposed to hypothetical'. (The root *jzm* is the same for *jazmī* and for *jāzim* 'declarative', but the notion of declarative is not reflected in al-Fārābī's use of *jazmī*.) If we are right in taking *Short Syllogism* to be a revision of *Syllogism*, then in this revision al-Fārābī reverted from his new term *ḥamlī* to a word that already carried the authority of the Baghdad Standard – though later he switched back to *ḥamlī*.

96 This is what al-Fārābī elsewhere calls the method of Examination, i.e. Induction. In his next sentence he mentions that this method works also for proving negative conclusions – a point that he tends to ignore.

97 Al-Fārābī says 'premise' although this is a conclusion rather than a premise. It was not uncommon to refer to propositions as premises.

98 At 48,7 al-Fārābī introduces a method with this title, in Arabic '*ijrā'u ḥukmi al-ᶜillati fī al-maᶜlūlāti*. There has been some debate about how to translate this phrase, as witnessed by the following proposals: 'To derive a judgment about a cause from the effects' (Rescher [134] p. 100); 'To apply the rule of the cause to the effects' (Sabra [138] p. 243); 'To extend a predicate from a cause to its effects' (Lameer [116] p. 218).

Al-Fārābī is very clear about what method he is describing, and his description leaves no doubt that Rescher's translation carries the right sense overall. It is less clear how to get that sense out of those Arabic words. Lameer [116] p. 223 quotes a very similar phrase attributed to a writer in the early ninth century, which raises the possibility that al-Fārābī chose the phrase as much for its associations in the literature as for its exact sense.

Lameer's 'predicate' for *ḥukm* (content) is almost right; Section 3.1 observed that it is completely correct for affirmative propositions. (So 'judgement' and 'rule' are wrong here.) Then *ḥukm al-ᶜillati* is literally 'content of the cause', or in al-Fārābī's application 'content true of the cause'. The opening noun *ijrā'* is literally 'causing to flow', which al-Fārābī has associated with a kind of transfer: the content flows so as to become true of the cause. But then the direction of movement is 'from' the effects, so 'to the effects' (Sabra and Lameer) is incoherent here. In fact the preposition before 'effects' *is fī*, which doesn't mean either 'from' or 'to'. Probably al-Fārābī is reading *fī* in its sense of 'regarding' or 'by reference to'.

99 This sentence appears in the manuscripts at 47,8f, where it clearly breaks the flow of the text. It fits naturally between lines 48,7 and 48,8. A possible cause of the dislocation is that the passage on 'drawing out' and 'driving out' between 48,7 and 48,13 was added in the margin, creating a danger that a copyist would attach parts of the passage to the main text in the wrong places.

100 'Driving out' (*ṭard*) is evidently a version of the 'drawing out' in the phrase quoted at 48,7. That phrase was already rather distant from its logical application, so we may never know why al-Fārābī uses 'driving out' here. See Lameer [116] p. 218f. It is also unclear what distinction al-Fārābī is making between the particular cases and the effects, given that at 48.8 he defined the effects as particular cases.

101 In mood *Felapton*, cf. Section 1.3 and the end of Section 3.21.

102 'Another way' refers back to [19.5], where it was noted that there are several ways of verifying that the cause satisfies the content. One was by syllogism, another was by examination of particular cases. This third method is in fact two methods, namely Accepting and Rejecting, cf. Section 3.21. Paragraph 19.9 will discuss Accepting, paragraph 19.10 will move to Rejecting, and paragraph 19.11 will comment on the simultaneous use of both methods.

103 'Whenever and wherever' has the effect of quantifying over all possibilities; cf. also 50,3.16; 52,9 below. Since there has been no mention of examining particular cases (and al-Fārābī is about to rule out the use of just one particular case), we should take literally his statement at 49,11 that the method is purely by examination of the possible concepts *B*, reaching *A* by some kind of conceptual analysis. This is what allows al-Fārābī to claim at 49,18f that the method is impregnable.

104 This is the second mood of the connected hypothetical syllogism, *Syllogism* 32,5f. The example of this mood in *Short Syllogism* 83,14 is not such a good fit, since it has the negations in different places (though it is still true that the contradictory opposite of the consequent is detached).

105 The phrase 'was put for the antecedent', which appears three lines later, reveals that this is strictly not a hypothetical inference where a part of the hypothetical premise is detached. It is a quantified hypothetical proposition, and some individual is introduced when the quantifier is removed before the detachment. It is not clear that al-Fārābī is aware of the difference.

106 Here al-Fārābī reminds us of the larger picture, that we are searching for possible values for the middle term *B*. The method of Rejecting is being used to test a particular candidate 'up for consideration' to be *B*. Confusingly the thing 'up for consideration' two lines earlier is an unspecified thing falling under the particular candidate for *B* that we are examining.

107 The manuscripts *B* and *H* omit the words 'Likewise . . . body'. These words contain an elementary logical error (reversing an implication), so one can see why a copyist might omit them. It is less easy to see any reason for adding them; so probably

al-Fārābī wrote them during a lapse of concentration. Rescher in his translation ([134] p. 106 l. 2) corrects the logical error silently.

108 The manuscripts *B* and *H* omit the sentence 'And if . . . an agent'. This may have been a consequence of abandoning the faulty text in the previous note; the point made in the sentence is sound but relies on the earlier text for context.

109 Literally 'convertible in predication'. Al-Fārābī describes two terms *A* and *B* as convertible in predication if every *A* is a *B* and every *B* is an *A*; when this holds and *A* is a species, he says also that *B* is a proprium of *A*. (Cf. his *Expressions* [58] 75,16–76,8.) He also speaks of the statement '*A* and *B* are true of each other' as a 'kind of predication'.

110 I.e. 'Every *B* is an *A*' doesn't entail 'Every *A* is a *B*'. but it does entail 'Some *A* is a *B*'. Cf. Part 6; by his definitions in that part, passing from 'Every *B* is an *A*' to 'Every *A* is a *B*' would not be a conversion, because it doesn't preserve truth; instead it would be a 'swapping'. *Short Syllogism* 80,8 uses the same terminology as the present passage.

111 Arabic has two common words for 'thing', namely *shay'* and *amr*. In his discussions of likening, al-Fārābī tends to use 'content' for *A*, *amr* for *B* and *shay'* for whatever *A* and *B* are true or false of. But in this sentence 'concept' is *shay'* and 'whatever' is *amr*, which is the other way round.

112 The 'or' is at 53,9 below.

113 This is not a categorical syllogism. What al-Fārābī means is the syllogism in the mood *Darapti* in the third figure (cf. Section 1.3), with singular middle term and conclusion 'Some agent is a body'. He states this conclusion correctly at 53,1. But here he has a reason for writing 'The agent is a body' instead; it gives him an excuse to discuss the use of indeterminate sentences in logic.

114 Al-Fārābī has already illustrated this way of introducing complex middle terms at 35,14f. The new point here is that when we form the middle term, we can omit some of the particular cases; the aim is to make it look like *Barbara*, and considerations of accuracy can be treated with tolerance.

115 Five lines later al-Fārābī will quote this passage; see Note 116 below.

116 The quotation follows the Baghdad Standard rendering ([109] ii 399,10f) of *Analytica Priora* 2.23, 68b9–12, almost verbatim. There is no reference to jurisprudence in the Greek; on this see Section 3.22 above.

117 'Up for consideration': *mafrūḍ*, a technical term of the art of debate, cf. Section 1.2 above. In debate it means a proposition that is stated for consideration at the beginning of the debate. In the present passage al-Fārābī may mean only that the proposition has been mentioned as a possible premise.

118 'Accepted': *maqbūl*, cf. Part 7 above.

119 This passage illustrates al-Fārābī's habit of writing 'universal' when he means 'universally true'. Cf. 40,8, 51.13,

120 The content (*ḥukm*) here is the predicate, cf. Section 3.1 above. The 'something' four words later can be either an individual satisfying the subject term (as at 54,15), or a universal such that the subject term is true of all of it.

121 The Qur'ān contains no absolute prohibition on drinking wine, though there are prohibitions of drunkenness and the like. But al-Fārābī was well within his rights to count this prohibition as accepted. In the *Risāla* [111] of the jurist al-Shāfiᶜī, Shāfiᶜī's interlocutor remarks that although there are very few legal rulings accepted by all Islamic scholars, a few stand out as unanimously accepted, such as 'that the noon-prayer has four cycles, and that wine is forbidden' ([111] p. 318).

122 In mood *Barbara*.

123 'Declarative' is defined at 12,11 above.

124 Qur'ān, *Sūrat al-ḥajj* 22,30.

125 Qur'ān, *Sūrat al-mā'ida* 5,6.

126 Qur'ān, *Sūrat al-naᶜām* 6,152.

127 Qur'ān, *Sūrat al-mā'ida* 5,1.

128 Literally 'by agreement', *bi-tawāṭu'in*. The word *tawāṭu'* normally means an agreement between people, and in this sense the Baghdad Standard uses it to translate *sunthḗkē* at *De Interpretatione* 16a19. But al-Fārābī's choice of the word in the present passage goes back to Aristotle's *Categories* 1a6, where Aristotle writes *sunōnuma* and the Baghdad Standard translates *mutawāṭi'* 'by agreement'. This translation must rest on a belief that when a word is unambiguous, this is because the community came together at some point and agreed to use the word with a single meaning. In a similar sense al-Fārābī in his *Demonstration* [71] 82,14 speaks of a word being unambiguous within a conversation, because the speaker and listener have previously come to an agreement (*mutawāṭi'*) about what the word should mean.

129 Al-Fārābī's point may be the one he makes at *Long Commentary on De Interpretatione* [59] 145,27–146,22, that a sentence containing an ambiguous term expresses more than one proposition.

130 One of the editors is familiar with a similar saying about one's children in present-day Tunisia. It may be intended to shame the children into taking proper care of their parents in old age; so the intended reference is to one's own children, though this is not explicitly stated.

Türker [157] 277.7f finds in her Istanbul manuscripts of *Syllogism* a further example: ' "Some people disbelieved the prophets", meaning some [of the prophets]'.

131 I.e. the subject term of the intended particular case is also a universal, but narrower than the subject term of the spoken universal proposition. This narrower subject term is the 'narrower universal' referred to in the next few lines, and the 'content true of the [narrower] universal' is the predicate of the intended particular case. For example if 'Children bring disappointment' was said instead of the intended

particular case 'Boy children bring disappointment', and Zayd is a boy child, then the intended particular case entails that Zayd brings disappointment.

132 The explanation that follows refers us back to the previous 'principle' in paragraph 20.2, viz. a universal premise being up for consideration as universally true.

133 Qur'ān, *Sūrat al-mā'ida* 5,38. Bukhārī [32] quotes several sayings of Muḥammad that make the offence more specific, including 'The hand should be cut off for stealing something that is worth a quarter of a dinar or more' (8:780).

134 In mood *Barbara*.

135 Al-Fārābī means that a more specific *phrase* is used instead of a more general one; the speaker's intended meaning is that expressed by the more general phrase. But he confuses the issue by describing this as putting a more specific *concept* in place of a more general one.

136 Two kinds of what, and mentioned at the outset of what? The least farfetched suggestion seems to be that he means two kinds of universal proposition, namely affirmative and negative, which appear in *Syllogism* at 14,3–5 and very briefly in *Short Syllogism* at 72,6. But if he meant that, wouldn't he just have said 'affirmative and negative'? This passage might be evidence that Parts 19 and 20 originally had a different introduction, perhaps one which distinguished between two ways in which a premise can be 'accepted'.

137 Qur'ān, *Sūrat banī isrā'īl* 17, 23.

138 The next sentence makes clear that the conclusion of the required syllogism is universal affirmative. Among the categorical syllogisms, the only mood with a conclusion of this form is *Barbara*, which was discussed in Part 11. But possibly al-Fārābī has in mind that a hypothetical syllogism of one of the forms in Part 14 might be used.

139 In mood *Barbara*.

140 I.e. induction, see Note 8 to Section 3.22.

141 More precisely, the task of finding the intended universal here is similar to that of finding the major premise in the version of inference to the unobserved by means of the observed that al-Fārābī has described as Synthesis.

142 There is a logical confusion here. It is not clear whether al-Fārābī is describing circumstances in which we can't either verify or refute the major premise under consideration, or circumstances in which we can't verify either the major premise or its corresponding negative statement. The text at 58,11 is easier to read as stating the former; but this would make 58,11–13 an unnecessary repetition, and in any case the circumstances needed for the former reading would be considerably more complicated than what al-Fārābī has written. On the assumption that al-Fārābī means the latter reading, the condition he needs here is still complex, as follows: every relevant universal *B* has both a particular case *C* such that we are unable to

verify that *C* is an *A*, and a particular case *C*' such that we are unable to verify that *C*' is not an *A*. He has simplified by assuming that the two particular cases are the same one. We have assumed that al-Fārābī's *aṣlan* in 58,10 is intended as a universal quantification over universals, and so we have moved its translation forward to where a modern reader would expect it. Otherwise we have kept close to the text.

143 Cf. paragraphs 19.5 and 19.6.

144 This is an example of usury (*ribā*). The Qur'ān forbids usury but without defining it (for example at *Sūrat al-baqara* 2,275f). Definitions are found in the *Ḥadīth* (Sayings of the Prophet), for example Bukhārī [32] (3:344) which begins 'Gold for gold is usury unless it is A for A; wheat for wheat is usury unless it is A for A'. This is commonly understood to forbid exchanging unequal quantities of wheat. The purpose is to protect a person (Zayd) from exploitation by another person (Khalid) in a position of relative power; for example Khalid might lend Zayd some wheat but demand an exorbitant extra amount when the loan is returned; or he might give Zayd high quality wheat in exchange for poor quality wheat, and demand an excessive compensation for the difference in quality.

145 'Take it as' (*nunzil*): this is an unusual turn of phrase, perhaps derived from *nazala* 'be a revealed truth'. But al-Fārābī uses it elsewhere (*Expressions* [58] 68,18; 84,6, *Demonstration* [71] 69,11.13).

146 Qur'ān, *Sūrat al-nisā'* 4,40.

147 I.e. induction, as at Note 161 to Section 3.22. This paragraph repeats the content of paragraph 20.11, but specialized to the case of exchange of wheat.

148 Throughout this passage the manuscripts *B* and *H* read 'plaster' (*jiṣṣ*) while *E* reads 'chick-pea' (*ḥimmaṣ*). Evidently some copier has tried to 'correct' al-Fārābī's choice of example. In such cases one chooses the *lectio difficilior*, which is 'plaster' since plaster is less like wheat.

149 In mood *Felapton*.

150 *Ethica Nicomachea* 1094b11–14.

151 *Ethica Nicomachea* 1094b23–27 roughly.

152 These seven words are missing from the manuscript *B*. If we are correct in accepting them, they were probably written to indicate that the version of transfer from the observed to the unobserved being discussed here is the Synthetic and not the Analytic.

153 This universal premise is what was called the major premise in the earlier discussions of likening and transfer, in symbols 'Every *B* is an *A*'.

154 'These arts' are presumably the arts that reason about practical affairs, such as the two that al-Fārābī has already associated with tolerance, namely ethics (cf. the quotation from *Ethica Nicomachea* at 60,14ff) and jurisprudence (61,8).

155 *Analytica Priora* 2.24, 69a13–15, quoted in Note 13 to Section 2.3.

156 This second kind is where the mind retains the notion of the exemplar, as at 63,2. The first is where the universal premise is separated out cleanly and can be used without reference to the exemplar.

157 First figure (for confirmation) at 54,15, third figure (for limited confirmation) at 52,18, (for refutation) at 58,16. Recall from Section 1.2 that the verification of an objective can be either confirmation or refutation.

158 Since there are only a handful of places where Aristotle mentions *parádeigma* or any similar kind of argument, al-Fārābī must be thinking of how transfer arguments are handled in the literature more generally.

159 I.e. induction and likening; likening brings together the methods that al-Fārābī has just described as 'the other methods that we listed after [induction]'.

160 I.e. categorical; see Note 95 to the translation.

Bibliography

Arabic names are listed according to the last item of the name, ignoring the prefix *al-*.

[1] Peter Adamson, *Al-Kindī*, Oxford University Press, Oxford 2007.

[2] Peter Adamson, 'Philosophical theology', in Sabine Schmidtke (ed.), *The Oxford Handbook of Islamic Theology*, Oxford University Press, Oxford 2016, pp. 297–312.

[3] Rafīq al-'Ajam (ed), *Al-manṭiq 'inda al-Fārābī (The Logic of al-Fārābī)*, Dar el-Mashreq, Beirut, vol 1 1985, vols 2, 3 1986.

[4] Alcinoos, *Enseignement des Doctrines de Platon*, ed. John Whittaker, Belles Lettres, Paris 1990.

[5] Alexander of Aphrodisias, *Alexandri in Aristotelis Analyticorum Priorum Librum I Commentarium*, ed. Maximilian Wallies, Reimer, Berlin 1883.

[6] Alexander of Aphrodisias, *Alexandri in Aristotelis Topicorum Libros Octo Commentaria*, ed. Maximilian Wallies, Reimer, Berlin 1891.

[7] Alexander of Aphrodisias, '*Fī in'ikāsi al-muqaddamāt* (On conversion of premises)', in Badawi [15] pp. 55–80.

[8] Ammonius, *In Aristotelis De Interpretatione Commentarius*, ed. Adolfus Busse, Reimer, Berlin 1897.

[9] Ammonius, *In Aristotelis Analyticorum Priorum Librum I Commentarium*, ed. Maximilianus Wallies, Reimer, Berlin 1899.

[10] Maroun Aouad and Gregor Schoeler, 'Le syllogisme poétique selon al-Fārābī: un syllogisme incorrect de la deuxième figure', *Arabic Sciences and Philosophy* 12 (2002) 185–96.

[11] Aristotle, *Prior Analytics, Book I*, trans. and ed. Gisela Striker, ClarendonPress, Oxford 2009.

[12] Aristotle, *Ars Rhetorica, The Arabic Version: a new edition, with Commentary and Glossary*, ed. M. C. Lyons, 2 vols, Pembroke Arabic Texts, Plumridge, Cambridge 1982.

[13] Averroes, *Kitāb al-ᶜIbāra*, in Averroes, *Talkhīṣ Manṭiq Arisṭū (Paraphrase de la Logique d'Aristote)*, vol. 1 ed. Gérard Jehamy, Al-Maktabah al-Sharqíyah, Beirut 1982, pp. 79–133.

[14] Abdurraḥmān Badawi, *Manṭiq aristū*, Dār al-Kutub al-Miṣrīyah, Cairo, vols. 1, 2 1948, vol. 3 1952.

[15] Abdurraḥmān Badawi, *Commentaires sur Aristote Perdus en Grec et Autres Épîtres*, Institut des Lettres Orientales de Beyrouth, Dar El-Mashreq, Beirut 1971.

[16] Carmela Baffioni (ed), *Epistles of the Brethren of Purity: On Logic, an Arabic Critical Edition and English Translation of Epistles 10–14*, Oxford University Press and Institute of Ismaili Studies, Oxford 2010.

[17] Ibn Bājja (Avempace), *Taᶜālīq ibn bājja ᶜalā manṭiq al-fārābī*, ed. Mājid Fakhrī, Dār el-Mashreq, Beirut 1994.

[18] Muḥammad ibn al-Ṭayyib al-Bāqillānī, *Kitāb tamhīd al-awā'il wa talkhīs al-dalā'il*, ed. ᶜImād al-Dīn Aḥmad Haydar, Mu'assasat al-Kutub al-Thaqāfīyah, Beirut 1987.

[19] Jonathan Barnes, *Porphyry: Introduction*, Clarendon Press, Oxford 2003.

[20] ᶜAlī bin Zayd al-Bayhaqī, *Tārīkh ḥukamā' al-'islām*, Al-Majmaᶜ' al-ᶜIlmī al-ᶜArabī, Damascus 1976.

[21] P. Bearman et al., *Encyclopaedia of Islam, Second edition*, Brill, Leiden 1960–2004.

[22] Ali Benmakhlouf, Stéphane Diebler and Pauline Koetscher, *Al-Fārābī, Philosopher à Bagdad au Xe siècle*, Seuil, Paris 2007.

[23] Gotthelf Bergsträsser, *Ḥunain ibn Ishāq über die Syrischen und Arabischen Galen-Übersetzungen: Zum ersten Mal herausgegeben und übersetzt*, Brockhaus, Leipzig 1925.

[24] Deborah L. Black, *Logic and Aristotle's Rhetoric and Poetics in Medieval Arabic Philosophy*, Brill, Leiden 1990.

[25] Susanne Bobzien, 'A Greek parallel to Boethius' De Hypotheticis Syllogismis', *Mnemosyne* 55 (3) (2002) 285–300.

[26] Susanne Bobzien, 'Hypothetical syllogistic in Galen – propositional logic off the rails?', *Rhizai: Journal for Ancient Philosophy and Science* 2 (2004) 57–102.

[27] Susanne Bobzien, 'Alexander of Aphrodisias on Aristotle's theory of the Stoic indemonstrables', in M. Lee (ed), *Strategies of Argument: Essays in Ancient Ethics, Epistemology, and Logic*, Oxford University Press, Oxford 2014, pp. 199–227.

[28] Boethius, *De Hypotheticis Syllogismis*, ed. Luca Obertello, Paideia, Brescia 1969.

[29] Boethius, *De Topicis Differentiis*, trans. Eleonore Stump, Cornell University Press, Ithaca 1978.

[30] Sebastian Brock, 'The Syriac commentary tradition', in Charles Burnett (ed.), *Glosses and Commentaries on Aristotelian Logical Texts: the Syriac, Arabic and Medieval Arabic Traditions*, Warburg Institute, University of London 1993, pp. 3–18.

[31] Kristen E. Brustad, *The Syntax of Spoken Arabic*, Georgetown University Press, Washington DC 2000.

[32] Muḥammad bin Ismā'īl Bukhārī, *Ṣaḥīḥ al-Bukhārī*, 9 vols including trans. by Muḥammad Muḥsin Khān, Hilal Yayinlari, Ankara 1976.

[33] John Buridan, *Summulae: De Suppositionibus*, ed. Ria van der Lecq, Artistarium vol. 10–4, Ingenium, Nijmegen 1998; trans. Gyula Klima in *John Buridan, Summulae de Dialectica*, Yale University Press, New Haven 2001.

[34] Walter Burleigh, *De Puritate Artis Logicae Tractatus Longior*, ed. Philotheus Boehner, Franciscan Institute, St Bonaventure NY 1955.

[35] Peter J. Cameron, *Combinatorics: Topics, Techniques, Algorithms*, Cambridge University Press, Cambridge 1994.

[36] Michael Chase, 'Did Porphyry write a commentary on Aristotle's *Analytica Posteriora*? Albertus Magnus, al-Fārābī, and Porphyry on *per se* predication', in Peter Adamson (ed), *Classical Arabic Philosophy: Sources and Reception*, Warburg Institute, London 2007, pp. 21–38.

[37] Saloua Chatti, 'Logical Oppositions in Arabic Logic: Avicenna and Averroes', in J.-Y. Beziau and D. Jacquette (eds), *Around and Beyond the Square of Opposition*, Springer, Basel 2012, pp. 21–40.

[38] Saloua Chatti, 'Existential import in Avicenna's modal logic', *Arabic Sciences and Philosophy* 26 (2016) 45–71.

[39] Saloua Chatti, 'The semantics and pragmatics of the conditional in Al-Fārābī's and Avicenna's Theories', *Studia Humana* 6 (1) (2017) 5–17.

[40] Saloua Chatti, 'Avicenna (Ibn Sina): Logic', in *The Internet Encyclopedia of Philosophy*. Available online: <https://www.iep.utm.edu/avlogic/>, accessed August 2019.

[41] Saloua Chatti, *Arabic Logic from al-Fārābī to Averroes*, Birkhaüser, Springer Nature, 2019.

[42] Riccardo Chiaradonna, 'Le traité de Galien Sur la démonstration et sa postérité tardo-antique', in Riccardo Chiaradonna and Franco Trabattoni (eds), *Physics and Philosophy of Nature in Greek Neoplatonism*, Brill, Leiden 2009, pp. 43–77.

[43] Gholamreza Dadkhah and Asadollah Fallahi, *Logic in 6th/12th century Iran* (Arabic texts with Persian notes and English introduction), Iranian Institute of Philosophy, Tehran 2018.

[44] Cristina D'Ancona, 'Greek sources in Arabic and Islamic philosophy', in Edward N. Zalta (ed.), *The Stanford Encyclopedia of Philosophy (Winter 2017 Edition)*. Available online: <https://plato.stanford.edu/archives/win2017/entries/arabic-islamic-greek/>.

[45] M. T. Dāneshpazhūh, *Al-manṭiqīyāt lil-Fārābī (The logical works of al-Fārābī)*, 3 vols, Maktabat al-Mar'ashī al-Najafī, Qum 1987–1989.

[46] Herbert A. Davidson, *Proofs for Eternity, Creation and the Existence of God in Medieval Islamic and Jewish Philosophy*, Oxford University Press, New York 1987.

[47] Augustus De Morgan, *The Connexion of Number and Magnitude: An Attempt to Explain the Fifth Book of Euclid*, Taylor and Walton, London 1836.

[48] Thérèse-Anne Druart, 'Al-Farabi', in Edward N. Zalta (ed), *The Stanford Encyclopedia of Philosophy* (Fall 2016 Edition). Available online: <https://plato.stanford.edu/archives/fall2016/entries/ al-farabi/>.

[49] D. M. Dunlop, 'Al-Fārābī's Introductory Sections on Logic', *Islamic Quarterly* 2 (1955) 264–82.

[50] D. M. Dunlop, 'Al-Fārābī's *Eisagoge*', *Islamic Quarterly* 3 (2) (1956) 117–38.

[51] D. M. Dunlop, 'Al-Fārābī's Introductory *Risālah* on logic', *Islamic Quarterly* 3 (1957) 224–35.

[52] D. M. Dunlop, 'Al-Fārābī's paraphrase of the *Categories* of Aristotle', *Islamic Quarterly* 4 (1957/8) 168–197, 5 (1959) 21–54.

[53] Sten Ebbesen, *Commentators and Commentaries on Aristotle's Sophistici Elenchi: A Study of Post-Aristotelian Ancient and Medieval Writings on Fallacies, vol. 1 The Greek Tradition*, Brill, Leiden 1981.

[54] Abdelali Elamrani-Jamal, *Logique Aristotélicienne et grammaire arabe* (Études musulmanes xxvi), Vrin, Paris 1983.

[55] Majid Fakhry, *Al-Fārābī: Founder of Islamic Neoplatonism: His Life, Works and Influence*, Oneworld, Oxford 2002.

[56] Asadollah Fallahi, 'Fārābī and Avicenna on contraposition', *History and Philosophy of Logic* 40 (1) (2018) 22–41.

[57] Al-Fārābī, *Kitāb al-mūsīqa al-kabīr (Great Book of Music)*, ed. Ghaṭṭās ᶜAbd-al-Malik Khashaba, Dār al-Kātib al-ᶜArabī lil-Ṭibāᶜa wa-al-Nashr, Cairo 1967; French trans, in Rodolphe D'Erlanger, *La Musique Arabe*, vols 1, 2 (of 6), Librairie Orientaliste Paul Geuthner, Paris 1930.

[58] Al-Fārābī, *Kitāb al-alfāẓ al-mustaᶜ mala fī al-manṭiq (Expressions)*, ed. Muḥsin Mahdī, Dār el-Mashreq, Beirut 1968.

[59] Al-Fārābī, *Sharḥ al-Fārābī li-kitāb Arisṭūṭālīs fī al-'ibāra (Long Commentary on De Interpretatione)*, ed. W. Kutsch and S. Marrow, Dar el-Mashreq, Beirut 1971.

[60] Al-Fārābī, *Kitāb al-Khaṭāba (Rhetoric)*, in *Deux ouvrages inédits sur la réthorique*, J. Langhade and M. Grignaschi (eds), Dar el-Mashreq, Beirut 1971, pp. 31–121.

[61] Al-Fārābī, *Al-tawṭi'a aw al-risāla allatī ṣuddira bih[ā] al-manṭiq (Introductory Risāla)*, in [3] vol. 1 (1985) pp. 55–62; trans. in Dunlop [51].

[62] Al-Fārābī, *Al-fuṣūl al-khamsa (Five Sections)*, in [3] vol. 1 (1985) pp. 63–73; trans. in Dunlop [49].

[63] Al-Fārābī, *Kitāb al-īsāghūjī (Eisagōgḗ)*, in [3] vol. 1 (1985) pp. 75–87; trans. in Dunlop [50].

[64] Al-Fārābī, *Kitāb al-qāṭāghūrīyās ayy al-maqūlāt (Categories)* in [3] vol. 1 (1985) pp. 89–131; Dunlop [52] gives a slightly different text together with an English translation.

[65] Al-Fārābī, *Kitāb pārī armīniyās ayy al-ᶜibāra (Short Interpretation)*, in [3] vol. 1 (1985) pp. 133–63. The trans. in Zimmermann (1981) pp. 220–47 indicates the pages in [3].

[66] Al-Fārābī, *Kitāb al-qiyās (Syllogism)*, in [3] vol. 2 (1986) pp. 11–64.

[67] Al-Fārābī, *Kitāb al-qiyās al-ṣaghīr (Short Syllogism)*, in [3] vol. 2 (1986) pp. 65–93.

[68] Al-Fārābī, *Kitāb al-taḥlīl (Analysis)*, in [3] vol. 2 (1986) pp. 95–129.

[69] Al-Fārābī, *Kitāb al-amkina al-mughliṭa (Sophistry)*, in [3] vol. 2 (1986) pp. 131–64.

[70] Al-Fārābī, *Kitāb al-jadal (Debate)*, in [3] vol. 3 (1986) pp. 13–107.

[71] Al-Fārābī, *Kitāb al-burhān (Demonstration)* in *Kitāb al-burhān wa-Kitāb sharā'iṭ al-yaqīn*, ed. Majid Fakhry, Dar el-Mashreq, Beirut 1987, pp. 19–96.

[72] Al-Fārābī, *Risālat al-tanbīh ᶜalā sabīl al-saᶜāda (Indication of the way to happiness)*, ed. Saḥbān Khalīfāt, Jamiᶜat al-Urdunīya, Amman 1987; trans. as 'Directing attention to the way to happiness' in Jon McGinnis and David C. Reisman, *Classical Arabic Philosophy, An Anthology of Sources*, Hackett, Indianapolis 2007, pp. 104–20.

[73] Al-Fārābī, *Qawl Al-Fārābī fī al-tanāsub wa-al-ta'līf (Proportion)*, in Dāneshpazhūh [45] vol. 1 (1987) pp. 504.1–506.6; French trans. as 'Discours d'al-Fārābī sur la proportion et l'agencement' in Benmakhlouf et al. [22] pp. 107–11.

[74] Al-Fārābī, *Kitāb sharḥ al-qiyās (Long Commentary on Prior Analytics)*, surviving part in [45] vol. 2 (1988) pp. 263–553.

[75] Al-Fārābī, *Kitāb al-ḥurūf (Letters/Particles)*, 2nd edn, ed. Muhsin Mahdi, Dar el-Mashreq, Beirut 1990.

[76] Al-Fārābī, *'Iḥṣā al-ᶜ ulūm (Catalogue of the sciences)*, ed. ᶜ Uthmān Amān, Dār Bibliyun, Paris 2005; Latin trans. by Gerard of Cremona in Alain Galonnier, *Le De Scientiis Alfarabi de Gérard de Crémone: Contribution aux problèmes de l'acculturation au XIIe siècle (édition et traduction du texte)*, Brepols, Turnhout 2017.

[77] Al-Fārābī (?), *L'armonia delle opinioni dei due sapienti: il divino Platone e Aristotele (Al-jamᶜ bayna ra'yay al-ḥakīmayn aflaṭūn al-ilāhī wa-arisṭūṭālīs) (Harmony)*, ed. Cecilia Martini Bonadeo, Plus, Pisa 2009; English trans. in Charles E. Butterworth, *Alfārābī, The Political Writings, 'Selected Aphorisms' and Other Texts*, Cornell University Press, Ithaca, NY 2001, pp. 117–67.

[78] Henry George Farmer, 'The music of Islam', in Egon Wellesz (ed), *Ancient and Oriental Music*, Oxford University Press, London 1957, pp. 421–77.

[79] Kate Fleet et al., *Encyclopaedia of Islam*, 3rd edn, Brill, Leiden 2007–.

[80] William W. Fortenbaugh et al. (eds), *Theophrastus of Eresus: Sources for his Life, Writings, Thought and Influence, Part One: Life, Writings, Various Reports, Logic, Physics, Metaphysics, Theology, Mathematics*, Brill, Leiden 1992.

[81] Galen, *De Placitis Hippocratis et Platonis, Libri Novem*, vol. 1, ed. Iwanus Mueller, Teubner, Leipzig 1874.

[82] Galen, *Scripta Minora III*, ed. Ioannes Marquardt, Iwanus Mueller, Georgius Helmreich, Teubner, Leipzig 1893.

[83] Galen, *Institutio Logica*, ed. Carolus Kalbfleisch, Teubner, Leipzig 1896.

[84] Galen, *Galen on Medical Experience, First edition of the Arabic version with English translation and notes by R. Walzer*, Oxford University Press, London 1944.

[85] Galen, *Three Treatises on the Nature of Science*, trans. Richard Walzer and Michael Frede, Hackett, Indianapolis 1985.

[86] Manuela E. B. Giolfo and Wilfrid Hodges, 'Syntax, semantics, and pragmatics in al-Sīrāfī and Ibn Sīnā', in Georgine Ayoub and Kees Versteegh (eds), *The Foundations of Arabic Linguistics III: The Development of a Tradition: Continuity and Change*, Brill, Leiden 2018, pp. 115–45.

[87] Manuela E. B. Giolfo and Wilfrid Hodges, 'Conditionality: syntax and meaning in al-Sīrāfī and Ibn Sīnā', in Manuela E. B. Giolfo and Kees Versteegh (eds), *The Foundations of Arabic Linguistics IV: The Evolution of Theory*, Brill, Leiden 2019, pp. 157–81.

[88] Mario Grignaschi, 'Les traductions latines des ouvrages de la logique arabe et l'Abrégé d'Alfarabi', *Archives d'Histoire Doctrinale et Littéraire du Moyen Age* 39 (1972) 41–107.

[89] Dimitri Gutas, 'Paul the Persian on the classification of the parts of Aristotle's philosophy: a milestone between Alexandria and Baghdād', *Der Islam: Zeitschrift für Geschichte und Kultur des Islamischen Orients* 60 (2) (1983) 31–267; repr. in Dimitri Gutas, *Greek Philosophers in the Arabic Tradition*, Ashgate, Aldershot 2000, ch. ix.

[90] Dimitri Gutas, 'Aspects of literary form and genre in Arabic logical works', in Charles Burnett (ed.), *Glosses and Commentaries on Aristotelian Logical Texts: the Syriac, Arabic and Medieval Arabic Traditions*, Warburg Institute, University of London 1993, pp. 29–76.

[91] Dimitri Gutas, *Greek Thought, Arabic Culture: The Graeco-Arabic Translation Movement in Baghdad and Early 'Abbāsid Society (2nd–4th/8th–10th centuries)*, Routledge, London 1998.

[92] Dimitri Gutas, *Avicenna and the Aristotelian Tradition: Introduction to Reading Avicenna's Philosophical Works, 2nd edn*, Brill, Leiden 2014.

[93] Kwame Gyekye, 'The term *istithnā'* in Arabic logic', *Journal of the American Oriental Society* 92 (1) (1972) 88–92.

[94] Kwame Gyekye, 'Al-Farabi on "Analysis" and "Synthesis"', *Apeiron: a Journal for Ancient Philosophy and Science* 6 (1) (1972) 33–8.

[95] Kwame Gyekye, 'Al-Fārābī on the logic of the arguments of the Muslim philosophical theologians', *Journal of the History of Philosophy* 27 (1) (1989) 135–43.

[96] Ahmad Hasnawi, 'Fārābī et la pratique de l'exégèse philosophique (remarques sur son *Commentaire au De Interpretatione d'Aristote), Revue de Synthèse* Paris 117 (1985) pp. 27–59.

[97] Ahmad Hasnawi, 'Boèce, Averroès et Abū al-Barakāt al-Baġdādī, témoins des écrits de Thémistius sur les *Topiques* d'Aristote', *Arabic Sciences and Philosophy* 17 (2) (2007) 203–65.

[98] Ahmad Hasnawi, 'Topique et syllogistique: la tradition arabe (Al-Fārābī et Averroès)', in J. Biard and F. Mariani-Zini (eds), *Les lieux de l'argumentation, Histoire du syllogisme topique d'Aristote à Leibniz*, Brepols, Turnhout 2009, pp. 191–226.

[99] Carl G. Hempel, 'Studies in the Logic of Confirmation', *Mind* 54 (213) (1945) 1–26 and 54 (214) (1945) 97–121.

[100] Wilfrid Hodges, 'Ibn Sīnā on analysis: 1. Proof search. Or: Abstract State Machines as a tool for history of logic', in A. Blass, N. Dershowitz and W. Reisig (eds), *Fields of Logic and Computation: Essays Dedicated to Yuri Gurevich on the Occasion of his 70th Birthday*, Lecture Notes in Computer Science 6300, Springer, Heidelberg 2010, pp. 354–404.

[101] Wilfrid Hodges, 'Ibn Sīnā on reductio ad absurdum', *Review of Symbolic Logic* 10 (3) (2017) 583–601.

[102] Wilfrid Hodges, 'Remarks on al-Fārābī's missing modal logic and its effect on Ibn Sīnā', *Eshare: An Iranian Journal of Philosophy* 1 (3) (2019) 39–73.

[103] Wilfrid Hodges, *Mathematical Background to the Logic of Ibn Sīnā*, Perspectives in Logic, Association for Symbolic Logic (in preparation).

[104] Wilfrid Hodges and Thérèse-Anne Druart, 'Al-Farabi's Philosophy of Logic and Language', in Edward N. Zalta (ed.), *The Stanford Encyclopedia of Philosophy* (Summer 2019 Edition). Available online: <https://plato.stanford.edu/archives/sum2019/entries/al-farabi-logic/>.

[105] Pamela Huby, *Theophrastus of Eresus: Sources for his Life, Writings, Thought and Influence, Commentary Volume 2, Logic*, Brill, Leiden 2007.

[106] Henri Hugonnard-Roche, 'Remarques sur la tradition arabe de l'*Organon* d'après le manuscrit Paris, Bibliothèque nationale, ar. 2346', in Charles Burnett (ed.), *Glosses and Commentaries on Aristotelian Logical Texts: the Syriac, Arabic and Medieval Arabic Traditions*, Warburg Institute, University of London 1993, pp. 19–28.

[107] Henri Hugonnard-Roche, 'La formation du vocabulaire de la logique en arabe', in Danielle Jacquart (ed.), *La formation du vocabulaire scientifique et intellectuel dans le monde arabe*, Brepols, Turnhout 1994, 22–38.

[108] Henri Hugonnard-Roche, *La logique d'Aristote du grec au syriaque: Études sur la transmission des textes de l'Organon et leur interprétation philosophique*, Vrin, Paris 2004.

[109] F. Jabre, *Al-naṣṣ al-kāmil li-manṭiq arisṭū*, Dār al-Fikr al-Libnānī, Beirut 1999.

[110] Al-Jawharī, *Tāj al-lugha wa ṣiḥāḥ al-ᶜarabīya*, ed. Aḥmad ᶜAbd al-Ghafūr ᶜAṭṭar, Dār al-Kutub al-ᶜArabī, Cairo 1956–1958.

[111] Majid Khadduri, *Al-Shāfiᶜī's Risāla: Treatise on the Foundations of Islamic Jurisprudence*, Islamic Texts Society, Cambridge 1997.

[112] Muhammad Ali Khalidi (ed.), *Medieval Islamic Philosophical Writings*, Cambridge University Press, Cambridge 2005.

[113] Ibn Khallikān, *Wafayāt al-aᶜyān wa-anbā' abnā' al-zamān*, Dār al-Thaqāfa, Beirut 1968?–1972?

[114] István Kristó-Nagy, *La pensée d'Ibn al-Muqaffaᶜ: un "agent-double" dans le monde persan et arabe*, Studia Arabica XIX, Paris 2013.

[115] W. Kutsch, 'Muḥaṣṣal – Ghayr Muḥaṣṣal', *Mélanges de l'Université Saint Joseph* 27 (1947–8) 169–76.

[116] Joep Lameer, *Al-Fārābī and Aristotelian Syllogistics: Greek Theory and Islamic Practice*, Leiden 1994.

[117] Tae-Soo Lee, *Die Griechische Tradition der Aristotelischen Syllogistik in der Spätantike*, Vandenhoeck and Ruprecht, Göttingen 1984.

[118] David Londey and Carmen Johanson, *The Logic of Apuleius*, Brill, Leiden 1987.

[119] Muḥsin Mahdī, 'Al-Fārābī, *Kitāb al-shiᶜr (Poetics)*', *Shiᶜr* (1959) 90–5; also in [45] vol. 1 pp. 500–3; French trans. in [22] pp. 112–18.

[120] Dominique Mallet, 'Le *Kitāb al-taḥlīl* d'Alfarabi', *Arabic Sciences and Philosophy* 4 (1994) 317–35.

[121] John Marenbon, *Boethius*, Oxford University Press, Oxford 2003.

[122] Stephen Menn, 'Al-Fārābī's Kitāb al-Ḥurūf and his analysis of the senses of being', *Arabic Sciences and Philosophy* 18 (1) (2008) 59–97.

[123] Ibn Miskawayh, *Tartīb al-saᶜāda*, ed. ᶜAlī al-Ṭūbajī al-Suyūtī, Cairo 1928.

[124] Andrea Moro, *The Raising of Predicates: Predicative Noun Phrases and the Theory of Clause Structure*, Cambridge University Press, Cambridge 1997.

[125] Ibn al-Muqaffaᶜ, *Al-manṭiq* (Logic), M. T. Dāneshpazhūh (ed.), Iranian Institute of Philosophy, Tehran 1978.

[126] Ibn al-Nadīm, *Al-fihrist (Catalogue)*, Dar al-Kutub al-ᶜIlmīyah, Beirut 2002.

[127] Ian Richard Netton, *Al-Fārābī and his School*, Curzon, Richmond Surrey 1999.

[128] Paul the Persian, 'Logica', in Jan Pieter Nicolaas Land (ed.), *Anecdota Syriaca vol.* 4, Brill, Lugdunum Batavorum (Katwijk) 1875, pp. 1–30.

[129] F. E. Peters, *Aristoteles Arabus: the Oriental Translations and Commentaries on the Aristotelian Corpus*, Brill, Leiden 1968.

[130] John Philoponus, *In Aristotelis Analytica Priora Commentaria*, ed. M. Wallies, Reimer, Berlin 1905.

[131] Dag Prawitz, *Natural Deduction*, Almqvist & Wiksell, Stockholm 1965.

[132] Ibn al-Qifṭī, *Ta'rīkh al-ḥukamā' (History of the Philosophers)*, ed. Julius Lippert, Dieterisch, Leipzig 1903.

[133] Fakhr al-Dīn al-Rāzī, *Manṭiq al-Mulakhkhaṣ*, ed. Ahad Farāmarz Qarāmalekī and Ādīneh Asḡarīnezhād, Tehran 1961.

[134] Nicholas Rescher, *Al-Fārābī's Short Commentary on Aristotle's Prior Analytics*, University of Pittsburgh Press, Pittsburgh 1963.

[135] Nicholas Rescher, *Galen and the Syllogism*, University of Pittsburgh Press, Pittsburgh 1966.

[136] Shalom Rosenberg and Charles Manekin, 'Themistius on Modal Logic: Excerpts from a commentary on the *Analytica Priora* attributed to Themistius', *Jerusalem Studies in Arabic and Islam* 11 (1988) 83–103.

[137] Ibn Rushd (= Averroes), *Maqālāt fī al-manṭiq wa-al-ᶜilm al-ṭabīᶜī (Essays on logic and physics)*, ed. Jamāl al-Dīn al- ᶜAlawī, Casablanca 1983.

[138] A. I. Sabra, Review of *Al-Fārābī's Short Commentary on Aristotle's Prior Analytics*, by Nicholas Rescher, *Journal of the American Oriental Society* 85 (2) (1965) 241–3.

[139] Joseph Schacht and Max Meyerhof, 'Maimonides against Galen, on Philosophy and Cosmogony', *Bulletin of the Faculty of Arts of the University of Egypt (Majallat Kulliyat al-Ādāb bi-al-Jāmiᶜa al-Miṣriyya)*, 5 (1937) 53–88.

[140] Sextus Empiricus, *Outlines of Pyrrhonism*, trans. R. G. Bury, Heinemann, London 1933.

[141] Ibn al-Sikkit, *Iṣlāḥ al-manṭiq*, ed. Aḥmad M. Shākir and ᶜAbd-al-Salām M. Mārūn, Dār al-Maᶜārif, Cairo 1956.

[142] Beata Sheyhatovitch, 'The notion of *fā'ida* in the Medieval Arabic grammatical tradition: *Fā'ida* as a criterion for utterance acceptability', in Amal Elesha Marogy and Kees Versteegh (eds), *Foundations of Arabic Linguistics. ii. Kitāb Sībawayhi: Interpretation and Transmission*, Brill, Leiden 2015, pp. 184–201.

[143] Abū Sa^{c}īd al-Sīrāfī, *Šarḥ Kitāb Sībawayhī (Commentary on the Book of Sībawayhī)*, vol. 3, ed. Aḥmad Ḥasan Mahdalī, Dar al-Kutub al-^{c}Ilmīya, Beirut 2012.

[144] Ibn Sīnā, *Al-burhān*, ed. A. Afīfī et al., Cairo 1956.

[145] Ibn Sīnā, *Al-ilāhiyyāt*, ed. S. Dunya, G. Anawati and S. Zayed, Wizārat al-Ṭaqāfa wal-Iršād al-Qāwmi, Cairo 1960.

[146] Ibn Sīnā, *Al-qiyās (Syllogism)*, ed. S. Zayed, Cairo 1964.

[147] Ibn Sīnā, *Al-^{c}ibāra*, ed. M. El-Khodeiri et al., Dār al-Kātib al-^{c}Arabī lil-Ṭabā^{c} wal-Našr, Cairo 1970.

[148] Ibn Sīnā, '*Risāla fī ta^{c}aqqub al-mawḍi^{c} al-jadalī*', in M. Mohaghegh and T. Izutsu (eds), *Collected Texts and Papers on Logic and Language*, Society for the Appreciation of Cultural Works and Dignitaries, Tehran 2007, pp. 63–77.

[149] Moritz Steinschneider, *Al-Farabi (Alpharabius), des Arabischen Philosophen Leben und Schriften, mit Besonderer Rücksicht auf die Geschichte der Griechischen Wissenschaft under den Araben*, Imperial Academy of Sciences, St Petersburg 1869.

[150] Tony Street, '"The Eminent Later Scholar" in Avicenna's Book of the Syllogism', *Arabic Sciences and Philosophy* 11 (2) (2001) 205–18.

[151] Gisela Striker, 'Aristoteles über Syllogismen "aufgrund einer Hypothese"', *Hermes* 107 (1979) 33–50.

[152] Riccardo Strobino, 'Varieties of demonstration in Alfarabi', *History and Philosophy of Logic* 40 (1) (2018) 42–62.

[153] Ibn Suwār, *'maqālatun li-abī al-khayri al-ḥasani bin suwār al-baghdādī fī 'anna dalīla yaḥyā al-naḥwī 'alā ḥud[ū]thi al-'ālami 'awlā bi-al-qubūli min dalīli al-mutakallimīna aṣlan'*, in Abdurraḥmān Badawi, *Al-aflāṭūnīya al-muḥdathah ^{c}inda al-^{c}Arab*, Maṭba^{c}a Dār al-Kutub al-Miṣrīya, Cairo 1947, pp. 243–5.

[154] Themistius, 'Traité en réponse à Maxime au sujet de la réduction de la deuxième et la troisième figures à la première' (trans. by Badawi from Arabic), in Abdurraḥmān Badawi, *La transmission de la philosophie grecque au monde arabe*, Vrin, Paris 1987, pp. 180–94.

[155] Paul Thom, *The Syllogism*, Philosophia Verlag, Munich 1981.

[156] Teun Tieleman, 'Methodology', in R. J. Hankinson (ed.), *The Cambridge Companion to Galen*, Cambridge University Press, Cambridge 2008, pp. 49–65.

[157] M. Türker, '*Fārābīńin bazı mantik eserleri*', *Revue de la Faculté de Langues, d'Histoire et de Géographie de l'Université d'Ankara* 16 (3,4) (1958) 165–286.

[158] Aḥmād bin al-Qāsim bin Abī Uṣaybi^{c}a, *^{c}Uyūn al-anbā'i fī ṭabaqāt al-aṭibbā'*, Dār Maktabat al-Ḥayāt, Beirut 1965.

[159] Philippe Vallat, *Farabi et l'École d'Alexandrie: Des prémisses de la connaissance à la philosophie politique*, Vrin, Paris 2004.

[160] Josef van Ess, 'The logical structure of Islamic theology', in G. E. von Grunebaum (ed), *Logic in Classical Islamic Culture*, Harrassowitz, Wiesbaden 1970, pp. 21–50.

[161] A. van Hoonacker, 'Le Traité du philosophe syrien Probus sur les *Premiers Analytiques* d'Aristote', *Journal Asiatique* 9 (16) (1900) 70–166.

[162] Kees Versteegh, 'Grammar and logic in the Arabic grammatical tradition', in Sylvain Auroux, Konrad Koerner, Hans-Josef Niederehe, and Kees Versteegh (eds), *Handbuch für die Geschichte der Sprach- und Kommunikationswissenschaft I*, Mouton de Gruyter, Berlin and New York 2000, pp. 300–6.

[163] W. Wright, *A Grammar of the Arabic Language.* Cambridge University Press, Cambridge 1967.

[164] F. W. Zimmermann, 'Some observations on Al-Fārābī and logical tradition', in S. M. Stern, Albert Hourani and Vivian Brown (eds), *Islamic Philosophy and the Classical Tradition, Essays presented by his friends and pupils to Richard Walzer on his seventieth birthday*, Cassirer, Oxford 1972, pp. 517–46.

[165] F. W. Zimmermann, *Al-Farabi's Commentary and Short Treatise on Aristotle's De Interpretatione*, British Academy and Oxford University Press, Oxford 1981.

[166] Mauro Zonta, 'Al-Fārābī's *Long Commentary* on Aristotle's *Categoriae* in Hebrew and Arabic: A critical edition and English translation of the newly-found extant fragments', in Binyamin Abrahamov (ed.), *Studies in Arabic and Islamic Culture* 2, Bar-Ilan University Press, Ramat-Gan 2006, pp. 185–253.

[167] Mauro Zonta, 'About Todros Todrosi's Medieval Hebrew Translation of al-Fārābī's Lost Long Commentary/Gloss-Commentary on Aristotle's Topics, Book VIII', *History and Philosophy of Logic* 32 (1) (2011) 37–45.

English–Arabic–Greek Glossary

Note: G = Greek. Where possible the Greek equivalents or near-equivalents of the Arabic terms are the words of Aristotle that the Arabic terms are used to translate in the Baghdad Standard translation of the *Organon*. But some Arabic logical vocabulary translates terms taken from other Greek authors such as Alexander of Aphrodisias; in such cases we indicate the Greek author in parentheses. A question mark indicates that there is some doubt how far the Arabic term matches the Greek.

absurdity: *khalf*, G *tò adúnaton*
accepted: *maqbūl*
Accepting (as a logical method): *wujūd*, G *kataskeuásai* (Alexander)
accident: *ᶜaraḍ*, G *sumbebēkós*
action: *fiᶜl*
actual: *bi al-fiᶜl*
affirmation: *ījāb*, G *katáphasis*
affirmative: *mūjib*, G *kataphatikós*
agreement: *ittifāq*
agreement (about the meaning of a word): *tawātu'*, G *sunthḗkē*
aim: *qaṣd*, G *skopós* (Alexander)
analogy: *see* likening
analysis: *taḥlīl*, G *análusis*
ancients: *qudamā'*
animal: *ḥayawān*, G *zô̧on*
antecedent: *muqaddim*, G *hēgoúmenon* (Alexander)
arrangement: *tarkīb*
aspect: *jiha*
attach: *aḍāfa*
available: *ḥaṣala*

bee: *naḥl*
believed: *maẓnūn*, G *hupolēptón*

categorical: *ḥamlī*, *jazmī*.
cause: *ᶜilla*, G *aitía*
clear: *bayyin*, G *phanerós*
complete: *tāmm*, G *téleios*
composed: *mu'allaf*, G *sugkeímenos*
composition: *ta'līf*
compound: *tarkīb*
compounded: *murakkab*, G *sumpeplegménos*
concede: *sallama*
conclusion: *natīja*, G *sumpérasma*
condition: *sharīṭa*, G *hupóthesis*
confirmation: *ithbāt*, G *?kataskeuázein* (Alexander)
conflict: *ᶜinād*
connected: *muttaṣil*, G *sunekhés* (Alexander)
consequent: *tālī*, G *hepómenon* (Galen)
content, information: *ḥukm*
contingent, *mumkin*: G *endekhómenos*
contradictory opposite: *naqīḍ*, G *antíphasis*
contrary: *ḍidd*, G *enantíos*
convention: *iṣṭilāḥ*
conversion: *ᶜaks*, G *antistrophḗ*
convert: *inᶜakasa*, G *antistréphein*
convertible: *munᶜakis*
copular: *wujūdī*
created: *ḥādith*, *muḥdath*

declarative: *jāzim*, G *apophantikós.*
defect: *khalal, ikhtilāl*
deficient: *nāqiṣ*
definition: *taḥdīd*, G *diorismós*
demonstration: *burhān*, G *apódeixis*
denial: *salb*, G *apóphasis*
deny: *salaba*
detached, excepted: *mustathnāt*
detaching, exception: *istithnā'*
dialectical: *jadalī*, G *dialektikós*
diminution: *tanaqquṣ*
direct: *mustaqīm*, G *euthús*
discover: *istanbaṭa*
disjunction: *infiṣāl*
divided: *muqassam*
doubted: *mashkūk fīh*

entail: *antaja*, G *sunágein* (Alexander)
essence: *dhāt*
every: *kull*, G *pâs*
examination: *taṣaffuḥ*
examine: *taṣaffaḥa*
example, exemplar: *mithāl*, G *parádeigma*
existence: *wujūd*, G *hupárkhein*
existing: *mawjūd*, G *hupárkhei*
experience: *tajriba*, G *empeiría*
explicit: *fī al-lafẓ*
expression: *lafẓ*
extreme (term): *ṭaraf*, G *ákron*

falling under: *(dākhil) taḥta*
false of: *kadhaba ᶜalā*
falsehood: *kadhib*, G *pseûdos*
figure (of syllogism): *shakl*, G *skhêma*
first: *awwal*, G *prôtos*
follow from: *lazima ᶜan*, G *sumbaínein* (Aristotle), *akoloutheîn* (Alexander)
forbidden: *ḥarām, muḥarram*
form: *hay'a*

generated: *mukawwan*
genus: *jins*, G *génos*

helpful: *nāfiᶜ*, G *khrḗsimos*
hidden: *khafiya*, G *ádēlos*
horse: *faras*, G *híppos*
human: *insán*, G *ánthrōpos*
hypothetical: *sharṭī*, G *ex hupothéseōs*

if: *in*, G *ei*
implicit: *fī al-ḍamīr*
impossible: *muḥāl*, G *adúnatos*
indeterminate: *muhmal*, G *aóristos* (Aristotle), *adióristos* (Alexander)
individual: *shakhṣ, shakhṣī*
induction: *istiqrā'*, G *epagōgḗ*
inference: *istidlāl*
inform: *akhbara*
information: *khabar*, G *?historía*
intellected: *maᶜqūl*
intention: *qaṣd*, G *skopós*
investigate closely: *istaqṣā*, G *akríbeia*
irremovable, *lā yanfakku minhu*

judgement: *ḥukm*
jurisprudence: *fiqh*

knowledge: *maᶜrifa*, G *epistḗmē*

likening: *tamthīl*
likening discourse: *qawl mithālī*, G *?parádeigma*
linked: *muqtarin*

major (premise): *kubrā*, G *pròs tò meîzon*
major (term): *akbar*, G *meîzon*
matter: *mādda*, G *húlē* (Alexander)
meaning: *maᶜnā*
measurable: *makīl*
method: *ṭarīq*, G *hodós, trópos*
middle (term): *awsaṭ*, G *méson*
minor (premise): *ṣughrā*, G *pròs tò élatton*

minor (term): *aṣghar*, G *élatton*
mobile: *mutaḥarrik*, G *kineîtai*
mood (of syllogism): *ḍarb*
most: *akthar*, G *tò polú*

nature: *ṭab*ᶜ, G *phúsis*
necessary: *ḍarūrī*, G *anagkaîos*
negative: *sālib*, G *apophatikós*
neighing, *ṣaḥīl*
none: *lā wāḥida*, G *mēdén*
not: *lā, laysa, ghayr*, G *ouk*

objective (*quaesitum*): *maṭlūb*, G *próblēma*
observation: *mushāhada*
observed: *shāhid*
openly visible: *ẓahara*
opposite: *muqābil*, G *antikeímenos*
opposition: *taqābul*, G *antíthesis*
order: *tartīb*, G *?trópos*

paradigm: *see* likening
part: *juz'*, G *méros*
particle (linguistic): *ḥarf*
particular: *juz'ī*, G *merikós*
perceived by the senses: *maḥsūs*, G *aisthétós*
perfect: *kāmil*, G *téleios*
permanent: *dā'im*, G *sunekhés*
persuasive: *muqni*ᶜ, G *pistós*
place: *makān*
posit (noun): *waḍ*ᶜ, G *thésis*
posit (verb): *waḍa*ᶜ*a*, G *tithénai*
possible: *mumkin*, G *endekhómenos*
potential: *quwwa*, G *dúnamis*
precision: *istiqṣā*, G *akríbeia*
predicate: *maḥmūl*, G *katēgoroúmenon*
premise: *muqaddama*, G *prótasis*
premise-pair: *iqtirān*, G *?suzugía* (Alexander)
prepared: *mu*ᶜ*add*, cf. G *paraskeuḗ*
prevented: *mumtani*ᶜ, G *kōlúei* (Aristotle), *adúnaton* (Ammonius)
principle: *mabda'*, G *arkhḗ*
produce: *antaja*
productive: *muntij*, G *sullogistikós* (Alexander)
proof: *bayān*
proposition: *qaḍīya*, G *prótasis*, *?axíōma*
prove: *bayyana*, G *deiknúnai* (Aristotle), *dēloûn* (Alexander)
proximate: *qarīb*
put up for consideration (*see* objective): *faraḍa*, G *?prokeiménos*

quality: *kayfīya*, G *poiótēs* (Alexander)
quantified: *maḥṣūr*
quantifier: *sūr*, G *diorismós* (Alexander)
quantity: *kammīya*, G *tò posón* (Alexander)
question: *mas'ala, su'āl*, G *erṓtēsis*

reason: *sabab*, G *aitía*
reduce: *raja*ᶜ*a*, G *?antistréphein* (Aristotle), *apágein* (Alexander)
refutation: *ibṭāl*, G *élegkhos*
refute: *baṭala*, G *anaireîn*
Rejecting (as a logical method): *irtifā*ᶜ, G *anaireîn* (Aristotle), *anaskeuásai* (Alexander)
reversal: *inqilāb*
rice: *aruzz*

scrutinize: *faḥaṣa*, G *sképsis*
sentence: *qawl*, G *lógos*
sentient: *ḥassās*
separated: *munfaṣil*, G *diairetikós* (Alexander)
similar: *shabīh*, G *hómoios*
similarity: *tashābuh*
singular: *shakhṣī*
some: *ba*ᶜ*ḍ*, G *tí*
standard: *mashhūr*
starting point: *mabda'*, G *arkhḗ*
stone: *ḥajar*, G *líthos*
subcontrary: *mā taḥta al-mutaḍāddayn*, G *hupenantíos* (Alexander)

subject: *mawḍūᶜ*, G *hupokeímenon*
syllogism: *qiyās*, G *sullogismós*
synthesis: *tarkīb*, G *?súnthesis*

take: *akhadha*, G *lambánein*
term: *ḥadd*, G *hóros*
theoretical: *naẓarī*, G *theōrētikós*
thing: *shay'*, *amr*
time: *waqt*, *zamān*, G *kairós*, *khrónos*
tolerance: *musāmaḥa*
tolerate: *sāmaḥa*
transfer (noun): *nuqla*, G *metábasis*
true of: *ṣaḥḥa ᶜalā*
truth: *ṣidq*, G *alēthés*

unaltered, the same: *bi-ᶜaynih*, G *tò autò*
under consideration: *mafrūḍ*, G *?hupékeito*
universal: *kullī*, G *kathólou*
unobserved: *ghā'ib*
unproductive: *ghayr muntij*, G *adókimos* (Alexander)

verb,:*kalima*
verification: *taṣḥīḥ*
visible: *mar'ī*

wall: *ḥā'iṭ*
wheat: *burr*
when: *lammā*, *matā*
white (colour): *bayāḍ*
white(-coloured): *abyaḍ*, G *leukós*
whole: *jamīᶜ*, G *hólos*
wished for: *maqṣūd*
work out: *istakhraja*

Arabic–English Index

Note: References are to the page and line numbers of the text (indicated in the margins of the translation).

a^cadda, prepares, 20,7.
abyaḍ, white(-coloured), 12,19.20; 13,5; 14,8.9; 15,17; 16;15.16.18; 17,4.7; 18.3; 30,8.9.11.12.13.14.15.16.17.18.20; 32,16.17; 33,11.
ᶜadad, number, 13,7.11; 19,4; 31,20; 32,10.11.14.20; 33,7; 58,21.
aḍāfa, pairs (a proposition with another proposition so as to form a premise-pair), 34,11.15; 37,2; 38,8.16.18; 39,2.4.5.7; 40,9.14; 41,6.
akbar, major (extreme, term), 35,15.
akhbara, informs, 12,11.
ᶜalā l-iṭlāq, absolutely, 11,6.8.12; 56,16; 63,5.11.16.
al-lāh, Allah, 59.9; 64,14.
amr, thing, concept, 128 times between pp. 8 and 64. See also *shay'*.
antaja, produces (conclusion), 100 times between pp. 20 and 41, and at 53,7.
ᶜaraḍ, accident, 19,8; 38,15.16; 39,12.13; 61,6.
arisṭūṭālīs, Aristotle, 22,11; 54,6; 60,14; 63,9.13; 64,2.5.12.
aruzz, rice, 60,2.4.5.6; 62,10.11.
aṣghar, minor (extreme, term), 19,5; 21,3; 35,16.
awsaṭ, middle (term), 21,1.5.7.9.10.11; 22,11.12; 24,10; 26,4; 35,14; 40,9; 42,17; 43,14; 47,9; 52,16; 53,9.
awthaq, most reliable, 57,19.
aẓhar, clearer, clearest, 36,5; 42,2.

baṭala, refutes, 47,17; 49,8; 58,17; 60,11.
bayāḍ, white (colour), 30,19.
bayyin, clear, 18,14; 20,2; 24,17; 34,2.4.7.10.12.13; 40,7.8.11.12; 41,3; 49,16; 50,16; 58,6.10.
bi al-fiᶜl, actual, explicit, 63,5.
burhān, demonstration, 61,1.
burhānī, demonstrative, 54,9.
burr, wheat, 58,21; 59,7.11.16; 62,10.

dā'im, permanent, 18,4.
dā'iman, permanently, 16,8.10; 17,12; 18,2.5.13.
dākhil taḥta, included in, falling under (as species or individual in genus), 35,2; 47,7; 48,8; 51,15.17.18; 52,1; 54,13; 56,1; 62,8. See also 43,1 (*dākhil fī*) and *taḥta*.
darā, knows, is aware, 34,2; 41,13.14.
ḍarb, form, kind, 13,8; 16,2.3.13.14.16; 46,4.5.
ḍarb, mood (of syllogism), 22,10; 23,4.11.17; 24,14; 25,4.6.9.10.11.12.15.20; 26,11.14.17; 27,1.13; 28,4.5.8.10.11.16; 29,4.7.10.16.20; 30,1.4.7.10.16.20.21; 31,1.10.11.12; 32,2.5; 33,13.16.17; 34,16; 35,18.
ḍarūratan, iḍṭirāran, bi l-ḍarūrati, bi-iḍṭirārin, necessarily, 19,9.17; 32,8; 33,16.20; 40,8; 42,5.6; 43,2.3.4.8; 44,1.4.8.18; 45,1; 46,12; 47,1.7; 50,1.7.11.14.16.20; 51,3.6; 53,1.
ḍarūrī, necessary, 16,13.16; 17,1.2.5; 33,16; 40,8; 42,5; 43,2; 44,1.4.5.8.20; 46,12; 47,1.7; 50,1.7.11.14.16.20; 51,3.6; 53,1.
ḍidd, contrary, 20,2; 61,5.11.

faḥaṣa, scrutinizes, 52,10.
faraḍa, assumes as premise, adopts as objective or as conclusion to aim for, 19,10; 25,18; 28,19; 34,20; 48,6.8.9.11.12; 51,2.4; 52,9.13.14.15; 53,6.8; 54,2.10.12.
faras, horse, 27,3.4.5.6.8.9.10.11.12; 41,4; 51,10.11.
fī al-ḍamīr, implicitly, 14,16; 15,8.12.
fī al-lafẓ, explicitly, 14,16; 15,8.12.

fiʿl, action, 58,6; 61,1. See also *kalima*.
fikr, reflection, 47,11.
fikrī, reflective, 11,3.
fiqh, jurisprudence, 61,8.
fiqhī, jurisprudential, 54,4.6.9.

ghādara, omits, 37,10.

ḥadd, term, 20,8.13.17; 21,5.7.8.10; 24,10; 26,4; 35,14.15; 40,9.12; 41,9.10.11.13; 42,12.13.14.17; 43,14; 47,9; 52,16; 53,9.
ḥadhafa, removes, suppresses, 37,10; 38,11.13; 39,8.
ḥā'iṭ, wall, 14,17; 36,12.13.15.17.19; 37,1; 48,15.
ḥajar, stone, 14,5.19; 16,15.17; 17,3.6.7; 18,1.2; 24,2.3.4.7.8.9; 27,1.2.3.6.7.8; 30,14.15.16.
ḥamlī, categorical, 11,7.8.13; 12,1.2.6.8; 13.6.14; 20,5.6.13; 21,8; 22,10; 31,6.9; 32,2.9; 33,19; 39,18; 40,5; 44,16.19; 51,11.
ḥarām, forbidden, 54,17; 57,7; 59,1.
ḥarf, particle (linguistic), 19,11.12.13; 25,19; 29,19; 31,9; 32,2; 33,10.
ḥassās, perceiving, perceptive, 20,15.16; 23,18; 24,1.2.5.6.7; 34,1.13.14.15.17.19.20.
ḥayawān, animal, 89 times between pp. 12 and 50.

ibṭāl, refutation, 11,3; 48,13; 49,5; 58,14; 60,14.
idhan, therefore, 21,5; 26,20; 27,12; 31,13; 32,5.6.7.20; 33,1.2.8.9.14.15; 34,1.6.9.19.20; 36,15; 37,1.2; 38,15; 39,16; 40,4; 42,3; 43,2.5.7; 44,1; 46,10.14; 47,2; 48,2; 49,10; 51,3.17; 53,16; 54,16; 60,2.12.
ījāb, affirmation, 14,9; 35,3.10.
ʿilla, cause, 24,10; 43,14.17.18; 44,2; 47,9; 48,5.7.8.9.11.12; 51,4; 52,4.5.9.13.14.15; 53,7.9; 54,2; 58,18.
ʿinād, conflict, 32,10.11.13.15.16.19; 33,2.9.
inʿakasa, converts, 17,10.14.17.18; 18,2.3.6; 25,3.8.10.14; 26,1.7.9.11.13.18.20; 27,2.4.5.7; 28,3.7.12.13.15; 29,9.12.13.15; 30,3.6.9.12.13.15; 44,21; 52,5.
infiṣāl, disjunction, 13,11; 19,11.12; 31,20; 32,1.
insān, human, person, 78 times between pp. 12 and 55.
iqnāʿ, persuasive point, 45,5.
iqtirān, premise-pair, 12,1; 22,1.4; 27,17; 32,8.
irtabaṭa bi, is linked together by, 19,11.
istakhraja, works out, 62,13.
istanbaṭa, discovers, 64,10.
istiqrā', induction, 12,5; 35,2.9.10.14; 37,4.6; 40,6; 41,7.8; 42,4.7.10; 43,8.9.10.11.13.14.15; 44,11; 45,2.3.6; 48,4; 53,12; 64,4.
istaqṣā, investigates, 41,7; 60,15.16; 61,1.2.3.4.5.7.17; 64,5,8.
ithbāt, confirmation, 11,3; 51,16.

jaʿala, takes as, 20,7; 27,10; 29,18; 30,19; 34,15; 42,3; 43,17.18; 46,16; 50,18; 51,5; 56,17; 57,1; 62,20.
jadalī, dialectical, 54,8.
jāzim, declarative, conveying truth or falsehood, 12,11; 54,17.18; 55,3.4.
jiha, aspect, 12,6.7.16; 15,6; 17,12; 36,4.11; 42,15; 45,10.16; 46,9; 49,1; 53,5; 62,1.4.11.12.13.
jins, genus, 39,17.
juz', part, component, particular case, 14,16; 15,4.5.10.11.19; 17,11.12; 18,7.8.11; 19,5.11.15; 20,3.7.8.14.15.16.17; 21,13.4.13.14; 31,15.16.17; 32,2.9; 36,9; 55,5.17; 56,9.11; 63,10.
juz'ī, particular, existential (quantifier), 113 times between pp. 14 and 64.

kadhib, falsehood, 11,10; 16,8.10; 17,1.4.8; 34,3.4.5.8.9.12.18.
kalima, verb, 12,13; 13,2.4.
kāmil, perfect, 24,17.18.19.
kammīya, quantity, 14,10; 17,16.17.18; 18,1.4.7.
kayfīya, quality, 12,9; 14,9; 17,11.13.18; 27,17.
khabar, piece of information, 12,12.
khalf, absurdity, 12,5; 33,19; 34,3; 40,5. See also *muḥāl, mumtaniʿ*.
kubrā, major (premise), 21,4.14.15.16.18; 22,11; 28,12; 29,12; 30,12; 31,14; 41,8; 42,5.6; 43,14.17; 44,2.18.19.
kullī, universal, 177 times between pp. 13 and 64.

lafẓ, expression, 13,18; 44,10.
lazima, follows, 19,8.17; 20,2; 23,1; 34,8.18.19; 38,17; 39,1.3.4.6.7; 42,5.6; 43,2.4.19.20; 44,1.4.5.8.18; 45,1; 46,12; 47,7; 49,19; 50,7.8.10.11.14.16.20; 51,1.2.6.8.9; 52,18; 53,1.11; 56,6; 58,16; 61,17.

mādda, matter, 16,13; 17,12.13.15; 18,2.4.5.13; 23,2.18; 48,14; 49,1.2.4.5; 60,16.
mafrūḍ, (thing that is) assumed or put up for consideration, 48,11f; 51,2; 54,10.12. See also *faraḍa*.
maḥmūl, predicate, predicated, 12,12.16.17; 13,1; 14,1.3.5.6.7.14.18; 17,11; 18,9.10; 20,8; 21,1.3.6.9.10; 48,3; 55,7.10.
maḥṣūr, quantified, 13,17.
makān, place, 14,16; 15,2.3; 22,11.12; 37,15; 42,6; 50,19.20; 55,4.6.13; 56,4.7; 57,9.14.17; 58,3.14; 59,5.7.11.13.17; 62,14.
makīl, measurable, 59,2.3.5.12.13.14.15; 60,1.2.3.4.5.6.7.9.10.11.12.13; 62,12.13.
malāk, foundation, 64,5.
maᶜ***nā***, meaning, concept, 11,11; 13,15; 14,13.14; 29,2; 36,4.10.13; 42,12.13.16.18; 43,1.3.4.5.6.7; 44,3.4.5.6.7.8.10.13.16.17.21; 45,1; 55,8.9.
maqbūl, accepted, 18,17.18; 54,5.12.14.16; 55,3.10.13.16; 56,3; 57,4.
maqṣūd, intended, wished for, 23,17; 38,9; 54,11; 55,13; 61,10.11; 62,15.
maᶜ***qūl***, intelligible, intellected, 18,18; 19,4.
mar'ī, visible thing, 32,3.6; 43,20.
maᶜ***rifa***, knowledge, 18,16.17; 19,6; 44,11; 56,10; 57,15; 60,18; 61,7.
mas'ala, question, 19,14; 47,3. See also *su'āl*.
mashhūr, standard, 18,17; 19,1.
mashkūk fīhi, doubted, 34,2.4.8.9.15.
mā taḥta al-mutaḍāddatayni, subcontrary, 15,15.19; 17,4.8.
maṭlūb, objective, 11,2; 19,10.11.14.16; 20,5; 21,2.3.4.5; 40,6.10; 41,1.17; 42,9.10; 45,4; 64,10.
maᶜ***ūna***, help, 44,11; 45,2.
mawḍūᶜ, subject, 12,13.17; 13,2.14.15.16.18; 14,1.4.5.6.8.13.17; 15,16.17.19; 16,1.2.4; 17,11; 18,9.11; 20,9; 21,2.4.6.7.9.11; 40,9; 41,9; 51,13; 55,6.10; 60,16 (posited); 62,8.18; 63,14.
mawjūd, exists, 13,10. See also *mawjūd fī*.
mawjūd fī, mawjūd li-, true of, 23,4.5.6.7.10; 36,2.7.8; 44,6.7.20; 45,11; 46,2.4; 47,5.16; 48,6.9.
muᶜ***add***, prepared, 20,8.10.
mu'allaf, composed, 37,18; 38,15; 39,12; 40,3.
muḥāl, impossible, 18,10; 34,17.19; 40,4. See also *mumtani*ᶜ.
muḥarram, forbidden, 54,14.16; 59,12; 60,2.3.7–13; 62,13.
muhmal, indeterminate, 13,17; 15,16; 16,5; 17,8; 21,13.15.16; 22,3.6.7.8; 42,18; 53,1.2.3.7.
mūjib, affirmative, 54 times between pp. 13 and 52.
mukawwan, generated, 36,14.15.17; 37,1.2; 48,14.
mumkin, possible, contingent. 16,13.15.18; 17,1.3.5.7; 42,2.3.
mumtaniᶜ, prevented, 16,13.14.17; 17,1.2.5.6; 34,18; 42,3; 58,15; 61,13. See also *muḥāl*.
munᶜ***akis***, convertible, 11,11; 44,16.18; 51,11.13.
munfaṣil, separated, 13,9.10; 31,10.11.12.19; 32,8.9.18; 40,4.
muntij, productive, 12,2; 22,4.8, 24,15.16.18.19; 27,16; 32,8.
muqaddama, premise, 65 times between pp. 11 and 63.
muqaddim, antecedent, 26,5; 31,18.19.20; 32,1.2.3.6.8; 50,19.20.
muqniᶜ, persuasive, 37,3; 45,6.
muqtarin, linked, 12,1; 20,13.14.15.17; 21,5.7.13; 22,10; 63,3.4.
musāmaḥa, tolerance, generous interpretation, 61,7; 64,8.
mushāhada, observation, 36,12.17.
mushtarik, sharing, ambiguous, 20,16.17; 55,9.11.
mustaqīm, direct, 33,20; 39,18.19; 40,5.
mutaḥarrik, moving, mobile, 19,13.14.
mutakallim, interrogator, 32,13; 43,10.
mutaqābil, opposite (to each other), 11,8.9.10; 14,12.13.18; 15,1.9.13.15.
muttaṣil, connected, 13,9; 31,10.11.13; 32,3.5; 40,4.

naḥl, bee, 41,6.
naqala, transfers (intrans. verb), 36,3; 47,18; 56,2; 57,10.11.12; 58,6; 59,6; 62,18.
naqīḍ, contradictory opposite, 18,10; 20,3; 34,4.9.10.14.15.20; contradictory pair of statements, 19,11.
natīja, conclusion, 19,9; 24,11; 25,10.11; 26,3,11.20; 27,5; 28,14; 29,13; 30,13; 33,20; 34,3.4.5.7.11; 35,9; 37,1.12; 38,9.16.18; 39,1.3.5.7.11; 40,8.9; 42,5; 44,20; 53,7.17.
nāṭiq, responder, 43,10.
naẓara, studies, 43,16; 47,4.5; 49,11.14; 50,21; 53,10.
naẓarī, theoretical, 30,1.2.3.4.5.7.
naẓīr, of same kind, 42,12.
nuqla, transfer (noun), 36,9; 45,7.8.10; 46,1.6.9.10.14; 48,4; 50,5; 52,7.11; 54,15; 62,19; 63,11.14.15.17.

qaṣada, intends, wants, 34,10.12; 51,16.19; 56,13; 57,5; 58,5; 61,4.5; 64,14.
qaṣd, intention, wish, 11,2; 45,4; 55,15.16; 61,6.
qiyās, syllogism, 138 times between pp. 11 and 63.
qudamā', ancients, 33,16.
qurina bi, is adjoined to, linked to, 12,17; 13,18; 15,17.19; 16,1.2.3; 19,11; 24,11; 31,9.16; 32,2; 33,10.

rafada, supports, 43,8.9.15.
rajaᶜa, reduces (something to something), 12,6.8; 25,4.8.12.15.20; 26,1.18; 28,4.7.10.16.18; 29,1.4.7.10.16.19.20; 30,3.7.10.16.20; 37,3; 54,7; 64,11.12.
ridf, consequence, outcome, 19,9.

sabab, reason, 24,10; 48,16; 61,11; 63,6.12.
ṣaḥḥa, is true, is verified, 40,14; 42,9; 43,11; 47,7.15; 49,18; 50,1.2; 52,3.10; 54,14; 56,1.5; 57,17; 59,11.12.13.14.15.16; 62,7.11.12.
ṣaḥḥāl, neigher, 27,8; 51,10.11.
ṣaḥīl, neighing, 27,10.
salaba, denies, 28,19; 34,14; 50,18.
sālib, negative, 51 times between pp. 13 and 33.
sallama, concedes, 34,14.
sāmaḥa, is tolerant, 53,2.7.15; 62,14.
shabīh, similar, 36,3.9; 42,12.13; 48,12; 62,3.19; 63,7.19; 64,3.
shakhṣ, individual, 13,16.
shakhṣī, singular, 15,15.16; 16,8; 19,3.
shakl, figure (of syllogism), 67 times between pp. 12 and 64.
sharīṭa, condition, 13,8.9.10; 14,15; 15,8.9.12; 31,18.20; 32,1.
sharṭī, hypothetical, 11,7.13; 12,5; 13,6.8; 20,6; 31,8.9.10.11.12.15.16.17; 32,2.5.9.18; 39,19; 40,4; 47,14; 50,17.
shay', thing, concept, 184 times between pp. 12 and 63. See also *amr*.
ṣidq, truth, 11,10; 16,8.10; 17,1.4.8.12.13.15.16.18; 18,5.13; 19,14.17; 20,1; 33,19; 34,2.7.10.11.12.16.21.
su'āl, question, 19,12. See also *mas'ala*.
ṣughrā, minor (premise), 21,5.14.15.16.18; 22,11; 25,11; 27,16; 28,3.6.9.15; 29,3.6.9.15; 30,3.6.9.15.21; 31,9; 32,1; 40,7.
sūr, quantifier, 13,17.18; 14,1.2.7.9; 15,18.19; 16,1.2.3.4.5.6; 17,10; 42,18; 53,2.3.

ta'ammul, meditation, 47,11; 56,8; 57,15; 59,8.
taḥdīd, definition, act of defining, 11,12. See also *ḥadd*.
taḥta, falling under (as species or individual in genus), 36,10; 41,8.9; 42,8; 43,1.4.6.7.18; 44,5; 45,9; 47,7.15.19; 48,11; 51,19; 52,6; 53,10; 57,11; 58,4.6.7.8.15; 59,6; 60,4; 61,12.13; 62,17; 63,7.14. See also *dākhil taḥta, mā taḥta al mutaḍāddatayni*.
tālī, consequent, 31,18.19.20; 32,1.2.3.6.8; 50,17.19.20; 51,2.
ta'līf, composition, 20,2.3.5; 23,1; 26,17; 35,17; 36,14; 37,9.10.13.14.15; 46.13.
tāmm, complete, 32,10.11.13.15.16.19; 33,2.10; 60,17.
tamthīl, likening, 12,7; 36,2.7.9; 42,7.10; 43,7.9.10.11.13; 44,11; 45,2.3.5; 63,9.15.
ṭaraf, extreme, 21,1.2.3.4; 24,10; 26,5.
ṭarīq, way, method, 40,5; 46,17; 47,3.4.18.19; 48,5.6.7; 49,6.18; 50,5.13; 51,4.7; 52,8; 57,20; 58,13.18; 59,14; 60,13; 61,15.
ṭarīqa, way, method, 46,15; 61,11.

tarkīb, synthesis, compounding, 46,15; 47,4.
tartīb, order, pattern, 17,11.12; 21,7; 23,17; 24,4; 25,5; 26,4.5; 27,13; 28,5.11; 29,2.5.11; 30,4.10; 37,13.
taṣaffaḥa, examines, 35,4.11.13.15; 41,11.15; 47,14.20; 48,2; 49,2.3.7; 53,13.14; 58,1.9.15; 59,14.15; 60,6.8.10; 61,13.14.
taṣaffuḥ, examination, investigation (Rescher), 35,2.9; 48,10; 57,20; 58,9; 60,3; 61,11.14.15.
tashābaha, are similar to one another, 13,15.16; 45,17; 46,11; 62,1.
tashābuh, similarity, 36,8.
taṣḥīḥ, verification, 11,2; 19,10; 35,3; 40,8.12; 41,9; 42,1.4.9.10.14; 43,9.12.14; 44,2.3.13; 45,2; 48,9.12.16; 50,5.6; 51,4.7; 52,2.7.9.15; 53,6; 54,2.3; 57,20; 58,5.13; 60,3.13; 61,12; 62,13.14; 63,1,
tawāṭu', *bi-tawāṭu'*, unambiguous, 55,8.11.
thabata, affirms, confirms, establishes, 35,4; 51,19.
waḍ^{c}, posit (noun), 32,17.
waḍa^{c}a, puts, 42,17; posits as assumption or premise, 18,10; 19,8; 25,17; 33,12; 60,10.
wajada, finds, 35,5.7.13; 42,12; 43,17; 47,1.6; 49,7; 58,12.15; 60,11. See also the passive form *wujida*.
wujida, is found, exists, is true (of), 58 times between pp. 12 and 63.
wujūd, existence, truth, finding, 19,12.13; 36,5.10.17; 39,2.3.4.5.6.14.15.16; 40.14; 42,9.12.15; 43,5.6.8.12.17; 44,2.4.16.18; 45,1; 48,1.5.6; 50,11.20; 51,4.7.14.16; 52,4.6.8.9.10.13; 53,6; 58,12.16.19; 61,15. (Note al-Fārābī's idiom *wujūd A fī B* = '*B* being an *A*'.)
wujūdī, copular, 12,18; 13,2.4.

ẓahara, is clear, explicit, 64,12.
zamān, time, 12,15.17.19; 13,2.3; 14,16.19; 15,1; 35,11.13.14.16.17.18; 45,10; 47,9; 48,7.

Index of Passages from Aristotle

Analytica Posteriora
1.12
78a14–21, 104
2.7
92a34–92b2, 97
2.19
100a3–9, 97
Analytica Priora
1.1
24a16f, 45
24a19, 49
24b18–20, 65
1.1–7, 33
1.4
25b32–26a21, 73
26a29f, 49
1.4–6, 71
1.6
28b20f, 79
29a6–10, 68
1.13
32b3–9, 120
1.15
34a25, 90
34b7f, 120
1.23–25, 102
40b17–42b26, 104
1.25
42a3f, 169
1.32
46b40–47b14, 102
1.42
50a5–7, 167
50a5–10, 104
1.44
50a40–50b2, 34
2.11
61b1, 27
2.15, 70
2.23, 91, 96, 97
68b9–12, 196
68b11, 127
68b20f, 98
2.24, 91
68b38–69a19, 101
2.25, 96, 97
69a26f, 112

Categories
1a6, 177

De Interpretatione
16a19, 197
17a2, 137
17a36f, 53
23a27, 52

Ethica Nicomachea
1094b11–14, 199
1094b23–27, 199

Rhetorica
1.2, 1357b26–36, 104

Topica
1.18
108b7–19, 101
2.2
109b13–25, 98
2.10
114b25–31, 101
114b25–36, 97
7.1
156a22–26, 98

Subject Index

Note: 'al-' at the beginning of an Arabic word is ignored in the alphabetical ordering. Dates are AD unless BC is specified.

abduction 102, 106
absurdity 6, 19, 23, 25, 59–62, 101, 136f, 141, 174
Abū Bakr bin al-Sarrāj al-Baghdādī (9th–10th c) 24, 92
Abū al-Barakāt bin Malkā (c. 1080–c. 1165) 12
Abū Bishr Mattā bin Yūnus (c. 870–940) 12, 13f, 90, 100
Abū Isḥāq Ibrāhīm Quwayrī 12
academies 9f, 14, 16, 57, 97, 105
accepted 25, 41, 96, 123, 154–6, 157, 159, 176, 177
accepting (method of) 21, 41, 54, 73, 80–2, 83, 87, 107, 108, 149–52, 159, 161, 172, 175
affirmative 1f, 21, 25, 28, 29, 33, 36, 39, 40, 48, 96, 108, 119, 121, 123, 152, 167, 174
al-ʿAjam, R. 17, 18
Alcinous (c. 200) 70
Alexander of Aphrodisias (2nd–3rd c) 11f, 13, 14, 25, 31, 41, 46, 54f, 57, 92, 95, 108, 167
ambiguous 86, 94, 110, 155, 166, 177
Ammonius Hermiou (c. 440–c. 520) viii, 9, 34, 94f, 101, 110, 166
analogy *see* likening
analysis (versus synthesis) 69, 79, 88, 107, 147f
antecedent 56, 62, 100, 101, 134, 151, 175
Anushirvan *see* Khosraw I Anushirvan
Apuleius (2nd c) 35, 97f
Aristotle *passim*; mentioned by al-Fārābī 126, 154, 160, 163f
Avempace (Ibn Bājja, c. 1085–1139) 16, 90
Averroes (Ibn Rushd, 1126–1198) 12, 14, 16, 27, 94, 100, 109
Avicenna (Ibn Sīnā, c. 980–1037) 12, 14, 27, 32, 39, 49, 58, 65, 72, 76, 85, 93, 94, 96, 98, 101, 102, 104, 105, 166, 167, 168, 171

Baghdad Standard translation of *Organon* 11, 25–7, 35, 49, 66, 70, 71, 88, 89, 102, 106, 109, 111, 165, 174, 176, 177
al-Bāqillānī (c. 940–1013) 105
Bobzien, S. 54, 100, 108, 168
Boethius (c. 480–524) 9, 12, 34, 55, 57f, 100, 109
Brethren of Purity 27
Bukhārī (810–870) 178f
Burley, Walter (c. 1275–1344) 105

candidate conclusion 7, 44, 95, 96
categorical 1f, 4, 7, 10–13, 25, 29–32, 41, 42, 46–50, 80–2, 83f, 86, 93, 96, 99, 108, 119, 124f, 134, 141, 148, 165, 166, 172, 173f, 176, 180
cause 57, 69, 77, 78, 82f, 105, 108, 128, 144, 148f, 151f, 153f, 158, 162f, 172, 174, 175
certainty 4, 57, 58, 76, 96, 104, 145f, 160
Chiaradonna, R. 109
Chrysippus (c. 279–c. 206 BC) 54, 99, 100
concession 3, 103; *see also* Responder
conclusion 2f, 4, 6, 7, 10, 25, 43, 44f, 50, 54, 59–62, 67, 70–2, 76f, 95, 96, 98, 100, 101, 124f, 134, 136, 137f, 140f, 153f, 157, 170, 171
condition of productivity 7, 10f, 20, 48, 51
consequent 56, 58, 134, 151, 175
content 26, 28, 63, 68f, 78f, 87, 105, 106, 107, 108, 137–9, 144f, 146–54, 156–64, 169, 173, 174, 175, 176, 177

contradictory 6, 33f, 35, 37, 44, 56, 59, 62, 94, 96, 98, 120f, 124, 136f, 151, 168, 175
contraposition 41
contrary 33, 96, 107, 120–2, 124, 161
conversion 6, 10, 13, 19, 22, 39–41, 45f, 51f, 95, 100, 122f, 145, 167, 176
convertible 40, 117; convertible in predication 176
copula 28
copular verb 25, 118, 165
created 42, 61f, 69, 72–4, 106, 140–2, 146–52, 173

David (6th c) 13
debate 3f, 15, 18, 26, 41, 60, 70, 75, 80, 92, 101, 103, 172, 173, 176
deduction *see* syllogism; natural deduction 60, 82, 108
definition 15, 20, 22, 27f, 40, 43–5, 46, 50, 52, 59, 80, 104, 117, 167, 168, 176, 179
De Morgan, A. 101
detach 56f, 134–6, 151, 175
dialogue 118; *see also* debate
al-Dimashqī (Abū ʿUthmān al-Dimashqī, 9th–10th c) 25f, 95
division 12, 64, 65, 102

Ebbesen, S. 34, 165f
ecthesis 51–3, 98f
Elias (6th c) 13
Eudemus (late 4th c BC) 41, 54
excepted *see* detach
exemplar 68, 88, 105, 107, 139, 158, 161–3, 169, 170, 171, 173, 180
existence 25, 108; *see also* created
extreme 46, 49, 125, 127–9, 167; *see also* term

Fakhr al-Dīn al-Rāzī (1150–1210) 99
al-Fārābī's books:
  Analysis 15, 18, 21, 41, 54f, 64, 66, 77, 78f, 80f, 82f, 102, 107, 108
  Categories 15, 17, 18, 39, 52, 53, 57f, 93, 95, 99, 108, 110
  Debate 15, 19, 57f, 59, 75, 77, 79, 96, 99, 102, 103, 106, 167
  Demonstration 4, 15, 96, 102, 104, 177, 179
  Eisagōgē 14f, 18
  Expressions 17, 30, 34, 40, 43, 57f, 88, 99, 176, 178
  Harmony (disputed attribution) 70, 171
  Indication of the Way to Happiness 17
  Letters/Particles 8, 17, 26, 74f, 88, 92, 102f, 168
  Long Commentary on De Interpretatione 25, 54, 89, 165, 167, 177
  Long Commentary on Prior Analytics 12, 14, 21, 59, 63f, 67, 89, 90, 94, 97, 98, 100, 102, 103, 104, 105, 106, 109
  Poetics 15, 18
  Proportion 8, 89
  Rhetoric 15, 18, 35, 42, 99, 104f, 173
  Short Interpretation 15, 27, 110, 165
  Short Syllogism 15, 18, 21–3, 26, 27, 33, 42, 45, 49f, 55, 59–61, 63f, 66, 68, 85, 88, 90, 91, 99, 100, 101, 104, 107, 165, 169, 170, 174, 175, 176
  Sophistry 15, 106f
figure (of syllogism) 4–8, 12f, 19, 22f, 44f, 46–8, 50, 70, 80, 97f, 117f, 125–7, 154, 164, 167, 170
Frege, G. 92

Galen (129–c. 200) 12, 49, 51f, 53, 54, 56, 57, 78, 82f, 99, 100, 102, 105, 108f, 172
George Bishop of the Arabs (c. 700) 89
Greek 3, 8, 9, 10, 11, 12, 14, 24, 25f, 33, 67, 78, 92, 93, 107, 109, 166, 167
Grignaschi, M. 18
Gutas, D. 13
Gyekye, K. 91f, 107

Hasnawi, A. 12, 100, 108f, 165
Haylā al-Malkānī 10
Hempel, C. 111
Hugonnard-Roche, H. 93
Ḥunayn bin Isḥāq (809–873) 11, 12
hypothetical sentence 28, 41, 54, 56–8, 99f, 117f, 165
hypothetical syllogism 19f, 22–4, 25, 42, 53–6, 61f, 66, 70, 80f, 83f, 91, 99f, 102, 104, 108, 117, 124, 133–5, 141, 148, 151, 167, 168, 172, 174, 175, 178

Ibn Abī al-Uṣaybiʿa (c. 1194–1270) 13, 16, 24, 89, 90
Ibn al-Biṭrīq (8th–9th c) 11
Ibn Khallikan (1211–1282) 89, 90
Ibn al-Miskawayh (932–1030) 13
Ibn al-Muqaffaʿ (mid 8th c) 10, 20, 33, 36, 49, 89, 93, 97, 166
Ibn al-Nadīm (late 10th c) 8, 11f, 16, 100
Ibn al-Qifṭī (1172–1248) 89
Ibn Ṣalāḥ Hamadānī (early 12th c) 47
Ibn al-Sikkīt (early 9th c) 93
Ibn Suwār (al-Ḥasan bin Suwār al-Khammār, c. 942–c. 1030) 11, 105f
Ibn al-Ṭayyib (Abū al-Faraj bin al-Ṭayyib, early 11th c) 13
Ibn Zayd al-Bayhaqī (c. 1097–1169/70) 89
indeterminate 2, 25, 31, 32, 38, 48, 93, 97f, 119, 120, 121, 122, 126, 144, 153, 166, 171, 176
induction 19, 21, 22f, 25, 62–7, 73, 75–7, 78–80, 82, 84f, 87, 102, 103, 104, 106f, 109, 111, 137, 139, 141–6, 153, 163, 170, 171, 172, 173, 174, 178, 179, 180
Isḥāq bin Ḥunayn (c. 830–c. 910) 100

Jawharī (10th–11th c) 104
judgement 26, 28f, 118, 174

kalām 73, 85, 87, 106f
Khosraw I Anushirvan (mid 6th c) viii, 13
al-Kindī (c. 801–c. 873) 12, 90

Lameer, J. 22, 89, 91, 106, 110, 174, 175
likening 19, 21, 22, 24, 31, 63f, 67–9, 73, 77–80, 82, 88, 91, 102, 104f, 107, 109, 117f, 138f, 143–6, 163, 170, 171, 172, 173, 176, 179, 180

Mahdī, M. 17
Maimonides (Moses ben Maimon, 1138–1204) 12, 14, 109
Majd al-Dīn Jīlī (12th c) 47
major *see* premise, term
manuscripts 11, 16–18, 42, 85, 90, 91, 113f, 167, 172–9
Mattā *see* Abū Bishr Mattā bin Yūnus
matter (in creation) 74, 149
matter (in logic) 31–3, 36–9, 40f, 45, 94–6, 98, 109, 121–3, 127
Menn, S. 92
method 6, 7, 9, 31, 42, 48, 51, 52, 62f, 67f, 73, 78, 87, 88, 97f, 105, 107, 111, 147–9, 150–2, 157–63, 167, 170, 173, 174, 175, 180
middle *see* term
minor *see* premise, term
modality 10, 25, 32, 34, 83f, 93, 109, 122, 165, 166, 167, 171, 172
mood (of syllogism) 4–7, 10f, 20, 22–5, 32, 42, 46–53, 54–7, 83f, 91, 96, 97–9, 104, 117, 126–37, 167f, 172
  Barbara 4, 5, 61, 64f, 68, 71, 75, 86, 98, 104, 169, 173, 176, 177f
  Baroco 5, 46, 51–3, 97, 98
  Bocardo 5, 53, 85, 168
  Camestres 5, 51, 98
  Celarent 5, 6, 23, 49, 98, 167f
  Cesare 5f, 51, 98
  Darapti 5, 24, 53, 95, 96, 101, 176
  Darii 5, 23, 48f, 168
  Datisi 5, 53
  Disamis 5, 53
  Felapton 5, 24, 53, 66, 85, 95, 96, 175, 179
  Ferio 5, 49, 52
  Ferison 5, 53
  Festino 5, 51

negation 33, 36; *see also* contradictory
negative 1, 25, 28, 29, 33, 36, 63, 94, 95, 96, 97, 119, 122f, 136, 167, 168, 174
Neoplatonists 9f, 12, 13, 14, 75, 90, 105

objective 3, 7, 44, 46f, 60, 63, 79, 80, 96, 117, 124, 125, 141f, 143, 145, 147–9, 164, 168, 180, 193, 195, 197
opposites 19, 22, 33–6, 119–21, 135, 166
opposition 27, 117, 166; square of opposition 33, 35f, 38f, 94, 96
Ouhalla, J. 94

Pappus (early 4th c) 107
paradigm 106; *see also* exemplar, likening

particular 1, 25, 29, 31, 38, 48, 51, 95, 119, 121, 122f, 126, 148, 152, 163, 174
particular case 30f, 63–7, 76, 78, 86–8, 91, 102f, 106, 107, 111, 137–9, 142, 144, 149, 154–62, 169, 175–9
Paul the Persian (mid 6th c) viii, 10, 13, 20. 33, 36, 49, 95
perfect syllogism 6, 50, 55, 95, 128
Peripatetics 28, 54f, 57, 74, 86, 100, 168, 170, 171, 172
persuasive 139, 146, 173
Philoponus, John (c. 490–c. 570) 12, 57, 95, 97f, 105
Plato (c. 429–347 BC) 4, 9, 70, 103
Porphyry (c. 234–c. 305) viii, 10, 11, 18, 34, 57, 101, 165f
potential 21, 64, 80, 117f, 137, 139, 147, 148, 163f, 167, 169, 173
predicate 1f, 25, 26, 28, 31f, 47, 98, 111, 118, 119f, 125, 155, 165, 174, 177
premise 2, 124f *and passim*
major premise 46, 49f, 68f, 75, 77, 79f, 86f, 98, 105, 144, 148–50, 171, 173, 179
minor premise 46, 49f, 75f, 98, 106
premise-pair 7, 25, 44–8, 55, 96f, 117, 124, 126, 140
Proba (mid to late 6th c) 10, 20, 33, 49, 97f
productive 6f, 10f, 20, 25, 45, 47f, 49f, 55, 96, 97, 126, 128, 130
Pseudo-Ammonius 57
pseudoconclusion 7, 10, 45, 48, 92, 96f

quality 25, 29, 48, 93, 119, 122
quantifier 1, 2, 25, 29f, 31, 93, 119, 121, 144, 153, 166, 175
quantity 25, 29, 40, 48, 93, 119, 122f
Questioner 3, 60f, 101, 103
Qur'ān 26, 85–7, 107, 110, 111, 177, 178, 179

reduction 6, 13, 42, 59, 64, 70, 80, 95, 100, 118, 128–33, 139, 154, 167
reduplicatives 105
refutation 63, 66, 78, 85, 149, 160, 180
rejecting 21, 26, 41, 54, 73, 80–2, 83, 87, 107, 108, 111, 149–52, 159, 161, 172, 175
religion 8, 9, 63, 74f, 85, 87, 106, 107, 173, 179
Rescher, N. 90, 91, 174
Responder 3f, 60f, 101, 103, 136

Saadia Gaon (c. 887–942) 74, 105
Sabra, A. 90, 174
Sarrāj *see* Abū Bakr bin al-Sarrāj al-Baghdādī
Scholastics 4
Sextus Empiricus (2nd or 3rd c) 99, 100, 106
al-Shāfiʿī (767–820) 111, 177
Sheyhatovitch, B. 92
al-Sīrāfī (c. 893–979) 56, 90, 168
Stephanus (early 7th c) 34
Stoics 54–6, 100, 108
subject 1f, 25, 26, 28, 29–31, 32, 33, 34, 46f, 56, 66, 96, 98, 111, 118–22, 155, 177
syllogism 43, 124 and *passim*; *see also* mood
synthesis (versus analysis) 24, 69, 79, 87f, 105, 107, 147f, 173, 178
Syriac 8–14, 19f, 24f, 89, 92, 93

Tarski, A. 94
tense 29, 118, 165
term 2, 4, 6, 21, 22, 39, 40f, 51f, 53, 62, 81, 86, 92, 104, 108, 110f, 125, 128, 143, 162
major (or first) term 46, 48, 137, 126, 167
middle term 46, 48, 64f, 68, 78f, 82, 105, 107, 125, 128, 137, 142f, 144, 149, 153, 167, 171, 173, 175, 176
minor (or last) term 46, 48, 125, 126, 137
Themistius (c. 317–c. 390) 9, 12, 57, 100, 101, 102, 109, 166
Theodorus (mid 9th c) 11, 89, 109f
Theophrastus (c. 371–287 BC) 12, 41, 54, 89
thing 27, 34f, 36f, 43, 68, 105, 106, 107, 118, 121–3, 146, 154, 157, 162, 166, 176, 177
tolerance 66, 83f, 87, 107, 109, 111, 152–4, 161f, 179
topics 12, 21, 39, 54f, 80–3, 100, 103, 108, 109

transfer 18f, 28, 69, 78f, 87f, 105, 106, 107, 138, 144, 146–8, 152–63, 174, 179, 180
Türker, M. 18, 91

universals 30f, 38, 86, 88, 93, 103, 119, 137, 138f, 143–5, 156–9, 162f, 169, 177, 178f
unobserved 68f, 78f, 86f, 105, 106, 107, 146–50, 152–4, 157f, 163, 173, 178, 179
unproductive 7, 10, 20, 32, 45, 47, 48, 49, 55, 97, 128
up for consideration 4, 26, 44, 60, 69, 82, 105, 137, 148f, 151–4, 168, 175, 176, 178
Uṣaybiʿa *see* Ibn Abī Uṣaybiʿa

Vallat, P. 90
van Ess, J. 107
verify, 3, 26, 63, 75–80, 87, 111, 117, 124, 137f, 142–63, 171–3, 175, 178–80
Versteegh, K. 92

Yūḥannā bin Ḥaylān (8th c) 13

Zimmermann, F. 24f, 92, 165

www.ingramcontent.com/pod-product-compliance
Lightning Source LLC
Chambersburg PA
CBHW072235290426
44111CB00012B/2110